THE PRACTICE OF HISTORY IN AFRICA

A History of African Historiography

Ebiegberi Joe Alagoa

Onyoma Research Publications

© 1995 Ebiegberi Joe Alagoa

ISBN: 978-37314-7-5

Published in 2006 by
Onyoma Research Publications
11 Orogbum Crescent, GRA Phase II
P.O. Box 8611, Federal Secretariat Post Office
Port Harcourt, Rivers State, Nigeria

E-mail: kala_joe@yahoo.com
Website: www.onyoma.org
Mobile: 0803-308-3385

Cover Design by
Samuel Marshall
One of the three unique terracotta masks recovered
from an excavation at the ancient settlement of Ke
in the Eastern Niger Delta, Nigeria

Printed by
Doval Ventures Limited
12 Ohaeto Street, D/Line
Port Harcourt, Rivers State
0803 307 5443

**Word Processing,
Type Selection and Layout:**
Jigekuma Ayebatari Ombu
at Hisis (Publishing) Ltd • Port Harcourt
0803 300 4589 • 0805 743 6265

Preface

The first flush of enthusiasm for the research and writing of substantive histories of Africa has waned in the west. Critical, even pessimistic, assessments of the oral traditional base of African historiography have largely replaced the earlier euphoria. Within Africa, university students, the rural and emerging literate urban communities continue to thirst after competent reconstructions of their history.

These essays offer a history of African historiography specifically from an internal African perspective extending back in time to Ancient Egypt. In addition, the essays attempt to present in outline, a history of all the different traditions of historiography that may be identified to have operated on the continent from antiquity to recent times.

An ambitious project of this type can go the way of comprehensive coverage. We have chosen the opposite route of presenting a framework of ideas only, which, we hope, delineates the shape of African historiographical practice. The object has been to create the base structure of a basket. Other practitioners must develop this base framework according to sizes and shapes as the basketry challenges them.

Ebiegberi Joe Alagoa
Choba, Port Harcourt
June 1995

Acknowledgements

I should acknowledge all those who have taught me history, from my grandmother in childhood, through my teacher in village school, to university graduate school, but desist from naming names in this instance.

My students at the University of Port Harcourt deserve to be acknowledged for serving as captive audience to some of the ideas in these essays in the various courses in Historiography, Methodology, and Philosophy of History which I had to devise and teach. Indeed, they instigated some of the ideas through the questions they raised in discussion. Similarly, my colleagues in the Faculty of Humanities stimulated my thoughts at the Faculty Seminars at which some of the essays were first presented.

The formal research was begun during my year as Fulbright Scholar, courtesy of The J. William Fulbright Foreign Scholarship Board and the United States Information Agency, at the University of Wisconsin-Madison in 1983/84, and the writing during a second period of five months as Senior Fulbright Scholar at Brown University, Providence, Rhode Island in 1993/94. In the interval, I had the opportunity to reflect on issues and organize my ideas during three months as a Deutscher Akademischer Austauscherdienst—DAAD—German Academic Exchange Service Visiting Scholar at the Frobenius Institute, of the Johann Wolfgang Goethe University, Frankfurt, Germany in 1989, and another three months as Resident Scholar at the Rockefeller Foundation Study and Conference Center at Bellagio, Italy in 1990.

I am grateful to the funding agencies and governments, and to the universities which generously offered me the use of their facilities, while I retain sole responsibility for the outcome of my research.

Ebiegberi J. Alagoa
Choba, Port Harcourt
June 1995

CONTENTS

Preface   iii

Acknowledgements   iv

1 Introduction: Terms of Discourse
Dorigha Kana / Fun tangha
An unwoven basket / Does not carry away dirt
Nembe proverb, Nigeria (Alagoa 1986: 30-31)   1

1.1 Definitions   1
1.2 Conditions   4
1.3 Traditions   8
1.4 Procedures   10

2 The Oral Tradition
M gbabulem eni oka; / M vuyalema ya apna bu aghalaghala
'I have killed an elephant' could be true; /
'I have carried it to the road' must be false
Ikwerre proverb, Nigeria (Ekwulo 1975: 24-25)   11

2.1 Definition   11
2.2 History   15
2.3 Philosophy   19
2.4 Practice   42

3 The Internal Written Tradition
If an apopokiri (fish) from the bottom of the river /
Says that the crocodile is sick, / It will not be doubted
Ashanti proverb, Ghana (Ojoade, 1988: 31)   45

3.1 Introduction   45
3.2 The Experience of Egypt   46
3.3 History of African Scripts and Communication Systems   84
3.4 Conclusion: African Scripts and Historiography   91

4 The Islamic Tradition
Nye olu si anwa ji owho / Nye ali si anwa ji owho / Owho magwu aye ji a
The man above claims to hold the staff of justice / The man below claims it too, / But the staff of justice knows who holds it
Ikwerre proverb, Nigeria (Ekwulo 1975: 6-7) — 95

- 4.1 Introduction — 95
- 4.2 Regional variations — 100
- 4.3 Ibn Khaldun: An African Philosophy of History in the Islamic Tradition — 143
- 4.4 Conclusion — 148

5 The Western Tradition
Ikagi / Nyingi di
Tortoise is / Parent to his mother
Nembe proverb, Nigeria (Alagoa, 1986: 52-53) — 157

- 5.1 Definition and History — 157
- 5.2 Conditions of Encounter with African Traditions — 167
- 5.3 Western Representations of African History — 177
- 5.4 African Practice of the Western Tradition — 185
- 5.5 'Africanist' Historiography — 205

6 Conclusion: Historiography in Transition
Even a bird with a long neck / Cannot see the future
Kanuri proverb, Nigeria (Ojoade, 1978: 174) — 211

- 6.1 African Traditions — 211
- 6.2 Alienation and Identity — 213
- 6.3 Tradition — 215
- 6.4 The Narrative Tradition — 218
- 6.5 Transition — 220

References — 221
Bibliography — 257
Index — 279

CHAPTER 1

Introduction: Terms of Discourse

Ḍoriḍha kana / Fun tanḍha
An unwoven basket / Does not carry away dirt
Nembe Proverb, Nigeria (Alagoa, 1986)

1.1   Definitions

What is *The Practice of History and A History of African Historiography?* It is necessary to lay down ground rules from the beginning. The definitions that we offer at this initial stage can only be on a broad and inclusive scale. They may appear even idiosyncratic, since they aim to embrace the perspectives of many cultures and periods from the ancient, to the modern and post-modern. It is not intended to rule anything out from the outset, but to investigate, describe and interpret in order to expose what is or is not valid. Critical assessment and appreciation can be made at the point where evidence is brought in. Fine distinctions then, belong to the substantive discussions of issues in other parts of this book.

An understanding of the project may be gained through a definition of each of the items in the title in either direction, from the beginning or the end. We begin at the end, and conclude with a consideration of the total concept.

The Project is a study of a variety of *historiography*. We conceive of historiography as embracing both the practice of the discipline of history as well as the experience and consciousness of historical processes by individuals and communities. It includes awareness of and or the formal or informal formulation of ideas concerning the shape of the past. It includes techniques and methods within a culture for recovering information concerning the past, and thoughts and speculation on the nature and consequences of past events and actions. We would be interested in the possibilities of learning about ideas concerning the past whether recovered or recoverable through the work of historians, lay or professional. The domain of historiography then, is conceived as coextensive with the methodology of history, as well as with philosophies of history, formal, folk or otherwise and eventually, with the practice of history in the context of philosophy and methodology. In this view, practice embraces the writing of history as well as manifestations in the life and activities of communities.

Historiography is qualified as to space, namely, *Africa*. 'African' in this context does not assume or impose on the project the definition of a single or distinctive variety of historiography. It implies the search for any and all types and forms of ideas and practices of history within the continent of Africa. Africa is conceived simply as the geographical space of the continent. It is not defined by race or any other category. The diversity of peoples, cultures and historical experiences is taken for granted, and a rich matrix of ideas and interactions within and without the continent should be expected.

What then, would be our perspective on African historiography? Our focus would be the *history* of the phenomenon of historiography in Africa. That is, historiography in African communities across the continent would be viewed in a time frame in the context of change, development and interactions with communities within the continent and interrelations with other continents. The historical orientation is paramount.

The Practice of History in Africa: A History of African Historiography therefore, represents one specific way of delineating the forms of historical consciousness within communities on the African continent over time from remote antiquity to modern times. The title, *The Practice of History in Africa*, is intended to clarify some of the explanatory definitions, in order to save the project from becoming overly pretentious or idiosyncratic. By the practice of history then, we mean, the consciousness of the historical process that we discover in the lives, customs, traditions, and cultures of communities, as well as the formal or informal doing or making of histories by historians, professional or lay.

In sum, the project is one to construct an authentic African historiographical basket that may be considered functional and efficient for providing the possibilities for future advance. At the least, such a product should be appreciated on its merit as a substantial contribution to the universal growth of historiography; as an object suitable for enjoyment on its own terms; or at the worst, as something worthless and to be deprecated and changed. In any event, in the spirit of the opening proverb, a basket has to be made before it can become useful or seen to be unusable.

1.2 Conditions

The conditions for a history of African historiography are to be sought in the history of the continent.

The research of prehistoric archaeologists and palaeontologists continues to push beyond the 100,000 year period the origins of human evolution to *homo sapiens* from fossils in the valleys and gorges of eastern Africa from the highlands of Ethiopia through the Olduvai, Tanzania and Kenya to South Africa and the Levant[1]. Evidently, the first human development of basic tools and other associated skills took place in this region of Afroasia.

Again, from the region of the Ethiopian highlands and neighbouring areas of eastern Africa flowed the waters of the Nile which created the environment for the rise of the first original beginnings of civilization. The civilization of Ancient Egypt came into being from over five thousand years ago, before about 4000 B.C., from the gathering of peoples into the fertile valley of the Nile from the surrounding areas of Africa affected by the desiccation of the Sahara[2]. This early concentration of population in the world provides, among its numerous original contributions, the first evidence of historical consciousness. Egyptian history, of course, covers several thousand years of high achievements in many areas, of which the historiographical has been one of the least studied. Its history went through many phases with contacts relating it to Asia, the Greeks and Romans, Arabs, and, of course, to the contiguous regions of Africa. These conditions of Egyptian history provide the promise and possibilities for a historiographical study.

The Nile Valley shared with the valleys of the Tigris and the Euphrates, the title of first founders of civilization, including the earliest forms of writing, namely, the cuneiform and hieroglyphics. The link between these regions of Africa and Asia has been known in Europe by the terms Ancient Near East and Middle East, but recently by the more appropriate term Afroasia. On the cultural criteria of language, Afroasiatic has been noted to have its roots in Africa. The Afroasiatic family was classified with a single Asiatic member, Semitic (Arabic and Hebrew), and four African subfamilies: Berber, Ancient Egyptian, Cushitic of the Horn of Africa, and Chad (including Hausa of Nigeria, Western Sudan)[3]. The flow of many innovations from Egypt, sometimes through its Asiatic members, was accepted by the ancient Greeks, but has since gone through periods of acceptance and rejection in Western Europe and America[4].

The rest of northern Africa has had a history similar to that of Egypt with intrusions from and contacts with the Middle East and the Mediterranean. Carthage, Phoenicia, Rome, and the Arabs have commingled with the Berbers at various periods. The historiography of these parts of Africa is, accordingly, related to the historiography of places and peoples outside Africa.

The Sahara Desert presented a challenge to contacts between the peoples of northern Africa and those to the south of it; but did not prove a complete barrier. From the time of Arab occupation of the Maghrib and the introduction of the camel, the Sahara became an ocean traversed along established routes with ports at both shores. The habitable shores to the south became the Sudan: the Eastern Sudan, the Central Sudan, and the Western Sudan, south of which lay the Guinea Coast region of West Africa with its forest and Savannah or Sahel kingdoms (Ghana, Mali, Songhai, Mossi, Asante, Benin, Yoruba, Hausa, Kanem-Bornu etc.), rich in gold and diverse tropical produce. The Sudan region became the meeting point of influences from the Guinea coastal south and the Arab/Berber, and, eventually, Islamic, north.

Eastern Africa has become prominent in prehistoric studies for the recovery of ancient hominid remains, but also established early contacts with the civilizations of Egypt and the Middle East, and across the Indian Ocean, with India and the Far East. The East African coastal region, eventually became the Swahili region, signifying its integration of indigenous African, and Asiatic cultural elements. Eastern Africa also became a major base from which the Bantu peoples of Central Africa spread south into South Africa.

The prehistory of the Bantu unifies Central, Eastern and Southern Africa. Originating from the border region between Nigeria and the Cameroon Republic, these peoples spread south into the basin of the Congo or Zaire River, and eventually over Eastern and; most of Southern Africa[5]. It is clear that they came into country occupied by earlier settlers, even if sparsely settled, such as the Bushmen, the Hottentotts and the Pygmies.

Direct contact between the nations of Western Europe and those of Africa south of the Sahara began from the age of Portuguese maritime explorations. European expansion into these regions of Africa began along the Guinea coast of west Africa, became concentrated in the Congo and Angola, and established as settlement in South Africa from the seventeenth century. European interest in most of the rest of Africa in these periods lay principally in trade in gold, tropical products, and in slaves. In the nineteenth century, European nations began to use the superiority conferred by the maxim gun, to seek dominion and to scramble for territory to colonise. European imperialism led to the establishment of colonial rule over most of Africa by the end of the nineteenth century; the notable exceptions being Ethiopia and Liberia.

In the twentieth century then, a potent factor in the historiography of Africa has been the impact of European colonial rule.

From about 1960, there was a wave of decolonization in which African peoples succeeded in regaining independence and created new nation states. These momentous transformations have left their imprint on the historiography of the continent, the most notable of these being, perhaps, the implantation of Christianity and the entrenchment of western formal education and traditions.

The institution of independent African nation states in the twentieth century has opened opportunities for doing 'independent', 'decolonised' histories, but within an international situation dominated by western technology and power.

1.3 Traditions

The historical conditions have created a number of historiographical traditions.

First, the Oral Tradition, which has preceded writing in all societies. This must be acknowledged every where on the continent, even in those areas which became literate and adopted other traditions as the dominant form. This occurred first in Egypt, later in the Maghrib, and over most of Africa in the recent periods of western colonial rule. It has remained the vital tradition in most of Africa south of the Sahara.

Second, we have to take account of an internal African Written Tradition, beginning with Egyptian hieroglyphics and its various forms through the Meroitic script of the Eastern Sudan, Ethiopic of the Ethiopian Highlands, and others in the Horn of Africa, and West Africa.

Third, the Islamic Tradition which has become an integral local tradition in all of northern Africa with a dominant Arab population; and an influential element in the Eastern, Central, and Western Sudan and in Swahili East Africa. In the Central and Western Sudan, the Oral Tradition has remained dominant and has selectively appropriated aspects of the Islamic Tradition.

Fourth, the Western Tradition, which reached northern Africa as early as Ancient Greek and Roman times, and eventually established itself as a Christian tradition with local roots in Egypt and Ethiopia, before being confronted and overlaid by the Islamic Tradition in Egypt. The Western Tradition reached its high point of influence from the period of European colonization in the nineteenth century. Like the Oral Tradition, the Western Tradition is present in all parts of Africa. But unlike the Oral Tradition, the Western Tradition is supported by the prestige of western dominance of the world in its effort to establish itself as the universal standard.

We note that the conditions of African history have created a situation in which these traditions of historiography no where operate in isolation. The contemporary situation is one in which the Western Tradition challenges all others for supremacy, and in most parts of Africa, one or more of the internal traditions struggle for survival or accommodation with it and other traditions. In Northern Africa, the dominant Islamic Tradition accommodated to the Oral Tradition, struggles with an intrusive Western Tradition. In the Sudan region also, the Islamic and Oral traditions have become integrated and have to come to terms with the challenge of the Western Tradition. A similar situation may be noted for the Swahili areas of East Africa. In the Guinea West African region and in Central and most of Eastern and Southern Africa, the Western Tradition contends with the Oral Tradition.

1.4 Procedures

We proceed from this point by order of the traditions of historiography identified above. The Oral Tradition comes first as the oldest and most widely distributed, followed by the internal African Written Tradition; the Islamic Tradition, and the Western Tradition. We conclude with a discussion of the possibilities for the future development of a new African historiography.

CHAPTER 2

The Oral Tradition

M gbagbulem eni bu ezi oka; / M vuyalema ya apna bu aghalaghala.
'I have killed an elephant' could be true; / 'I have carried it to the road' must be false.
Ikwerre Proverb, Nigeria (Ekwulo, 1975: 24-25).

2.1 Definition

The oral tradition is one common to all peoples and times. The differences that exist between peoples and times relate to the extent of their dependence on the oral tradition, or the nature of the traditions that operated in particular cultures. The invention of writing in a society, for example, would reduce the degree to which reliance is placed on oral testimony, but cannot eliminate oral communication altogether. Certain segments of such societies usually remained wedded to oral communication, and certain areas of activity remained for which oral communication continued to function as the principal means of preserving knowledge. Indeed, at the point where writing becomes significant, the most valuable elements of the oral corpus get transferred into writing, and the oral heritage rides tandem with the written tradition, even if in a subsidiary role. This is seen in the case of the Greek epics, the Hebrew scriptures, and other texts which began their life in the oral tradition.

The above generalization applies to each of the traditions of historiography in Africa, each of which developed out of its own prior period of oral communication, and still retains a minimum level of orality within it. The western tradition whose practitioners now insist on written documents above all else had its origins in Greek and Roman historiography which was mainly based on oral testimonies. It developed along these lines and only achieved its present orientation from the nineteenth century. The Islamic tradition, although a tradition rooted in a written mode of expression, remains within the oral system in its use of its special authoritative *hadith*, being accounts of the statements or life of the Prophet Mohammed. The nature and history of the oral tradition in historiography is perhaps best illustrated in the historiography of Africa.

Forms

The oral tradition is a very broad category of cultural phenomena which come into being without benefit of writing through oral expression. In societies without writing, where all communication was carried out orally, the category was indeed, a wide one. Some of the forms were not intended to communicate history or information about the past, but to entertain or produce pleasure. These forms of oral utterance are termed *oral literature*. As is usual with literatures everywhere, oral literature in Africa embraces a large variety of genres, including myth, legends, poetry of various types[1]. These literary traditions, of course, provide information to the historian of oral societies. However, the traditions that have a focus on the past have been classified into two categories, namely; oral tradition, and oral history.

Oral tradition, has been specified to those oral testimonies concerning the past that are reported accounts. That is, accounts for which the informants or raconteurs were not themselves participants, eye-witnesses or contemporaries of the events reported. In the event, such accounts have been transmitted from one person to another, often over considerable periods of time. Vansina's definition of oral traditions and the methodology of their exploitation for the construction of modem histories in the western tradition remains a standard[2]. Recently, Vansina revised his interpretation of the traditions as mainly source material for the use of modem historians, and defined them as *history* in their own right; that is, that the transmitters of the oral information themselves functioned as historians in their communities and had interpreted the accounts they received[3]. The forms of the oral tradition, comprising, in turn, a large variety of genres, constitute the major interest of African historians since they contain the information for the centuries of the histories of many African communities for which no other reliable body of historical documents exist.

Oral history identifies those oral testimonies concerning the past told by participants in the events, or by persons who were eye-witnesses to them or belonged to the generation or period in which the events took place. The informants, in these cases, do not report information passed to them, but assume the posture of first-hand reporters or interpreters of the events.

These were the oral accounts favoured by Graeco-Roman historians and whose study has been revived in recent times by the historians of Europe and America[4].

The oral tradition of Africa, therefore, embraces both *oral tradition* in terms of reported accounts from the recent or remote past as well as *oral history*, being the testimonies of contemporaries of the events. We contend that the Homeric epics, the Biblical accounts, the *hadith* of the Islamic tradition, the ballads, saga, and epics of many national literary traditions, belong to the category of oral tradition written down and transformed from the oral tradition at the point where it was giving place to a written tradition. It is in this sense that it may be claimed that the oral tradition has been a universal tradition. The oral tradition is universal also in the form of *oral history*, since this form of the oral tradition co-exists with the written tradition and complements it in every culture.

We note that the oral tradition embraces forms of information preserved in the life of peoples outside the literary system. Data of this type may be subsumed under terms such as folklore or the ethnographic record. In the oral societies of Africa, much information of a historical character was embedded in ritual incantations, festivals, dances and masking, drumming and declamatory utterances and in various economic, social and political institutions and activities[5].

2.2 History

The history of the oral tradition in African historiography necessarily begins in ancient Egypt. The role of the oral tradition in Egyptian historiography was first reported by the father of western historiography, Herodotus, who visited Egypt during the 27th Dynasty (525-444 B.C) in the First Persian Period[6]. By this period, Egyptian historiography was already fully in a phase of written historical consciousness, but still retained the oral tradition alongside the written practice. The written records on papyri and monuments were supplemented and amplified by oral accounts remembered mainly by the priests or reduced to writing. Herodotus, indeed, encountered the phenomenon of variant versions characteristic of oral traditions in his discussions with priestly historians at different places. Thus, he recorded two accounts of the duration of Egyptian history: one in which

> 'the priests read to me from a written record the names of 330 monarchs, in the same number of generations, all of them Egyptians except eighteen, who were Ethiops, and one other, who was an Egyptian woman'[7]

And a second in which the priests stated that

> '341 generations separate the first king of Egypt from the last I have mentioned and that there was a king and a high priest corresponding to each generation'[8].

He also recorded the tradition that:

> 'Egypt was, ... ruled by gods, who lived on earth among men'

in its early history. Herodotus also recorded the tradition that a king Neco of Egypt had sent Phoenician sailors to circumnavigate Africa by way of the Indian Ocean and back through the Mediterranean. Although he came from a tradition in which only oral history was practiced, Herodotus was sympathetic to the African oral tradition of Egypt and the oral traditions of Asia. It was, indeed, in this that Herodotus was criticized as 'father of lies' by Greek and Roman historians, and began to be fully appreciated in the western tradition only after the period of western knowledge of 'primitive populations'[9].

The inscription of Egyptian oral tradition into a written tradition reached its final form in the history written by the Egyptian priest, Manetho, apparently on a commission by the Greek pharaoh, Ptolemy II Philadelphus (285-246 B.C). Little is now known of Manetho, except that he was 'high priest and scribe of the sacred shrines of Egypt, born at Sebennytus and dwelling at Heliopolis'[10]. He has also been characterized as 'Manetho the Egyptian, who attained the acme of wisdom', and 'in Manetho we have a native Egyptian who was manifestly imbued with Greek culture'[11]. It is clear that Manetho knew Egyptian hieroglyphic literature and historical records as well as Egyptian oral traditions, and was able to translate this knowledge into a historiography accessible to the Greeks of Alexandria. It was this depth of knowledge that made Manetho's *Aegyptiaca* superior to the histories of Egypt written by Herodotus and other Greek authors before him.

Unfortunately, Manetho's book has not come down in an authentic form. Only the excerpts of it quoted by other authors have come down, and the epitomes made out mainly by the Jewish scholars of Alexandria and later Christian scholars who tried to use it to prove the antiquity of the Jewish nation, and to establish the chronology of the Bible. Indeed, Manetho's contribution to Egyptian historiography is now accepted to reside mainly in the dynastic chronology it established. Manetho identified thirty dynasties down to the eve of the conquest of Egypt by Alexander the Great. The users of his book added a thirty-first dynasty composed of the Greek rulers of Alexandria. Manetho himself divided the period before the first kings or pharaohs, the pre- and proto-dynastic periods of modem Egyptology into periods of (1) the gods, (2) demi-gods, and (3) of spirits of the dead. These must be the periods recorded by Herodotus also as a period of rule by gods.

According to a recent study, 'there is growing doubt being expressed about the use of the Manethonian tradition as a valid source for Egyptian chronology'[12]. But the conditions for its transmission have to be kept in mind for any fair assessment of Manetho's contribution: 'So far as we are able to check Manetho from the contemporary monuments, his division into dynasties is entirely justified ... but unhappily his work has come down to us only in copies of copies; and, although the framework of the dynasties remains, most of the royal names, originally Graecized, have been so mutilated by non-Egyptian scribes, who did not understand their forms, as often to be unrecognizable, and the regnal years given by him have been so corrupted as to be of little value ...'[13]

At the time of Manetho's *Aegyptiaca* the oral tradition he relied on was already on the retreat against the Greek tradition. This Hellenic period of Egyptian history (332–30 B.C) gave place to the Roman (30 B.C–395 A.D.), the Byzantine (395–640 A.D.), and eventually, the current Arab or Islamic period from 640 A.D. Respect for Egyptian religion passed away, and with it the educated priestly class and the practice of ancient Egyptian culture and tradition. Elements of ancient Egyptian tradition only survived among the illiterate peasantry, in the Coptic language, and in some forms of the Coptic religion.

We may observe a similar retreat of the oral tradition against the Christian western tradition and the Islamic tradition in the rest of northern Africa, in the Maghrib, and the Horn of Africa. In northern Africa, the Berber became increasingly Islamized, but continued to represent the ancient heritage of Carthage and the basic indigenous tradition of the land. In Ethiopia, the indigenized Christian and encroaching Islamic traditions incorporated the oral tradition. Similar assimillations and coalescences of the oral tradition and external traditions took place in many parts of Africa: in the creation of a Swahili tradition in East Africa, and in various degrees of accommodation achieved in the Central and Western Sudan, and in continuing tensions in the Eastern Sudan.

Africa south of the Sahara remains the last bastion of a living oral tradition, inspite of regions such as Angola and southern Africa where historical disruptions such as the Atlantic slave trade in the seventeenth century, and the Shaka Zulu Mfecane revolutions and mass migrations in the nineteenth century, tended to obliterate memories of previous times. From the last decades of the nineteenth century through the middle of the twentieth century, European colonialism and white settler pressures have been most significant challenges to the survival of the oral tradition in Africa. These and other trials of the oral tradition have been much discussed[14]. Here, we proceed to represent our ideas on an African philosophy of history in the oral tradition[15].

2.3 Philosophy

It is possible to define an African philosophy of history in the oral tradition along the lines proposed for philosophy itself[16]. According to this scheme, an 'implicit philosophy', ethno-philosophy, Negro-African traditional philosophy, or folk philosophy exists side by side with a *philosophia perennis* or analytical philosophy of the type practised in the Western Tradition. Tempels, Griaule, and Kagame are the apostles for the definition of an African philosophy in the first category; while a new crop of African scholars trained in western universities practise the second in many departments of philosophy in African universities or outside the continent[17].

Western philosophers of history already recognize a history of their discipline developing from a period of the practice of a speculative philosophy of history to the current analytical or critical stage[18]. Practitioners of the speculative variety dealt with the subject of history in its content. They directly confronted the course of historical events and attempted to discover meanings and universal rhythms and patterns. While many modem philosophers of history are willing to accord this activity the label of philosophy of history, others such as Collingwood, refuse to do so on the grounds that it is not a second order activity. That is, that a philosophy of history should be concerned with thought about historical thought, and not with the object of the historian's thought. We are in sympathy with a historical view which recognises the possibility of changes, even transformations, in the shape and concerns of disciplines. We note that Collingwood did, indeed, recognise such shifts in the development of philosophy, which he believed derived from the subject at the centre of society's interests. Accordingly, the change from a philosophy based on science, theology, and language to a philosophy of history suggested to him a position of centrality for history in the interests of western society. Since Collingwood, new schools of philosophy have arisen to redefine philosophy of history, including, recently, the philosophy of narrativity, placing emphasis on the autonomy of the historical text[19].

The history of western philosophy of history suggests that a wide definition should be given to the territory of an African philosophy of history. It should include what is 'implicit' in institutions, customs, practices, structures, and ethnology in general. In particular, it must derive its validity from what is expressed in language, and oral texts. The project for a definition of an African philosophy of history is, therefore, a search for African ideas or wisdom encapsulated in history and experience. In such a project, it would be necessary to search as much as possible of what Mudimbe has termed 'the primordial African discourse in its variety and multiplicity'[20].

The variety and multiplicity of African cultures and knowledge enforces a regional approach. We use texts and examples from a restricted area of the Niger Delta region of Nigeria, with a few supporting materials from other regions of Nigeria and West Africa. This strategy falls in line with the successful practice of Tempels, Griaule, and Kagame in providing evidence of African ethno-philosophy or folk philosophy in chosen regions of Africa among specific groups. Inspite of the obvious difficulties of generalising from a small region of Africa to the whole, the demonstration of a specific system of philosophical ideas about history within the corpus of one oral tradition should be relevant to the discussion of the possibilities of an African philosophy of history in general.

The Evidence of Ethnology

The world-view of some Niger Delta communities is basically historical. Their systems of belief contain within them entities conceived in historical terms as the ground on which the identity of the community is established. The earth is, for example, a common object of worship or veneration among

African peoples. The Igbo of southeastern Nigeria, bordering the Eastern Niger Delta, conceive of Earth as a dominating female spirit: Ala, Ali, Ana or Ani. In the Niger Delta, the earth-spirit resides specifically in 'the settled earth', *Amakiri (ama*=city, *kiri*=earth). Here it is the spirit of the earth on which the city is founded that is venerated, not earth in general. City-earth, then, is a historical entity bound up with the foundation and fortunes of the community in a continuing relationship.

In the Nembe area of the Eastern Niger Delta, each established community identifies a spot marked by a life tree, *iginiga (Neubouldia laevis)* marking 'the place of creation' *suotugu*. This spot is identified with a spirit or principle of creation or destiny, not in general terms, but specifically for the historical community or city in which the *suotugu* is sited. The spirit is, accordingly, named *ama-teme-suo (ama*=city, *teme*=create, *suo*=spirit or destiny), 'city-creating spirit/destiny'. It may be noted that other historically conceived spirit beings are recognised in Niger Delta belief systems: the chief of them being *ama-nyana-oru (ama*=city, *nyana*=own, *oru*=spirit or god), tutelary deity. The *ama-nyana-oru* was the most visible object of worship in Niger Delta communities, and features prominently in the historical traditions, virtually as participant in decisions and historical events. There is, of course, no conflict between the principles of *ama-teme-suo* and *ama-nyana-oru*. If a hierarchy has to be established, *ama-teme-suo* as creating-destiny must be considered prior and superior to *ama-nyana-oru*, as guardian or god overseeing the affairs of a created community. The priority of *ama-teme-suo* appears to be established through the use of *ama-teme-suo kule*, the drum praise poem of *ama-teme-suo*, as the anthem or identifying slogan of the cornmunity[21].

These ideas suggest an approach to history which did not exclude spiritual entities or beings from the sphere of human activities, and therefore, of history. It was not, normally, the gods deciding the direction or outcome of events, but rather assisting or participating in them. It was in this sense that dead ancestors were venerated as continuing their role in history from the spirit world into which they had been translated. Indeed, some of the *ama-nyana-oru* may be interpreted as heroes of the community deified after their death[22]. It was this idea of the continuing relevance of the dead in the historical process that underpinned the creation of monuments and ritual institutions in the names of founders of lineages or war-canoe house chieftaincies (*wari* or houses), and kings. Thus structures were erected over the graves of such ancestors, known as *okpu* among the Nembe, which served as shrines for the pouring of libations and the performance of other ritual acts, but also as museums for the preservation of memorabilia, regalia etc. as well as for meetings of the lineage or group. Some communities of the Eastern Niger Delta went beyond the erection of structures over the graves of ancestors to the creation of artistic representations of the essences of particular ancestors. The Kalabari made wooden sculptural figures, *duein fubara (duein*=the dead, *fubara*=forehead or face), faces or foreheads of the dead[23]. The Okrika represented their dead ancestors in fired clay pottery, named *okpo*[24].

The representation of individual ancestors was a step beyond the erection of buildings which became communal monuments and museums for the history of the group through time. However, the Niger Delta *duein fubara* and *okpo* did not attempt a realistic recording of the physical features of the ancestor. Rather, they aimed at a general historical representation of his character and achievements. The figures, accordingly, were stylized humans bearing symbols which the community could read as historical documents.

Beyond the hierarchy of individually recognized ancestors lay the group of ancestors from a period of history too remote to distinguish as historical individual figures. In Nembe, a ritual square was designated 'place of the great ancestors', *opu-gbololo-ongu-tugu (opu*=great, *gbololoongu*=ancestors, *tugu*=place). This designation is, of course, a clear indication of a historiographical admission of the limits of the ability of the oral tradition to remember the remote past or to recover full knowledge of it.

The ethnological record of Eastern Niger Delta communities, then, had historiographical ideas embedded in the world-view of gods and ancestors, represented in material structures and artistic symbols, and built into their social and political institutions such as the war-canoe house. Festivals succeed in bringing together many elements. The *idu* festival for example, is an apparent historical re-enactment festival celebrated in honour of the supreme being or creator spirit on the platform of the *amanyana oru* among the Nembe people[25].

The performances combine theatre, the affirmation of historical solidarity of lineages, of economic interest groups or professional guilds, the celebration and display of the mythical foundations of the society in ritual, dance, and song. The historiography depicted in the festival is, therefore, both visual art and performing art, religion, and social activity. It eventually impinges on the category of text in the linguistic expression of myth, belief and history in songs, prayers and other ritual utterances.

We may note that the religious festival is not the only area where African communities enact their history in the process of doing many other things. One other notable activity is the sometimes purely, or mainly, artistic activity of the mask or masquerade. In the Eastern Niger Delta, it is a specialised and elite domain, or developed to be that, by the nineteenth century[26]. The Ekine, Owu Ogbo or Sekiapu Society in many Eastern Niger Delta communities became a badge of cultural citizenship, knowledge, and of artistic talent. Political leaders took membership in it, and endowed it with authority to exercise discipline over citizens in certain matters. But for our specific purpose, the most important aspect of Ekine or Sekiapu activity was the display of knowledge of the drum praise poetry, *kule*, during mask dances in the central city square. Ekine or the mask dancing society became, in this way, the principal custodian of this variety of historical fixed text.

Ethnology in these cases represent historiography in concrete, visible signs, suggesting both the relevance of history to society and individuals as art, social ideology, symbols of identity, and the solidarity of groups. Ethnology also provides the context of the texts which articulate the historiography and its principles in a more explicit form.

The Evidence of the Text

African historical texts come in many forms. The formal narrative traditions constitute the largest and best known variety. Most commentators on the oral tradition refer to this category of the text or testimony. Jan Vansina made a great advance for African historiography when he established oral traditions as valid historical documents or testimonies, and later, as history[27]. That is, that the formal traditions recited, told, or performed by informants are, in fact, histories or reconstructions of the past in accordance with local canons of historiography. What texts, then, can we identify as philosophical or second order thoughts on the local historiography? We wish to present proverbs as the best candidate for this role. However, proverbs, like other categories of texts in the oral tradition, perform the role both of documents and of interpretations of, and comments on, historical events and actions.

In the specific case of the Nembe from whom examples are predominantly used for this analysis, all the various forms of oral texts also exhibit the dual functions of document and historical comment to varying degrees. The formal narrative traditions, because of their extreme flexibility, are the ones recognized in the culture as history *par excellence*. They bear the generic name of *egberi*, 'story', along with folktales or fiction. However, the formal historical account is *elemu-kura egberi* (meaning, stories about the past). What is intended primarily as fictional accounts are termed *lugu egberi* (stories of fable-land). However, the demarcation is not always precise, and it is thought necessary in recounting *lugu* (fables, tales), to specify a location or definition of dimension. Thus, after the opening announcements of an *egberi* session, the raconteur states for each narrative whether the account is located in *ama lugu-ama* (city of fable-land), *ama Oba-ama* (in the city of the Oba of Benin), *ama-duei-ama* (in the city of the dead), *ama-nama-ama* (in the city of animals), *ama-owu-ama* (in the city of water spirits) etc. Accordingly, the location of an *egberi* in a real geographical environment is the clearest means of making it an account of human history, inspite of the additional problems arising from the possibilities of gods and the dead participating in it.

Other forms of oral traditional text in Nembe are mainly fixed texts and are not normally considered historical accounts even when they comment on history or document history. However, they are cited to validate or refute formal narrative accounts. The proverb, *kabu*, used as the major text here, is perhaps, the most prolific. But the riddle, *duu* is also capable of use[28]. Songs, *numo*, are, of course, both texts and commentaries[29], but the drum praise poem, *kule*, distills an essence from history and creates it into a slogan for action in the present and an inspiration for the future[30]. Inspite of the absence of clear boundaries between the various categories of text, the formal traditional narrative is assumed to represent oral traditional historiography, and the proverb text as a philosophical commentary on it[31].

The discussion deals with the following issues of historiography in the oral tradition, namely, problems and standards of transmission ; the judgment of truth and criteria by which to determine its presence or absence; the necessity for rigour in the historical discourse, and its rewards; the meaning of time and of chronology; the value of historical knowledge and the case for the relevance of history.

(i)   **Transmission: Informants / Historians**

To the question, who is best qualified to be an informant on the past? The proverbial evidence is apparently overwhelming in favour of the old against youth:

1.   *Noin nẹngia / Bẹrẹ nẹngia*
       More days / More wisdom (historical knowledge).[32]

2.   *Okosibo kirigho timite eriye / Togu soutieka erigha.*
       What an old man sees seated / A youth does not see standing.[33]

3.   *Watakiri vulizo nda olu / Ikpe wusime a anya.*
       If a child lifts up his father, / The wrapper will cover his eyes.[34]

4.   *Agbara watakiri vugwu risi a / Raawhu nekwe mba.*
       A god whose chief priest is a child / Can easily get out of hand[35].

5. *Okne atitikpo etekne / Nnwo atiti nwee manya riagbo.*
    However big the male lizard is, / The wall-gecko drinks the wine as the senior[36].

Text 1 is as explicit as a comment can be, that the old are the best qualified to act as historians because they have greater experience and have had greater opportunity to learn to be wise. There is a clear equation of history with experience and wisdom. Text 2 extends the metaphor to the ability for discrimination over matters in the present, and, possibly, the ability to project into the future. The elder sees farther because of the greater range of hindsight available to him. The physical advantage of added height gained by standing makes no difference since understanding comes not simply through sight, but through past experience transformed into wisdom. Texts 4 and 5 confirm a preference for age as the determinant of efficiency and effectiveness, and in the award of rewards or status in society. Text 3 states that should a youth presume to challenge an elder to a wrestling contest, he might succeed in lifting him, but cannot throw the elder. The elder's wrapper would cover the youth's eyes and frustrate his efforts.

The case for the elder as the true historian appears open and closed, against practical experience of ignorant elders. At least one text has been recorded among the Itsekiri of the Western Niger Delta on the possibility, indeed, the existence, of ignorant elders:

6. *The spirits do not kill an old man for not knowing the history of his time*[37].

This exception saves the African discourse from the charge of naiveté and over-simplification. The preference for age is founded on the view of the nature of history as experience, but not all old men and women gain from the opportunities they have had. However, the youth are not encouraged to challenge the elders to tests of knowledge or power, but to cultivate the spirit of humility, and learn from the experience of the elders, so that they do not become ignorant elders in their time.

(ii) **Truth and Falsehood**

The evidence of the proverb commentary is clear that African communities placed great store on the reliability of accounts. According to Ojoade, 'some of the most memorable Birom proverbs pay tribute to the great importance the people place in truth and justice'[38]. He cites the following:

7. *Truth never finishes*

8. *Truth never rots*

9. *Truth never rusts*

10. *Truth is worth more than money*

11. *Lies have their end, but truth lives for ever*

Truth had to be such a prized commodity because of the awareness of errors and falsehood. There was no complacency or lack of vigilance against falsification by design or error or ignorance.

The Kuteb of Central Nigeria warned against errors even of the best qualified authorities in the words of the following proverb:

12.   *Even a four-legged horse stumbles and falls*[39].

How then can we seek truth? The Ikwerre of the Niger Delta caution against judgments based on appearances:

13.   *Nsni be ji nonu nhne / O hnaa nu izemini*
      The keen ear / Is not as big as an umbrella.

14.   *Kpa anya hna nu risi / Buo kpa o hnu n'osno.*
      A large eye / Does not mean keen vision[40].

Two criteria for seeking truth are suggested. First, the force of direct eye-witness testimony:

15.   *He who sees does not err* (Kikuyu)[41].

16.   *If an apopokiri (fish) from the bottom of the river says that the crocodile is sick, it will not be doubted.* (Ashanti)[42].

Such an apparent totality of acceptance of eye-witness testimony obviously runs counter to commonsense experience of deliberate falsehood or of mistakes of observation or other sources of error. The oral tradition recognized such situations and recommended confirmation by a second witness as a practical solution:

17.   I have seen the one who stole the hen; I don't tell because I am alone. (Sena)[43].

18.   Ḅarịgha nama / Korogha
      An animal does not fall / Without a second shot[44].

Because of the difficulties in the definition of truth arising from human weakness, appearance, and corroboration, further ways were required to distinguish truth from falsehood. One such means was a judgement of the probability of the account or claim from 'the nature of things'. If a statement is manifestly improbable from the nature of things in the real world of experience, there was no compulsion to accept it as true:

19.   Wopnara maa nda a, / Ke olu si anwa nyakaru rekpa esau.
      The eldest son does not know his father, / Yet the youngest one claims to have carried seven bags for him[45].

20.   M gbagbulema eni bu ezi oka, / M vuyalema ya apna bu aghalaghala.
      'I have killed an elephant' could be true / 'I have carried it to the road' must be false.[46].

The truth of the claims in the two cases above is open to doubt, indeed, disbelief, because they so clearly go against the logic of experience and probability. Disbelief is unavoidable especially in the conditions implied by text 19, of a family where the father died when the eldest son was too young to recollect his features, and in text 20 where no assistance was available to the hunter. We note also the general philosophy of truth propounded by Wiredu from Akan linguistic expression, as a moral concept meaning, that which 'is so'[47].

(iii) **Diligence, Rigour**

The problems imposed by the effort to arrive at objective truth require rigour in the assessment of accounts. Text 18 suggesting a second shot at game may be interpreted both as a requirement for the corroboration of testimony as well as for the need for a second opinion, taking more than one look below the surface. Other texts are more explicit in recommending close study of history in detail. The historian is likened to the African python with its presumed keenness of sight, and instructed to develop a capacity to listen to the footfall of the ant:

21. *I bnotee nsni n'ali / I joonu ikiri ochi ndna.*
     If you keep your ear close to the ground / You will hear the footsteps of the ant[48].

22. *Tọrụma kirima kirima / Tọrụma kirima kirima.*
     Eyes to the ground / Eyes to the ground[49].

It is clear from texts 21 and 22 that the rigour expected of the historian embraces all the faculties and senses of eye and ear.

Text 21 poses the rewards of such diligence to be the possession of above ordinary knowledge and experience.

(iv)   **Time**

The oral tradition recognises the passage of time and change as the essence of history, the primacy of the present for the validation of the past, and the necessity for taking account of the future in present planning and action, and even a notion of eternity. Concerning the passage of time and the wear and tear that is the consequence and evidence of it, the Ikwerre say:

23.   *Awha be kparu nkita / Buo awha o kaa.*
       The year a basket is made Is not the year it wears out.[50]

A Nembe text bears testimony to a concern for the relevance of accounts of the past to present realities. What is the possible relationship between our accounts of the past and our present concerns and circumstances? The text suggests that the historian's account corresponds to current 'seasons' and 'tides':

24.   *Egberigbabọ / Dịn mindi gbagha.*
       A story teller / Does not tell of a different tide / season.

Text 24 suggests that the historian would validate his account on current 'tides' or situations, with the possibility that the present 'tide' might be the basis for the particular account of the past because of its relevance.

What then is the past? Is it merely a creation of the present in its own image? The answer would appear to be provided by the next text, providing a past that forms the base and ground, the foundation and origin of present reality:

25.   Kiri pagaterẹ / Tịn paga.
      The earth came into being / Before the trees[51].

The future is a more difficult concept since it is not yet known, unlike the past that had been experienced but was no more. The Ikwerre text defines the future as a time to be expected and planned for:

26.   Dikne choru be bisi anwa evulu n'anwu, / O bita antnuru joomuyanu a evulu nga o zi budnu.
      A man who wants a ram slaughtered at his graveside / Should keep a ewe to produce the ram while he is alive[52].

If the future is not yet and has to be imagined in expectation, is it possible to obtain reliable knowledge of it? The specific case of text 26 suggests the possibility of using hindsight of past experience to plan in the present to achieve foresight. However, such foresight of the future must remain imperfect:

27.   Even a bird with a long neck cannot see the future (Kanuri)[53].

Indeed, the future is beyond sight and full knowledge. If so, can one relate to eternity in human terms? In the words of the Nupe text, eternity can only be discussed in relation to God:

28.   *God will out-live eternity. (Nupe)*[54].

We note that the African oral tradition does not place emphasis on the measurement of time, or even on the calculation of an exact chronology. In addition, although the three human dimensions of time, namely, the past, present, and future are well defined, there is no strict demarcation. The various dimensions of time flow into each other in imagination.

It is noteworthy that St Augustine, the African Bishop of Hippo (354–430 A.D) formulated a philosophy of time within the western tradition with obvious similarities to the ideas of the African oral tradition. First, St Augustine ruled out the possibility of exact measurement of time, since the present which alone has reality, does not occupy space, and is always in the process of changing into the past and passing out of existence, while the future which had no existence was constantly becoming manifest as the present.

Accordingly to St Augustine, time is only conceivable on the basis of the impression it makes on the mind in the present as memory (the past), intuition (the present) and expectation (the future)[55]. Like the Nupe, St Augustine secured all time, that is, eternity, in God, since God preceded all times, and created all times.

It is instructive to bring together some of the images presented in the oral texts as representations of time. In text 25 we have the stability and reality of the earth on which life in the form of trees come into being. There is reality and stability but also continuity and change. Second, text 2 presents the seated elder, secure on the solid earth, the standing youth representing an effort of the present to penetrate the future. However, text 27 presents an even more elevated image than the standing youth, namely, a flying bird 'with a long neck'. Even these levels of physical elevation and extension are insufficient to achieve a vision of the future.

These texts confirm that time has remained one of the most difficult problems for the African oral tradition.

(v)   **The Value of Historical Knowledge**

The texts are more anxious to warn against the negative consequences of ignorance than recount the positive benefits of knowledge:

29.   *Ama nimighabọ / Ḍubu ọgọnọ.*
      A stranger in town / Walks over hallowed graves[56].

30.   *Boyo nimighabọ / Nọndọ.*
      One ignorant of his origins / Is nondo (non-human)[57].

31.   *Rizo nwee nye znikwa a ya ezni / Niiznu sno n'abna ali.*

      The fly who has no adviser / Will follow the corpse into the grave[58].

Text 29 suggests that knowledge of local history is a necessary part of being a member of a community. It is only a stranger who would also be assumed to be ignorant. The consequence and evidence of such ignorance is, the desecration of taboos, such as walking over graves. Thus knowledge equips the individual to act in accordance with customs, ignorance lays one open to error.

The consequence of ignorance, according to text 30, can be as severe as loss of humanity. Absence of history, or the knowledge of it, could lead to loss of humanity itself, since the creature, *nondo,* is a mythical ape-like being reported in tales as a denizen of the mangrove forests in the Niger Delta. This text shows the enormity of the offence committed against African peoples by colonial historians who denied Africa a history. It was a position which amounted to taking away from Africans their place in the family of human-kind.

Text 31 lays on the individual the responsibility to obtain from those with the necessary experience, knowledge of things. Failure could lead to drastic consequences, such as loss of life.

In all three cases, the positive opposite of the cases presented is historical knowledge possessed and used to perform creditably in society, secure in an identity as a responsible human person, confident in the wisdom and experience of the elders.

The following text presents the case for knowledge in a direct form:

32. *Anya diali / Bu anya eke.*
     The son of the soil / Has the python's keen eye[59].

'The son of the soil' is the man who is not 'a stranger' (cf. text 29), who knows his origins, unlike the fellow in text 30, and has taken care to discover and acquire knowledge from those qualified to impart it. The consequence is, that he sees clearly and steadily, like the python. The African python referred to in text 32 is unlikely to be acknowledged keen-sighted by zoologists, but its record of success in securing prey is sufficient evidence in support of the thesis of the text, that experience pays.

Finally, a number of texts dealing with miscellaneous issues related to historical knowledge:

33. *Avnuru ji ize neepne olu / Be magwu isisi lu ilu.*
     The family that climb with their teeth / Know the bitter trees[60].

34. *Imeni peibo biobara ; / Imgba peibo biobaragha.*
     He who eats the flesh forgets; / Who eats the bone does not[61].

35. *Kala qwqma egberi naa / Egberi sun.*
     A story known to children / Becomes a foolish story[62].

36. *Ọwọma kalaị timi yọ ghọ / Segi furo pugha.*
    A crocodile's stomach / Is not opened before children.[63]

37. *Nama nyingi mọndị eteli / Yaị ka mọndị eteli.*
    The path a mother-animal takes / Is the path the baby-animal takes[64].

38. *Wan dibọ / Bịla iregha.*
    A child born of the duiker / Does not name the elephant in parental fondness[65].

39. *Nwii a naa sua loo te / A son who did not get to know his father. (Khana)*[66].

The pair of texts 33 and 34 deal with the problem of the relative instructive value of bitter and pleasant experiences, and the relative chances of their being remembered. Does human memory give priority to pleasant experiences or to the unpleasant? Text 34 contends that pleasant experiences are forgotten before the unpleasant. Text 33 contends that unpleasant experiences provide wisdom of a sort, presumably what to avoid. On the other hand, does oral tradition select its material in such a way that a superior genealogy or prouder progenitors than one's natural ancestors are recounted? Text 38 says 'No', apparently as a prescriptive principle rather than as a statement of practice.

The texts 35 and 36 relate to the possibility or necessity for keeping certain historical information secret. Both texts accept the necessity for keeping categories of information secret. The types of traditions are not specified, but the class of persons from whom information may be kept secret is specified: the children, the young.

Texts 37, 38, 39, all explore aspects of the relationship between the young and their parents in the matter of the transmission of experience. Text 37 assumes that the young will follow the footsteps of their parents as a matter of course. The text may, in fact, be equally interpreted as a reference to heredity as to the transmission of experience. However, text 39 specifies knowledge passed from father to son, since the context of this Khana expression is recorded to apply to 'a son who shows gross ignorance of community traditions or customs'. Clearly then, the oral tradition of historiography was one in which parents were expected to instruct their young in community history. This implied the reciprocal responsibility of each individual to take the steps necessary to acquire historical knowledge of family and community. How then, does one acquire the knowledge to become a competent citizen? Through 'imitation', which neatly summarizes the multiple means by which oral historiography is transmitted and absorbed through all the senses. One 'imitates' parents in the family, elders in the community, and 'neighbours' with proven practical abilities:

40. *Igbede bukwu snonce ibne gbaa mono / Any young palm-fruit that does not imitate its neighbours cannot produce oil*[67].

This summary sample of proverb texts is sufficient to indicate the existence of thoughtful discourse on historical experience in African oral traditions. It does not represent the totality of philosophical expression among Africans even on the topics discussed. Other forms of tradition texts may be exploited, and the expressed thoughts of living traditionalists can also be explored through discussion with them. Eventually, of course, modern African philosophers of history will emerge to articulate thoughts springing from the African environment and the African experience.

2.4 Practice

The history of the oral tradition in antiquity in Ancient Egypt and northern Africa has its modern parallel in Africa south of the Sahara. Here the oral tradition was challenged by the introduction of the Islamic tradition from about the eleventh century from North Africa and Afroasia across the Sahara, and the intrusion of the Western tradition from about the fifteenth century along the Atlantic and Indian ocean coasts. Both traditions penetrated the oral tradition mainly through religious conversion and education, although there was Arab settlement in the Eastern Sudan, the Horn of Africa and the East African coast and European settlement in South Africa. The converts to Islam and Christianity became the first to adopt the written traditions of their new faiths. In every case, however, the converts took steps to transcribe the oral tradition into writing.

The Islamic tradition produced the first historians transcribing oral traditions in the form of chronicles and histories, *tarikh*, in Arabic writing from the mosques and universities of Timbuktu and other cities of the Western and Central Sudan from the sixteenth to the seventeenth centuries.

The beginning of African historical writing in Western scripts came towards the end of the eighteenth century, but mostly from the end of the nineteenth century. This coincided with the intensification of Christian missionary enterprise and the onset of European imperialism and colonial rule. The Christian missionaries as the first agents of western education, encouraged members of their congregations to transcribe the oral tradition, sometimes in local languages. Indeed, some of the new historians were the first generation of African clergymen. From the early twentieth century, African political activists also began to challenge the imperialist propaganda denying Africa a history by producing polemic texts confronting it[68]. It was from the 1950s that the first African academic historians trained in western universities began to operate in the western tradition and to acknowledge the legitimacy of the oral tradition, and to make efforts to record and use it in a systematic manner.

A recent symposium in Lagos brought together the work and thought of African scholars in many disciplines with and on the oral tradition.[69] A substantial amount of work continues to be done on the continent in the collection and analysis of oral texts for the reconstruction of community histories and for other purposes. Senegalese historians report projects for the collection of detailed village traditions over regions; Nigerian scholars reported the use of oral traditions for archaeology and the history of technology, and the increasing awareness of oral traditions by government agencies in the cultural domain. The literary scholars already show a tendency to take theoretical directions in the definition and interpretation of oral traditions independent of the directions favoured by the historians. We note that the African oral tradition has been durable also in the Diaspora across the Atlantic in the hostile environments of slave society and of subsequent histories of struggle in North, Central, and South America[70].

The history of the transformations and uses to which the oral tradition was put therefore become a part of the acoount of the Islamic and western written traditions which sprang up from the African environment as outlined in the succeeding chapters.

CHAPTER 3

The Internal Written Tradition

If an apopokiri (fish) from the bottom of the river / Says that the crocodile is sick, / It will not be doubted.
Ashanti proverb, Ghana. (Ojoade, 19818: 31).

3.1 Introduction

It is necessary to remember that there was a very early tradition of writing in Africa prior to the arrival of the written historiographical traditions of Islam and of the West. The pioneer Egyptian invention of writing naturally provides the centre of a history of the African written tradition, but we must give attention also to other forms of communication systems in other parts of Africa from ancient times through the nineteenth century.

Under written tradition therefore, we will discuss all forms of linguistic, syllabic, functional, symbolic or sign communication systems. Some of the systems may be very distant from the alphabetic systems of the West, but still need to be investigated for their contribution to the mnemonics of historical consciousness in the communities where they operated. Indeed, it is likely that many of the systems, if not all, operated tandem with the oral tradition, in complementary symbiotic relationship.

3.2 The Experience of Egypt

The experience of Egypt constitutes a crucial link in the history of historiography for Africa as for the rest of the world, providing as it does, the first example of the move away from the oral tradition, as well as the accommodation of a written tradition to the oral tradition. Accordingly, the discussion of the Egyptian experience will take a great part of this chapter, under the following sub-sections:

(i) an outline history of ancient Egypt, to provide a background to the discussion,
(ii) an account of the orientation of Egypt to the rest of Africa, its ideas about Africa, and of the period of a southern Nubian or Ethiopian dynasty,
(iii) the impact, status and the mechanics of writing and the production of historical documents and other texts by scribes and the literati;
(iv) the nature and sources of ideas of history, to be followed by a discussion of the major categories;
(v) mythology;
(vi) calendars and chronology;
(vii) documents—king-lists, annals, daybooks;
(viii) Manetho, and other historians of Egypt before and after him;
(ix) the contribution of Egyptian literature in general to the generation of ideas or a philosophy of history.

(i)   *Outline History*

The work of prehistorians from many lands from the nineteenth century to recent times has revealed the outline of continuous development of the physical features of the Nile Valley through the geological ages of the Miocene, Pliocene, to the Pleistocene. Similar advances have been made in the study of the cultural sequences through a continuum from the Paleolithic or Stone Ages to the Neolithic when copper began to be used alongside flint. The study of burials, pottery, ivory, basketry and other artifacts have established the "essentially African" grounding of these early proto- or pre-dynastic periods which provide the roots for the civilization of the Egypt of the Pharaohs, conventionally divided into Dynasties after Manetho[1]. The history of the land of the Nile moved from these early beginnings in Africa in contact with the neighbouring Asian lands of Mesopotamia, Sumeria, Babylonia and others to make the great leaps of the Dynastic periods, including the invention of writing, among others, creating thereby a unique Afroasiatic civilization.

To the ancient Egyptians, their land was *Keme*, "the Black Land", from the black mud of the Nile inundations, providing a justification for its description by Herodotus as the gift of the Nile. In contrast, the dry desert land was *Dashre*, "the Red Land". Indeed, Egypt was defined by the configuration it received from the geography of the Nile valley, its Delta, and the rising highlands that etched it from the deserts to east and west. The long narrow valley from the First Cataract from Aswan between the islands of Elephantine and Philae or

Upper Egypt, was differentiated from the Delta, or Lower Egypt. Egypt thus became the nation of "the Two Lands", the southern Upper Egypt from which the only source of water and the sustenance of agriculture and life came, and the northern Delta or Lower Egypt to which the Nile flowed: the one oriented mainly to the continent of Africa, and the other also to the Mediterranean and Asia.

The history of ancient Egypt may be summarized under the thirty or thirty one dynasties of the first native historian, Manetho. He took account of the pre-dynastic or Prehistoric Period by postulating two periods of rule by gods and demi-gods (the Greater and Lesser Ennead). Modern scholars have devised broader groupings of rulers to denote periods of unity as kingdoms and periods of disunity as intermediate periods:

Old Kingdom (incorporating Manetho's First to Eighth Dynasties: c.3100–2130 B.C.);
First Intermediate Period (Ninth to Tenth Dynasty, c.2130–2040 B.C.);
Middle Kingdom (Eleventh to the Twelfth Dynasties: c.2130–1786 B.C.); Second Intermediate Period (Thirteenth to seventeenth Dynasties: c.1786- 1567 B.C.);
New Kingdom (Eighteenth to Twentieth Dynasties: c.1567–1085 B.C.);
Third Intermediate Period (Twenty-First to Twenty-Fourth Dynasties: c.1085–715 B.C); and
Late Period (Twenty-Fifth to Thirtieth Dynasties: c.747–343 B.C.)

Inspite of the problems identified in the dynastic system of Manetho, it has remained the basis of Egyptian chronology[2].

The eight kings of the First Dynasty, dated c. 3100–2890 B.C., with their cemeteries in Abydos, represent the period of the earliest unified rule and the emergence of the hieroglyphic script. Netjerikhet of Djoser of the Third Dynasty (c.2686–2613), built the Step Pyramid, Snefru of the Fourth Dynasty (c. 2613–2494 B.C.) built the first true pyramid, and Khufu of the same dynasty the Great Pyramid of Giza, followed by other kings in the same locality. The Fifteenth Dynasty (c.1674–1567 B.C), were the "Desert Kings" or *Hyksos*, kings who entered the Delta, from the east, eventually expelled by the kings of the seventeenth Dynasty (c.1674–1567 B.C.) from Upper Egypt. The New Kingdom is dated from the Eighteenth Dynasty (c.1567–1320 B.C.), beginning a period of expansion into Syria-Palestine and Nubia. A period of decline soon set in, and a succession of foreign dynasties came into existence for example, the Twenty-Second Dynasty (c.945–715 B.C.) "from a northwestern tribe, the Meshwesh"; the Twenty-Fifth Dynasty (c. 747–656 B.C.), from Kush, being the Ethiopian Dynasty of some accounts; the Twenty-Seventh Dynasty or First Persian Period (c. 525–404 B.C.).

The Thirtieth Dynasty ended the period of ancient Egyptian civilization. Thereafter, Alexander the Great of Macedon took over from the Thirty-First Dynasty (343–332 B.C.), to end the Second Persian Period and begin the Greek Period (332–30

B.C), followed by the Roman Period (30 B.C.–305 A.D.), and by the Arab Period. What remained of the ancient Egyptian heritage was embodied in the Coptic language and the culture of the Copts.

(ii)   **Orientation to Africa**

The people of the Nile and its Delta distinguished themselves from all other peoples outside the region beyond the First Cataract. They were the only true "men", *piromis / rome,* all others were "vile", "miserable" foreigners. The Egyptian "gentlemen" clearly distinguished themselves from the Setyu, Asiatics across the Isthmus of Sinai, but also from the neighbouring peoples of Africa[3].

West of the Delta, a Libu tribe was first mentioned in the time of Memeptah (c. 1220 B.C, Nineteenth Dynasty). Two other groups were noted in earlier periods as Tjehnyu and Tjembu. All these African groups of the western desert from the Mediterranean coast to the oasis of Siwa, Bahriya, Farafa, Dakhla, and Kharga came to be known by the collective term of Libyan.

By way of the Red Sea, the Egyptians came into contact with the coast of Africa facing east. This was the land of Pwene or Punt, rich in spices, myrrh, and other exotic products.

Along the course of the Nile, the First Cataract formed a boundary between Upper Egypt and Lower Nubia, but there was continuous movement of the formal borders, and interactions between the peoples along the Nile through the centuries. There were peoples of Berber tongue as well as Nehasyu, Nubians living along the banks, and Medjayu, desert Nubians who came to serve in the Egyptian police. The boundary itself moved beyond the Second Cataract to the fortresses of Semna and Kumma, in the land of Kush or Cush, or Wawae/Wawat, and eventually to el-Kenisa only 350 miles to Khartoum beyond the Fifth Cataract in the time of the warrior kings Thutmose I and II (Eighteenth Dynasty, c.1567–1320 B.C.). This was the Ethiopia of the Greeks and Sudan of the Arabs, all terms indicating the black pigmentation of its inhabitants.

To the Egyptians, it was *Ta-sety* "Land of the Bow", "the Southern Lands", as well as Kush[4], while the Roman term Nubia may have also derived from the Egyptian word for gold, *nbw*. The Egyptians identified various regions and groups with which they did business at different times: the "Land of Yam" south of Wawat, Irjet and Satju in the Sixth Dynasty; and the Medjay and Blemmyes of the Eastern Desert in later periods (possible ancestors of the Beja).

It was, in the main, a history of Egyptian exploitation of the south for its natural and human resources over a period of about five hundred years, closing with about fifty years of Nubian rule of Egypt in the Twenty-Fifth Dynasty (c.747-656 BC). Nubia served as the link between Egypt and Africa south of the First Cataract. Through it Egypt obtained gold, copper, stone, carnelian, diorite, jasper, amethyst, ivory, ebony, incense, oil, throw sticks, ostrich eggs and feathers, lions, antelopes, ostriches, gazelles, giraffes, monkeys, leopards and leopard skins. Egypt also took prisoners, hostages, mercenaries, and slaves from Nubia to serve in its armed and civilian labour forces. Nubia did receive from Egypt material goods such as beer and wine, linen cloth, copper axes and others, but mostly skills and ideas, such as the influences that lead to the creation of the Meroitic script.

The balance sheet of Egyptian-Nubian interaction cannot be fairly drawn until the Meroitic script has been deciphered and the voice of the Southern Lands can be heard along with the Egyptian from its hieroglyphic records. As things stand, only the rulers of the Twenty-Fifth Dynasty: Kashta, Piy (Piye, Piankhi), Shabako, Shabitko, Taharqo and Tanutamani are able to speak through their Egyptian records. Their rule, based at the four centres of Memphis and Thebes in Egypt and Napata and Meroe in Kush (with their pyramids at Kurru and Nuri), is celebrated for its sense of history. They initiated a revival of ancient Egyptian art, but with a new southern element added to it.

(iii)   **Writing**

The earliest hieroglyphic signs appear on stone and pottery of the late Pre-dynastic Period, and on the famous palette of King Narmer, the first Pharaoh of the First Dynasty. The appearance of writing may therefore be dated to c. 3100–3000 B.C.[5] Egyptian traditions ascribe the invention of the hieroglyphs to the divine hand of Thoth, "lord of writing", and its historical origins are unknown. Cuneiform, the script used to write Sumerian and Proto-Elamite in Mesopotamia is estimated to have appeared about a century earlier, but could not have been the direct ancestor of Egyptian hieroglyphics, except through stimulus diffusion. The two systems differ, the Sumerian being syllabic (with both consonants and vowels), while the Egyptian is consonantal (representing only consonants), and "clearly derived from indigenous sources".

Although Egyptian hieroglyphs have not been used to write as many languages as the Sumerian, it had a much longer period of use than any other known system of writing covering a period of about four thousand years. It may have stimulated the development of Cretan and Hittite "hieroglyphs" in the second millennium B.C. It has been identified as the direct ancestor of Protosinaitic and Meroitic. Its claims to a contribution to modem alphabetic writing derives from its influence on the scripts of the Near East, such as Protosinaitic, which provided the stimulus for the Greek alphabetic system.

Four distinct scripts came into being in Egypt: hieroglyphics, hieratic, demotic, and Coptic, resulting from circumstance and history.

Hieroglyphics dated to about 3100 B.C has its last dated example in A.D. 394 at Philae. The term 'hieroglyph', however, derives from the Greek, *ta hieroglyphica,* "the sacred carved letters". It was a mixed system of miniature pictures and alphabets, in which aesthetic, calligraphic, religious, 'sportive', and cryptographic considerations played a part in the form of a text. Thus the script was believed to confer divine power, and was capable of cryptographic elaboration to over 6,000 hieroglyphs, although the standard number did not exceed 1,000 , and was less than 700 in Middle Egyptian.

Hieroglyphics then, was the sacred original script of ancient Egypt used for prestigious religious and monumental inscription to ensure that the lives and names of the personages so inscribed would endure for ever. Writing was, in effect, an act of inscription on the rolls of history.

Hieratic was a simplification of the hieroglyphic for writing on rolls, papyrus, pottery, stone (ostraca) with black and red ink for day-to-day business, administration, literary, scientific, and religious writing. Although used from the earliest periods of writing, the Fourth Dynasty provides the largest samples of it, but it became a purely religious script from the Late Period (c. 600 B.C.), thus its name *hieratika* , "priestly", in Greek.

Hieratic differed from hieroglyphics by being written invariably right to left. From the Middle Kingdom, hieratic began to be written in horizontal lines rather than in columns. It was supplanted by demotic in the Twenty-Sixth Dynasty.

Demotic, *sh s t,* "the writing of letters" in Egyptian, and *demotika,* "popular (script)", in Greek, was the typical day-to-day script for writing on papyri and ostraca in horizontal lines with rightward orientation. It had peculiar and independent cursive character and increasingly moved outside everyday business into literature and even monuments, and thus its appearance on the Rosetta Stone in the Ptolemaic

Period alongside hieroglyphics and Greek. Its latest use is 450 A.D at Philae.

Coptic came into use in the Roman period as signifying the script used by the *Copts, Aiguptios,* in Greek, and *gubti,* in Arabic. Coptic represented a departure from the old scripts of Egypt, being an effort to write the Egyptian language in Greek alphabets. Accordingly, it borrowed Greek alphabets for sounds available in that script, and adapted demotic signs for sounds not available in the Greek.

Coptic became the preserve of the Christian monasteries from whose libraries the majority of texts were derived that assisted in the decipherment of hieroglyphics and the study of ancient Egyptian by modem Egyptologists. Coptic documents appear on papyri, ostraca, wooden tablets, parchment, paper, and on monuments. It was written from left to right and its scribes produced codex documents in the Greek tradition, and has remained alive in the sacred context of the Coptic Church of Egypt.

What was the state of literacy in ancient Egypt? Literacy in hieroglyphics could not have been high, but would have increased in the Greek and Roman Periods with the popular scripts such as Coptic, although the priests apparently made the ancient scripts deliberately elaborate to keep them secret. A literate rate of 1 per cent in the Pharaohnic Period and 1 0 per cent in the Graeco -Roman Period has been suggested.[6] Writing skills were required by royalty and public officials in the military, civil administration, and in religion, and above all, by the professional scribe.

Scribal skills were acquired at elementary schools, and advanced skills acquired in apprenticeship from masters and on the job. The evidence of school texts of classical literature attests to the existence of formal training, while extant texts extol the work of the scribe as "pleasant and wealth-abounding".

It is significant that writing came into being ready-made from the beginnings of Egyptian society. The language is, as a result, the one with the longest documented history in the world, over about 4,000 years. The fact that vowels began to be written only in Coptic means that the exact forms in which the words were vocalized is uncertain; but the system is relatively unambiguous in its meaning. In addition, Egyptian papyrus made incalculable contributions to the development of Greek literature and civilization. In the view of one scholar, "without it Greek spiritual life would have been much poorer and more primitive"[7]. It served as the viable medium for the production of books before parchment and eventually paper by the Chinese about 100 A.D.

These developments had momentous consequences for the practice of history, but the limitation of literacy to a small elite meant that the base of the practice remained in the oral tradition.

(iv)   **Nature of Historical Sources**

The earliest historical records of the Dynastic Period reflect the oral tradition of the Pre-Dynastic Egypt of Upper and Lower Egypt. Indeed, the confinement of literacy to a small elite ensured that the oral tradition remained in good health, and the written tradition remained, in part, a transcription of the oral tradition.

The written documentation, then, resembled categories of the oral tradition, but also related to artistic representation, and often accompanied works of art.

In terms of genres, lists were predominant: king-lists, lists of priests, and geanalogies. These developed into the royal annals, and day-books.[8] Egyptian historical efforts included biographical entries on kings and great or wise men, and voluminous archives of administrative, legal, business, literary, scientific, medical and other material was produced that is only inadequately represented by what has survived.

The oldest specimens have come down in stone monuments, slabs, stelae, mace heads, palettes, even rock inscriptions. The stone slab seven feet and two feet high, of which the Palermo Stone formed a part, represents a list of kings made in the Fifth or Sixth Dynasty partly from the oral tradition, going back to very early times. Similarly, a Memphite genealogy of priests carved on white lime-stone slab extends from the Twenty- Second or Libyan Dynasty to the beginning of the Eleventh Dynasty, a period of over a thousand years or sixty generations. The "King Scorpion" ceremonial mace head of limestone from Hierapolis represents scenes interpreted as the conquest of Lower Egypt by an early ruler of Upper Egypt. This interpretation is confirmed by the great dark-green slate palette of King Narmer (Menes?), showing this first king of united Egypt "about to brain a kneeling captive". There is a rock stele of King Shekhemkhet of the Third Dynasty in Sinai, and records of events or activities of historical significance to the Egyptians were also made on small tablets of stone, ivory, or wood.

The full flowering of historical documentation on stone came from the time of the first Step Pyramid of Netjerikhet (Djoser), first king of the Third Dynasty, through the emergence of the true pyramid in the Fourth Dynasty in the reigns of Snefru and Khufu. The stone structures of tombs and temples provided wall space for the inscription of historical messages for visitors and for posterity. Royal tombs provided an example for private citizens with the means or royal patronage to leave memorials of their achievements. Autobiographical data, legal documents, treaties, accounts of public works and religious observances were recorded in these places.

The pyramid provides the most visible monument to the Egyptian striving for immortality. It was a mountain of stone to prevent the desecration, destruction or removal of the embalmed body of the king or noble; but eventually, to preserve his memory for ever. In terms of the range of recording, however, the papyrus and other handier material, such as leather, provided a more suitable medium, especially for the hieratic and demotic cursive scripts. The Turin Papyrus of Kings (the Turin Canon) recorded in the Nineteenth Dynasty, listing gods, demi-gods, and more than 300 kings from the Old Kingdom to the end of the Second Intermediate Period, is probably the most remarkable example of these documents. After that, we have to await the formal history of Manetho, the priest, in the Greek tradition, but from indigenous Egyptian traditions and records.

The Egyptian sense of history is revealed in the efforts they made to copy records and preserve them over centuries and millennia, through times of war, invasions, and civil disturbance. In the New Kingdom, for example, deliberate efforts were made to copy styles of architecture and art of the Old Kingdom, restore temples, and to copy old documents from papyri to stone. We can do no better than cite the case of the Memphite theology copied by King Shabako (c.716–701 B.C.) of the Twenty-Fifth or Ethiopian Dynasty onto a thick slab of black granite. The king recounts his work and motives:

> "His majesty wrote this document anew in the house of his father Ptah. His majesty had discovered it as a work of the forefathers which had been eaten of worms and was not [completely] legible from beginning to end. Therefore his majesty wrote it anew, so that it is more beautiful than it was before, in order that his name might endure and his monument be fixed in the house of his father Ptah forever."[9]

(v)   **Mythology**

Egyptian mythology represented a synthesis of the speculative thought and the experience of communities about nature, the environment, and about divinity, humanity, and life (and therefore, about history).[10] This species of historical thought was crystallized at various centres of religious and state activities in the course of Egyptian history.

The earliest creation myths were those of On, or Heliopolis to the Greeks. According to the Heliopolitan Theology, in the beginning was the uncreated primordial ocean, Nuu/Nun *(Nw/ Nwn)*. Out of Nun emerged the sun-god, Atum, from whose spittle or semen were created Shu, god of air/atmosphere and his wife Tefenet, who gave birth to Geb, earth-god, and Nut, sky god. Geb and Nut in turn bore the gods Osiris and Seth, and the goddesses Isis and Nephtys. Atum, the sun-god, and his eight descendants formed the Great Ennead or "Nine".

In the theology of Khmun or Hermopolis, generation began with the self-created Thoth (known to the Greeks as Hermes). By his word on the primeval mound, Thoth called into being four male deities each with his female partner:

> "(1) the primeval water (2) spatial infinity (3) darkness, and (4) a being who is called 'obscurity' and also 'lack' or 'loss' "[11].

Thus Thoth's Ogdoad or "Eight" gave their name to the city of Khmun and created the egg out of which the sun itself came into being.

From the First and Second Dynasties from the unification of the Two Lands, the priests of Memphis also elaborated theologies to place their god, Ptah, on the top of the pantheon. In this new theology, embracing the essentials of the earlier theologies, Ptah, as To-tenen (the emerged land) became the primeval mound, creator of the primeval ocean Nun and his wife Nuwet/Nunet, parents of the lotus, Nefer-tem, from which emerged the sun, Atum. Atum brought into being Horus, Thoth and the other gods of the Ennead. Accordingly, Ptah became the spring of creation, the other gods being "merely functions of Ptah".[12]

At Thebes, Amun, the "hidden" or "obscure" god of the Hermopolitan theology was developed from the Eleventh Dynasty into a central position. Amun was eventually "identified with Re, the sun-god", and the head of the Heliopolitan Ennead and the Ogdoad of Hermopolis.[13]

It was in accord with the Egyptian tradition of the continuity of divine rule with the emergence of human dynasties that myths of the origin of the gods predominated over myths about human origins. Children were shaped by the god Hnum, patron of potters. An early legend from about 300 B.C created the human race, *rmt*, from tears *(rmy.t)* of rage from the eye of Re.[14]

The story of the Deliverance of Mankind, going back to the Old Kingdom was recovered from the New Kingdom tomb of Sethy I (Sety I), Nineteenth Dynasty (c.1320–1200 B.C.). Re as "king over men and gods together", summoned the Ennead to discuss a plot against him by mankind, who had fled into the desert. Re was advised to send the goddess Hat-Hor to slay the conspirators. Re relented after he saw the extent of the first day's destruction. He devised a stratagem to stop Hat-Hor from completing the assignment. He sent messengers to collect and pulverize a red substance, *dedy*, to give seven thousand jars of beer the colour of blood, to be poured four palms deep over the fields Hat-Hor would pass to accomplish her mission. The following morning, Hat-Hor saw the blood-red fluid, tasted it, drank herself drunk, and forgot her assignment!

Egyptian mythology was not fully systematized or integrated. Apparently incongruous elements from different sources cohabited to offer differing perspectives. It was the uniformity and symmetry of the environment that provided an organizing principle for the Egyptian tradition of art, thought and creativity[15]. The Nile's two banks were uniformly fringed by mountains and deserts, one the symmetrical balance of the other, and its valley uniformly flat and open. Relatively minor phenomena stood out and became significant in such an environment.

The Nile provided a stable base as emerging from Nun, the underground primordial water source. It provided compass orientation also: upstream for "face" or south, downstream for "back" or north, left for east, and right for west. The periodic inundations and dry recessions symbolized life and death. In these flatlands of the valley and the delta, the sun was another constant presence and source of orientation as well as symbolism of life and death. Its rising from the east each morning symbolized birth, and its setting in the west, death beneath the waters of Nun. In the delta, in particular, the sun provided the major indicator of compass direction; and the east became "God's land", *ta-netjer,* and the west, the region of afterlife and death.

Indeed, the sun-god, Re, was represented not only as a disk of fire, but as varied forms of divinity. Re was the first divine king and represented in art as a bearded ruler crowned with the sun-disk; as Re-Atum in Heliopolis; Re-Harakhte or Re-Horus-of-the-Horizon; as Montu-Re in the form of a falcon; Sobek-Re as a crocodile god; Khnum-Re as a ram god; and as Amun-Re, king of the gods at Thebes.

In the established cosmogony of Ancient Egypt, therefore, the sun-god became dominant with minimal attention paid to the moon and stars. The sky-god, Nut was balanced by the earth-god, Geb, separated by the god of air/atmosphere, Shu. The waters of Nun lay beneath Geb, with its own subterranean "sky", Nunet, and "air/atmosphere", Dat. Inspite of variations in the theologies of regions and religious centres over time, a symmetrical and balanced system could be constructed in accord with the unique environment and genius of Egypt.

The Egyptian myth of creation then, had some elements in common with other world creation myths such as the Hebrew story of Genesis. Nun, the deep watery abyss and the first hillock or primeval mound rising out of it, like the first productive land out of the Nile inundation represent possible early models for later accounts, although the Hebrew account breaks new grounds by raising the Creator above the first dark nothingness.

The Egyptian procreation universe contained within it two pairs of mated gods and goddesses forming the "Eight" or Ogdoad of the Hermopolitan mythology; namely, Nun or water; and Naunet or counter-heaven; Huh or formlessness and Hauhet; Kuk or darkness and Kauket; Amun or obscurity and Amaunet[16].

The developed mythology of the Memphite Theology advanced the myth to the point of creation through thought and word, heart and tongue. The Memphite Theology placed Ptah as a first principle of creation above Atum who produced the supreme council of the gods, the Ennead or "Nine" of the after-creation: Atum, Shu and Tefnet, Geb and Nut, Osiris and Isis, Seth and Nephtys.

In its mythology of creation and origins then, Ancient Egypt developed overlapping accounts or theologies which did not destroy each other as incorporate each one into the other over time; and the creation of the gods implied the generation of humanity.

(vi) **Calendars and Chronology**

Egyptian calendars and chronology were among the subjects that attracted the attention of Herodotus during his visit to Egypt in the 27th Dynasty (525–404 B.C). Herodotus held discussions with the priests of Memphis, Thebes, and

Heliopolis, and concluded that their methods of keeping a record of times and chronology were superior to those of the Greeks of his time in three areas :

(i) keeping written records of events at the time of their occurrence
(ii) the use of genealogies to construct chronologies, and
(iii) the organization of calendars.

In the area of chronology, Herodotus recounted the story of the discomfiture of a visiting Greek historian, Hecataeus of Miletus, by the priests of Thebes. The Greek was unable to convince the priests that he was related "with a god sixteen generations back"[17], since they kept records of the genealogies of their own priests by making statues of them in addition to written documentation.

Herodotus accepted the claim of the priests that "the Egyptians by their study of astronomy discovered the solar year and were the first to divide it into twelve parts ... (and) make the year consist of twelve months of thirty days each and every year intercalate five additional days, and so complete the regular circle of the seasons"[18]. Herodotus considered this practice superior to the Greek practice of intercalating "a whole month every other year".

Modem scholars have charted the course of the development of calendars in Egypt out of four basic sources:[19]
(i) An agricultural calendar derived from the three seasons of the inundation of the Nile

(ii) A lunar calendar for the regulation of festivals and rituals,

(iii) The use of "the coming forth of Sirius" (Sothis to the Greeks), and

(iv) The civil calendar or schematic calendar for administrative and fiscal and economic uses, the Egyptian calendar that so impressed Herodotus and has exercised the most influence on the development of calendars.

The **agricultural calendar** based on the Nile floods divided itself into three seasons: first, the period of inundation and sowing (comprising the months of Thoth, Phaophi, Athyr, and Choiak); second, the period of tending to harvest (comprising the months of Tybi, Mechir, Phamenoth, and Pharmuthi); and third, the season of low waters before the next inundation (comprising the months of Pachons, Payni, Epiphi, and Mesore). Since the flood was controlled from its sources by complex phenomena, the seasons were irregular and variable. The year reckoned by this calendar thus varied between 336 to 415 days in length.

Parker identifies the *lunar calendar,* as "the first Egyptian calendar of record", a survival from African roots (comparable to systems in Loanga, among the Masai, and Wadschagas). [20]

By this calendar, the year normally ran only 354 days, and the twelve months were named after the most important festivals or the gods for which they were celebrated. If the first month of the year fell within eleven days of the rising of Sirius (Sothis), it was intercalary, and an intercalary month was added, an event that occurred about every three years. According to Parker, a modified lunar calendar was formulated after the civil calendar was instituted.

The star Sirius, the brightest in the Egyptian sky, played a crucial role in Egyptian time reckoning. In the lunar year, the beginning of the year was marked by the rising of the star. Possibly from the fifth or fourth millennium B.C. the rising of Sirius/Sothis became associated also with the beginning of the inundation of the Nile, inspite of the inevitable variability. The intercalations of a thirteenth lunar month tended to keep the New Years Day approximately attuned to the rising of Sirius/Sothis, and within the periods of Nile inundation. These calculations were sufficient to keep a calendar of agricultural and religious events, but not the regulation of an advanced economy and centralised administrative system, hence the formulation of the civil calendar from at least about 2500 B.C.

From that date three calendars operated together: the lunar calendar, the agricultural calendar based on the Nile inundations and the civil calendar. The **civil calendar** became dominant in Egypt because of its centralised administrative structure and the relative advantages enumerated by Herodotus. Its regularities appealed to astronomers down to Claudius Ptolemy of Alexandria, Egypt, (2nd century A.D.) and Copernicus (sixteenth century A.D.). It was used for over three millennia in Egypt, and used with slight modifications by the Coptic Church in Egypt and Ethiopia, the Persians, and the Parsees of India for another two millennia.

In the west, the landmarks of development were the Julian calendar of Julius Caesar from 46 B.C, the Alexandrian of Emperor Augustus from 30 or 26 B.C, the first on the advice of the Greek Egyptian astronomer, Sosigenes. The "strange hodge-podge" Gregorian Calendar of Pope Gregory, instituted in 1582 A.D, has survived so far.

(vii)   **Documents / Archives**

Why did the Egyptians take such great care of their records over so many centuries and millennia? This must remain a basic question in any consideration of Egyptian ideas of history. It was, indeed, a basic element of the Egyptian practice of history. We focus here on the genres of archives created and preserved, and on histories of documents. Here, the statement of King Shabako of the Twenty Fifth or Ethiopian Dynasty (c.747–656 B.C.) on the stone slab in the British Museum where he had had copied, the only extant version of the Memphite Theology, serves as a veritable manifesto for archivists and historians.

"His majesty wrote this document anew in the house of his father Ptah. His majesty had discovered it as a work of the forefathers which had been eaten of worms and was not (completely) legible from beginning to end. Therefore his majesty wrote it anew, so that it is more beautiful than it was before, in order that his name might endure and his monument be fixed in the house of his father Ptah forever" [21].

This document is thought to have originated from a time in the Old Kingdom up to one thousand eight hundred years from Shabako's time, which could itself have been copied from an earlier version from the pre-dynastic period before the end of the 4th millennium B.C. Thus the document had been preserved as a fragile papyrus roll over thousands of years before Shabako inscribed it on the apparently permanent stone material in the hopes of ensuring its survival "forever". Its subsequent history, however, suggests that attitudes of appreciation were more important than material in the preservation of documents and archives. In the Christian Era, when a proper sense of the value and relevance of such documents was lost, the stone was used as a "nether millstone" and up to a third of the text was destroyed.

In this discussion of documents and archives, therefore, we identify historical documents by their genres rather than by the materials on which they were created or preserved, following Redford's categories of king-lists, annals, and day-books[22].

King-lists comprise groupings of rulers arranged in a sequence of succession, and indicating durations of reigns. The only surviving original example of a true Egyptian king-list is the Turin Canon of kings, apparently copied on papyrus in the Nineteenth Dynasty (c. 1320 - 1200 B.C.) in the reign of Ramses II in the New Kingdom. The kings are listed in the following form: a title "king of Upper and Lower Egypt", a cartouche containing a name or names, and a number or numbers indicating years, months, and days of reigns; and sometimes also the length of life. There is, in addition, a division of individual names into sections (representing the Dynasties established by Manetho a millennium later). Section titles include a Greater and a Lesser Ennead indicating an early period of mythical rulers. From the Dynastic period of human rulers over a united Egypt, an obvious criterion for the demarcation of a section was the place of residence of the kings. The scribe supplied historical information through the use of epithets such as "he who inaugurated stone (work)" to Djoser. The scribe of the Turin Canon indicated periods for which no kings were shown in the original document from which he had copied it.

A considerable number of other "lists" of kings and ancestors exist on papyri, ostraca, and stela in royal and private tombs, and temples, mostly in cultic contexts. There are a number of such assemblages of names associated with Abydos and Memphis, but the vast majority of examples relate to the Theban tradition, from the Middle Kingdom through the New Kingdom. Various office holders listed the kings under whom they held office in their tomb or statue inscriptions and in other documents. Some genealogies of priests and other office holders also supplied supplementary information on royal successions and chronologies as suggested by Herodotus.

However, the character of the Manetho Dynastic list is evidence of the travails of the king-list tradition through the millennia of Egyptian history. For example, a revival of interest in the past is apparent in the Eighteenth Dynasty and the conquests of Thutmoses I and III opened Egypt to the outside world, and the practice of making offerings to the dead in the tombs and temples provided occasions for continuing the tradition of creating king-lists. However, certain circumstances threatened the tradition at various times: changes of dynasty, periods of external conquest or of internal unrest, periods of interregnum, periods such as the reign of Akhenaten which were formally declared anathema and consigned to forgetfulness and oblivion.

It is, therefore, remarkable that "the tradition of a 'running king-list', attested by the Turin Canon continued unimpaired down to the Ptolemies"[23] and became enshrined in the synthesis prepared by the historian Manetho.

Annals appear in Ancient Egyptian as *gnt* (singular), *gnwt* (plural), apparently derived from "a prepared wooden tablet"[24], with the meaning of an inscribed text or record. The word occurs in Old, Middle and New Kingdom contexts in passages related to reliefs, inscriptions on the jambs of monumental gates, and in the epithets of divinities. In most contexts, the annals of a king were "established", "published", by a principal god, and inscribed by another on a branch or tablet. Amun, Atum, Ptah, Harweris, Horus, Khonsu, Re, and sometimes Thoth and the goddess Seshat appear in the principal role. The role of scribe belonged to Thoth, but was sometimes assigned to the goddesses Seshat, Sefkhet-abwy, and to the gods Khonsu and Horus.

In a few cases, annals appear in contexts with the meaning of destiny, and established at the beginning of a reign at the coronation, or even before the birth of the ruler. According to the following texts:

> "It is thy *ku* that creates annals through thine activity", and another refers to annals "intituled in the womb before he (the king) was born"[25]. The coronation contexts imply the establishment of legitimacy by divine authority, over lengths of years, usually in millions of years , "forever and aye". Annals were related also to the jubilee festival. Annals, then, had a mystical element, since the gods were implicated in pronouncing and inscribing them, but also because there were also "the annals of the gods and goddesses in the House of Life".

Other characteristics of annals definitely identify them as written records of the past derived from "the predecessors", "the ancestors", "those who were aforetime", "from the time of Re", and "of earlier times".[26] The archaic nature of the annals as records of the past is confirmed by the references which characterise them as difficult to decipher. Annals, then, were records of accession and coronation, *sd* - or jubilee festivals, temple foundations, notices of Nile inundations, battles, and miracles, arranged in regnal years and preserved for reference. The best known examples are the Palermo Stone and the Cairo fragments.

The **day-book**, *hrwyt*, was a literary offshoot of the annal, in the form of a diary, journal or list recording events by days or specified dates. It did not, however, achieve an official status, and documents of the same form or type were described by other titles as well, such as "roll of days". The extant examples suggest its ordinary day to day origins.

In the tomb and pyramid temples on the necropolis, the priests kept records of duties and assignments; in the king's house, officials recorded movements and significant daily events; in the treasury, shipyards, storehouses, military installations and expeditions, accounts of receipts, expenditures etc. were kept by date; in the judiciary, collections of dated copies of deeds, wills and other legal documents came to be described as day-books; and so were dated dispatches of the chancery.[27]

(viii)   **Manetho**

Manetho, the high priest, born in Sebennytus, and living at Heliopolis falls in the Greek period of the Ptolemies (305–30 B.C.). He was credited with great wisdom in Egyptian lore and well groomed in Greek.[28] His name has been derived from the Egyptian god of letters, as meaning "Truth of Thoth"; and his office in Heliopolis with knowledge of the work of "the goddess Seshat, the Lady of Letters, the Mistress of the Library".[29] His history of Egypt was, in part, an attempt to correct the errors of earlier Greek histories of Egypt. Manetho specifically criticised Herodotus for factual errors due to ignorance of local traditions and records. Manetho's commission from Ptolemy II Philadelphus (285–246 B.C.) to write his *Aegyptiaca* was part of the policy of the first two Ptolemies to cultivate the goodwill of the Egyptian priesthood and intellectual classes, and to profit from Egyptian wisdom. It was part of the mandate of the Library and Museum of Alexandria, and an advance on the commission of Ptolemy I to the Greek historian, Hecataeus of Abdera (c. 320 B.C.), to write his own *Aegyptiaca*.

Manetho's *Aegyptiaca*, therefore, represents a high point of Greek efforts to understand the Egyptian tradition, and the high point of the development of the Egyptian practice of history. It represents a movement from the collection and preservation of historical records to their use in the construction of formal accounts of the past. However, the loss of the original of Manetho's work in three books, and its survival only in the form of a king-list, creates difficulties for a proper assessment of the full extent of his contribution to historiography.

Manetho's rich background qualified him to correct the errors of Greek historians and to instruct the Greek population in Egyptian religion and culture. He was, indeed, the heir to the whole tradition of Egyptian historical source preservation and sense of history. However, he apparently worked from the records and books in the depository of the temples only, and did not necessarily inspect monuments on the spot or interrogate informants.[30] The depositories of temple archives and libraries in Manetho's time would have contained king-lists, annals, mythological reference works, wisdom, astrological, and omen literature, ritual books, directories and inventories, and temple day-books. A temple repository, however, would not normally keep government documents: reports, day-books, census lists, etc. By all accounts, Manetho used oral traditions, possibly in codified texts in the temple archives and library. Some of these traditions may have been popular interpretations of inscriptions on or of monuments, stelae, reliefs, etc. Manetho's division of the earlier section of his history into periods of the gods, demi-gods, and spirits of the dead, is an obvious indication of his reliance on oral traditions and the tradition of the ancient king-lists (cf. Greater Ennead, Lesser Ennead, and Heroes).

The *Aegyptiaca* is likely to have been cast in the form of a king-list extended by narrative. The original arguably influenced its early reduction into an *Epitome* extending the dynastic lists from thirty to thirty one. This became the basis of the versions adopted by the Christian authors, Julius Africanus and Eusebius who attempted to use Egyptian chronology to prove the antiquity of the Jewish nation, and the Biblical accounts of Moses. It was Josephus who, in his *Contra Apionem* used the original Manetho. He reproduced extracts and a critique by another expert. Jewish and Christian writers identified the Hyksos invaders with the Israelites, but were alienated by Manetho's apparent identification of them as lepers.

Greek and Roman writers took only a limited interest in Manetho's *Aegyptiaca* and we find only scattered references in "Plutarch, Theophilus, Aelian, Porphyrius, Diogenes Laertius, Theodoretus, Lydus, Malalas, the Scholia to Plato, and the

Etymologicum Magnum".[31] The accounts of Herodotus, Hecataeus, and other writers remained more accessible.

Manetho has no influential native successors. There is little known of Ptolemy of Mendes (close to Manetho's home in the Nile Delta), in the Roman period, and Apion, against whom Josephus wrote. Manetho's synthesis achieved the status of a standard of reference, so that succeeding interpretations earned the derogatory designation of Pseudo-Manetho. It came to provide the framework and grounding for the chronology of Egyptian history from the turn of the nineteenth century in the discipline of Egyptology.

(ix) **Philosophy of History**

The Egyptian experience of history lays bare a sense of history ingrained in many aspects of life. What did they think about history in general and its recovery as an intellectual activity? Three lines of investigation may be pursued: first, a search through the wisdom, instruction meditation, complaints and lamentations, and dialogue literature; second, a study of the ideas expressed or incorporated in Manetho's *Aegyptiaca*, the apical synthesis of the Egyptian practice of the art of historiography; and, finally, a discussion of some modern western assessments of the Egyptian sense of history.

The quantity of ancient Egyptian literature recovered from papyri, ostraca, and inscriptions is now quite large, but must represent only a small percentage of the total output of the millennia of cultural flowering in the Nile Valley. Narratives, songs, and poetry are represented, but no texts of dramatic or epic literature have yet been recovered.[32]

The one genre for which the Egyptians had a specific term, *sboyet*, instruction or teaching, is featured here as representing the closest examples of philosophical texts, and generally referred to as *Wisdom Literature*. Lamentations, and complaints or *literature of pessimism*, and dialogues, may be considered a sub-genre of Wisdom literature, and considered here for thoughts on history or on its practice or effects.

The literature identifies and celebrates individual wise men, scribes, prophets, and singers: Hardedef, Imhotep, Neferti, Khety, King Amenemhet, Ptahhemdjehuty, Khakheperresonbu, Ptahhotep, Kaires, Ipuwer, Amennakhte, Amenemope, Anii, Piyay, Hory, Wen-nefer, and others. In *The song of the Harper*, two wise men are distinguished and memorialised:

"Now I have heard the sayings
Of Iyemhotep and Hardedef
Which are quoted
In the proverbs so much"[33]

In another text, scribes and their writings and books are represented as more enduring than pyramids and stelae:[34]

> "As for those learned scribes from the time of the successors of the gods, even those who foretold the future, it has befallen that their names endure for all eternity, though they be gone, having completed their lives, and though all their kindred be forgotten".

The pyramids which they built were not of copper with stelae of iron. They knew not how to leave heirs that were children who should pronounce their names, but they made heirs unto themselves of the writings and the books of instruction which they made.

... Books of instruction became their pyramids, and the reed-pen their child....

There were made for them doors and halls, but these are fallen apart. Their mortuary servants are gone, and their stelae covered with dirt, their chambers forgotten. But their names are pronounced because of these books of theirs which they made ... More profitable is a book than a graven stelae, than a chapel wall (?) firmly established.

A man is perished and his corpse has become dust ... But writings cause him to be remembered in the mouth of the reciter. More profitable is a book than the house of the builder, than chapels in the necropolis.

Is (any) here like Herdedef? Is there another like Imhotep? There have been none among our kindred like Neferti and Khety, that chief among them. I recall to you the names of Ptahemdjehuty and Khakheperre-sonbu. Is there another one like Ptahhotep or Kaires?

Those sages who foretold the future, that which came forth from their mouths happened... They are gone, their name(s) are forgotten. But writings cause them to be remembered. "

The *sboyet* were instructions of a sage, usually to his son, but included discourses on general matters intended mainly for use as school texts. The thoughts they express cover issues of life in general, and ideas on history must be picked out with a fine tooth comb.

The Instruction of Ptahhotep (Erman)/*The Maxims of Ptahhotpe* (Simpson), are attributed to the vizier of King Isesi of the Fifth Dynasty (c. 2350 B.C.) although the extant copies date only from the Middle Kingdom with revised versions from the New Kingdom. In an opening dialogue, the vizier sought royal permission to instruct his son in "the words of the judges, the counsels of those who were aforetime". The king orders Ptahhotep/Ptahhotpe to "teach him / what has been said in the past"[35]. The exchange suggests the common African idea that wisdom comes from age and experience flows from it. That is, that wisdom is equated with historical knowledge. At several points in the discourse, the transmission of knowledge from the past is specifically identified as coming from father to son: "a man learns from his father"; "a son should accept what his father says"; "Your teaching is in your son, a hearer"; "A son who hears is a follower of Horus"[36].

The submission of the young to the wisdom of the fathers was, indeed, the basis of the tradition of the *sboyet*, for sons to follow the instructions of their parents and to pass it on to "the children of your children"[37].

The unknown father of King Merykara / Merikare (Ninth and Tenth Dynasties: c. 2130 - 2040 B.C.) instructed him:

> "Copy your forefathers... their words endure in writing ... read and copy knowledge"[38], and "The soul comes to the place which it knows, and it will not overstep the ways of the past; no magic can oppose it, and it will reach those who will give it water"[39]. History, then, is elevated to supreme arbiter, conferring its benefits on those who would tend it with care. Yet the wise teacher was equally aware of the imperative call of the future, and of eternity: "the soul goes to the place it knows and does not stray on yesterday's road", and "one generation of men passes to another"[40]. Indeed, the pressing march of time toward the future and eternity thus provides a major motivation for action: "a man works for his predecessor, through the desire that what he has done may be embellished by another who shall come after him"[41]. The teacher instructs King Merikare: "maintain your monuments in proportion to your wealth, for a single day gives to eternity, an hour does good for the future, ..." because "it is good to act on behalf of posterity"[42].

The *Wisdom literature* firmly establishes its continuity with the oral tradition in the New Kingdom precursor of the Hebrew Book of Proverbs, *The Instruction of Amenemope* where the tradition of respect for parents is extended to respect for all elders:

"Do not stretch out your hand to touch an old man,
Nor snip at the words of an elder"
"Do not reproach someone older than you
For he has seen the Sun before you ...
Very sick in the sight of Re
Is a young man who reproaches an elder"[43]

The *Literature of Pessimism:* Lamentations, Complaints, Meditations, and Prophecies, proceed from the position that times are out of joint and the course of history has come unhinged from its normal moorings. In the words of *The Man who was tired of life,* "None remember the past"[44]. According to the prophet Ipuwer, scribes "are killed and their writings are taken away", and "the statues are burned and their tombs destroyed"[45].

However, not all wise men reacted by extolling conservative ideas and bemoaning their abandonment. Khakheperre-sonbe reacted to unhinged times by crying out for liberating ideas:

> "Would that I had unknown speeches, erudite phrases in new language which has not been used, free from the usual repetitions, not the phrases of past speech/which (our) forefathers spoke" ..."What I say has not been said"[46].

The recurring themes in Manetho's *Aegyptiaca* may be used as a key to discover some binding elements of Egyptian historiography.[47] The numerous examples of these themes in literature, and inscriptions on monuments suggest a continuity with the *sdd*, oral tradition or orally transmitted folklore. A pervasive theme also reflected in the *Literature of Pessimism* is that of "Dissolution and Restoration" comprising accounts of "Times of Trouble" followed by rulers claiming to be carrying out unprecedented works of restoration. These accounts predominate in the period after the New Kingdom. The causes cited for the troubles include invasion by the Sea People, Hykssos and other Asiatics from the east, Libyans, and Nubians; internal rebellions and revolutions, such as that of Akhenaten.

A related theme is that concerning the intrusion of "impure ones", mainly from the north, and of their expulsion, often from the south. In Manetho, the theme is exemplified by the story of the plague-ridden people driven out to the quarries, organised by the rebel-priest, Osarsiph (identified with Moses), who invited shepherds from Jerusalem to rule Egypt for thirteen years before being driven out by King Amenophis and his sons from exile in Ethiopia.

These stereotypical themes have historical parallels, and confirm the link between the *sdd*, oral tradition, and the written tradition of Egyptian historiography.

Western assessment of the intellectual contribution of ancient Egypt in historiography have tended to be hypercritical through the use of overly technical definitions of the field or over-concentration on particular factors of the Egyptian environment or history[48]. In *The Origins of History*, Herbert Butterfield considered the characteristic Egyptian historical annal to be, eventually, "an obstruction to historical writing", and begins the discussion of the history of the discipline with the Hebrew and Greek contribution. Collingwood's classic, *The Idea of History*, defines philosophy of history in a peculiarly strict sense that put out of consideration, the early and original contributions of ancient Egypt along with the contributions of other early Afroasiatic civilizations. Even Ludlow Bull's positive discussion of the Egyptian concern with the past concluded that the Egyptian view of history was defined by "a static quality", because of the comparative geographical isolation of the Nile Valley, and the belief that "the conditions of their existence... had always been, always would be, governed by the gods, whose will and purposes were utterly inscrutable".

Redford took great care, in his defined "field of historical source criticism", to detail the history of the specific genres of Egyptian historical practice while ruling out the existence of "history-writing in a classical sense". He recognised the development of abstractions from the Egyptian regard for, and consciousness of, the past; and isolated:

(i) ideas of changelessness and cycles in the course of history
(ii) a desire for permanence and continuity
(iii) an appreciation of longevity or "length of years"
(iv) a passion for order in the form of concrete achievements
(v) a respect for divine precedent
(vi) ideas of divine participation in, and even of
(vii) divine causation, in history, *hprt*, "that which has happened".

John Wilson's assessment of the speculative thought of ancient Egypt takes account of its role as a pioneer, its very early flowering, and its impact on neighbouring civilizations whose later contributions to western thought is generally acknowledged. According to him, "the very size of Egypt left its mark on her neighbours" (including the Hebrew and the Greeks), while he considers their appreciation of "all the wisdom of the Egyptians", to have been "vague and uncritical".

It is clear that, on balance, western appreciation of the pioneer contributions of Egypt to the history of ideas, especially in the field of historiography, has fallen short of the appreciation accorded Egyptian achievements in the arts and architecture.

3.3   African Scripts and Communication Systems

The Egyptian legacy of storage of information and communication through writing influenced the invention of similar systems in neighbouring regions of Africa. Egyptian hieroglyphics provided the most direct example of stimulus diffusion in the development of the Meroitic script. Other scripts came into being much later through the indirect influence of the Egyptian system, for example, *Punic* and *Lybian; Coptic* through the Greek alphabet and demotic; and *Ethiopic* by way of the South Arabic systems of writing.

In other parts of Africa indigenous systems of information storage through mnemonic devices were also known.[49] Following the introduction of the Arabic script through the expansion of Islam from the seventh century A.D. and of the Roman script in the wake of European expansion and imperialism from the end of the fourteenth century, a few African communities invented new original scripts, with possible influence from the Arabic and Roman systems. Each of the African systems served the needs of the cultures and societies that invented them.

(i) **Meroitic Script**

The Nubian kingdom raised inscriptions in hieroglyphs in the Egyptian language until the second century B.C when they produced a distinct script using a local language thus moving further away from Egyptian influence as the centre of the kingdom moved from Napata to Meroe. Two forms or scripts have been distinguished, one using twenty three symbols adapted from Egyptian hieroglyphs, and the second a shorthand or cursive script with some symbols derived from the Egyptian demotic script. The hieroglyph-based style was used mainly for inscriptions on the walls of tombs and temples, while the demotic-based script was more common, appearing on graffiti, ostraca, and papyri.

The Meroitic script differed from Egyptian scripts in its internal structures. Meroitc scripts were phonetic, using twenty three consonant signs, two syllabic and vowel signs. Words were also divided by three dots in the hieroglyph-based script, and two dots in the demotic.

Although the script was deciphered in all its essential forms by Francis L. Griffith since 1909 from a text in both Egyptian and Meroitic scripts, the language itself remains unknown. The problem with the Meroitic script is the understanding of the language of the script.[50] Until the language is known, the texts cannot be read inspite of our knowledge of the script itself. Research is now focused on the study of the language through comparison with Nubian and other African languages.

(ii)   **Punic and Lybian Scripts**

The Phoenicians carried Semitic scripts to parts of the western Mediterranean, including North Africa. The *Carthaginian or Punic* script was a phonetic script with twenty two letters written from right to left.

The *Lybian* scripts dated towards the close of the first millennium B.C include examples in Tunisia, and the *Numidian* script, whose modem version, the *Berber* script, is still used by the Tuaregs. The Spanish variety of the script is known as Turdetanian.[51]

(iii)   **Ethiopic**

Ethiopic established around the kingdom of Axum is related to the Semitic systems of Southern Arabia, from about the fourth century A.D. The Cushitic language of Ethiopia eventually created distinctive features including "a visually different appearance, a new arrangement of letters, another direction of writing (from left to right) and, most important, a systematic and obligatory vocalization".[52] It has become a syllabic script similar to scripts in India, consisting of twenty seven consonants and seven vowel indications.

(iv) **Coptic**

Coptic, from Greek Aiguptos, Arabic gubti, meaning "Egyptian", was merely the new script replacing Egyptian hieroglyphics in the Roman and Christian periods of Egyptian history.

Standard Coptic or Sahidic comprised twenty four letters of the Greek alphabet and six characters from the Egyptian demotic script. It was an alphabetic script representing vowels and consonants. In sum thirty two signs were used, twenty five from Greek and seven from demotic.[53]

Coptic may be dated from the end of the first century A.D to the thirteenth century. It continued to be used as the liturgical language of the Coptic Church and in the Nubian Church in a modified form.

Coptic boasts a large literature mainly from the monasteries on Biblical and religious subjects. Most of the texts are written in ink with reed pens on papyri, ostraca, wooden tablets, parchment, and paper.

(v) **Somali Scripts**

Somali scripts were all invented in modern times by people open to the influence of Arabic and Roman alphabetic writing.[54]

The best known is the *Ismaaniya* script invented in about 1920 by Ismaan Yusuf Kenadiid, who knew both Arabic and Italian. The script, fully alphabetic, is composed of original signs for nineteen consonants and ten vowel sounds.

A second script invented in about 1933 by Sheikh Abdurahman Sh. Nuur was used only in the Gadabuursi district, and has not received wide publicity or attention. The *Gadabuursi* script employs twenty one consonants and seven vowels.

Both *Ismaaniya* and *Gadabuursi* are written from left to right.

(vi) **The Mende Script of Sierra Leone**

The *Mende* script invented by Kisimi Karnala, a Muslim tailor, in 1935 in three and a half months, consists of about one hundred and ninety signs. It is related to the *Vai* script of the neighbouring Liberian region.

(vii) **The Vai and Related Scripts**

The *Vai* script was a syllabic system invented in about 1814–1816 in the reign of Manja (King) Gotolo by Dualo Bukele.[55] Bukele saw a Spirit in a dream which wrote the signs in the sand, and urged him to teach it to the community without monetary reward: "freely ye have received, freely give"..."the only fee for tuition should be one bottle of palm wine, a portion of which must be poured on the ground in the name of the Spirits of the book party. Upon the completion of the study a single fowl of white plumage should be given to the teacher". Bukele recruited friends (Momolu Duwau Wogbe, D. Tamia, Jaa Zaawo, Zolu Tabaco, J. Belekole, and Kahnie Bala) who assisted him to set up schools at Tombe and Gawalu.

The script became known to the western world in 1849, was studied by the German linguist, S.W. Koelle soon after, and taught at the Hamburg University around 1924. Accordingly, the script underwent several revisions by Vai teachers and scholars who made translations of the Bible and the Koran, and transcribed the traditions of origin of the Vai people. The script thus became an instrument for the practice of history among the Vai.

The *Vai* script is an early example of a writing system in Africa outside the Egyptian tradition. It became a syllabic system using "some 226 syllabic signs plus a very few word signs".[56]

Other scripts in the same West African region show evidence of diffusion of ideas from the practice of the Vai system of communication. These include the *Mende* script, the *Basa* syllabary and the *Kapelle / Kpelle* script of Liberia; and the *Toma* (187 signs) and *Gerze* (87 signs) of Guinea.

(viii) **The Bamum Script of Cameroon**

The *Bamum* script was invented by King Njoya in about 1895-96 as a means of communication within the court. King Njoya and his chiefs apparently adapted words from French, German, and English.[57] Starting with as many as 510 signs, the script contracted to a syllabary of some 70 signs. It thus began to move towards alphabetization.

(ix) **Nigerian Scripts**

The Nigerian examples of invented scripts show the same originality as the other scripts outside the Egyptian system, with no more than indirect influence from the Arabic or Roman orthographies. Indeed, Kathleen Hau has suggested, in a series of papers in the *Bulletin de l'Institut Fondamental d'Afrique Noire* that the origins of these scripts may go back into periods before the arrival of Arabic and Portuguese to the Western Sudan and West African coast.[58] She recommends a systematic search for evidence in the arts of the Edo of Benin and of the Yoruba, and of other groups, for early systems of sign communication.

The best known system of signs in Nigeria is the *nsibidi* of the Cross River basin among the Ekoi groups, Ibibio, Efik, and Igbo.[59] It was practised mainly in the context of the secret societies of *Ekpe, Ukpotio, Ukwa, Isong Esil,* and others. The signs were tattooed on the faces and bodies of women, on calabashes, walls, and on road junctions etc. to convey instructions or warnings. Accordingly, a number of the signs were widely known in the communities, but the majority of the signs remained the possession of the members of the secret societies that operated *nsibidi*, who conducted long discussions by means of the signs. Up to 500 signs have been recorded. However, among the Ibibio, it was apparently used to inscribe historical information in ancestral shrines.

A less well known and more recent script among the Ibibio of the Itu area is *Oberi Okaime:* being a script, new language, and system of numerals.[60] It was revealed to one Michael Ukpon by the Holy spirit of God (Seminant), in dream sessions and written down by Akpan Akpan Udofia of Ididep between 1927 and 1936.

Oberi Okaime was a new communication system supernaturally revealed for the use of a religious community among whose members it was taught and used to communicate its doctrines and Holy Books. The script had only 32 symbols, and numeral signs from one to twenty.

Like the *Vai, Oberi Okaime* was taught in formal systems of instruction in special schools, just as both were delivered through dreams. *Oberi Okaime* was also similar to *the Bamum* in being a new language as well, except that the Ibibio case was believed to have been brought out through revelation and not through conscious effort of invention.

3.4 African Scripts and Historiography

From Egypt, Africa shares in the prestige of the origins of writing in the ancient Near East, Afroasia, to which it gave so much in contribution. It is not surprising that the African communities taking part in the history of the Afroasiatic region also received feedbacks leading to the creation of early systems of writing: *Meroitic,* in the Sudan; *Ethiopic,* in the Horn of Africa; and *Lybian* in North Africa.

For other parts of Africa, the earliest efforts at keeping information and ideas for future reference or communication were effected through the arts: rock paintings and engravings from prehistoric times, signs and inscriptions on pottery, ivory, wood, cloth etc. But a great deal of symbolic messages were tattooed on bodies, written on sand or clay, tree trunks etc. and lost to posterity. However, historians of Africa are yet to pay serious attention to the evidence of the past inscribed in works of art that survive from the distant or even the recent past.

We may note also the evidence in Africa of the universal relationship between religion and writing. The Egyptians credited the invention of writing to the god Thoth. Similarly, the inventors of other scripts credited them to other supernatural agents: the *oberi okaime* to Seminant, the *Vai* to "spirits", and the *Toma* to God. Where human inventors are remembered, dreams and visions provide the media of transmission from the supernatural. The *oberi okaime* and the *nsibidi* also remained the property of a religious community.

The impact of internal systems of writing on African historiography has been minimal, overlooked, or neglected. The influence of the systems outside the Egyptian orbit have been minimal, in most cases because of the limited use of the scripts by secret societies, except in the case of the *Vai* script which has potentials not yet exploited by historians so that the *nsibidi* and *oberi okaime* are unknown to, or neglected by many Nigerian historians.

Egyptian hieroglyphics has been the basis of an entire discipline, Egyptology, separated from African historiography. Accordingly, its contributions to African historiography have been overlooked, and many scholars cannot conceive of an internal written tradition as something applicable to Africa. African historians have to make conscious efforts to embrace the history of ancient Egypt and acquire the skills necessary to incorporate it into the historiography of the rest of the continent.

We note that most of the 'recent' scripts outside the Egyptian system were invented by persons who were either illiterate or only minimally literate in the Arabic/ Islamic or Roman scripts. They were, however, often aware of the prestige of these systems of communication, and had a desire to endow on their communities the expected benefits of writing. According to one account of the invention of the *Toma* script of Guinea, God granted Wido his wish to catch up with other cultures only on condition that the Toma remained faithful to their own traditions:

" 'God takes he no pity on the Tomas? Other races know writing. Only the Tomas remain in their ignorance'. God answered him: 'I fear that when you are able to express yourselves you shall have no more respect for the beliefs and customs of your race'. 'Not at all', answered Wido, 'we shall still keep living as in past days. I promise it'. 'If such is the case', answered God, 'I am willing to grant you the knowledge ...[61]

After his strenuous efforts to expound the virtues of literacy over the oral tradition, Goody had to admit that even in the western written tradition, writing continues to be "an addition, not an alternative, to oral transmission". In the cases of Islamic literacy cited by Goody from West Africa to Madagascar, there was no case in which the alien script gave rise to a local one, merely the use of the foreign script to serve magical, astrological and other purposes.[62]

What, then, have been the contributions of these prestigious written traditions to African historiography?

CHAPTER 4

The Islamic Tradition

Nye olu si anwa ji owho / Nye ali si anwa ji owho / Owho magwu aye ji a.
The man above claims to hold the staff of justice / The man below claims it too, / But the staff of justice knows who holds it. Ikwerre proverb, Nigeria (Ekwulo, 1975: 6-7).

4.1 Introduction

The origins of the Islamic tradition of historiography are to be found in, first, the oral traditions of the Arabs; second, the twenty year mission of the Prophet Muhammad beginning from his *hijra* in 622 A.D. through the one hundred and thirty year ministry of the four "orthodox" caliphs (Abu Bakr, 'Umar, 'Othman, and 'Ali); and third, in the achievements of the classical period of some three hundred years from about 750 A.D. following the rise of the Abbasid caliphate.[1]

The pre-Islamic Arab legacy lay in "a vast store of narratives, legends, poems, and proverbs which had been handed down from generation to generation by oral transmission".[2] The prose narratives consisted mainly in stories of the "Days of the Arabs", *aiyam al-arab,* recounting largely wars and blood feuds. Genealogies going back to common ancestors, accounts of the dignity, prestige, and glory of leaders and tribes, and the play of blind Fate or destiny featured in these histories in which "a day" implied a memorable or notable series of events in the life of a group, often the story of a blood feud.

Muhammad initiated a turning away from the insular Arabism of the oral tradition towards a written tradition of universal historiography. He attempted to build on the Arab oral tradition some basic elements of the historical traditions from the holy books and traditions of Judaism and Christianity. His revelatory historiography went back to a Creation of the world, and forward to a future Day of Judgment or Day of Resurrection which those who had heeded the warnings of the prophets (Noah, Lot, Moses, Hud, Salih, Jesus, Muhammad) went to paradise, and the condemned went to hell. Eventually, the monotheism of Islam provided the motive force for change from the blind Fate of the early Arab tradition to the Providence of Allah in the new world history. The early pagan "Days of the Arabs" became *jahiliya* "a term of contempt and condemnation"[3], inspite of the fact that the new historiography was to remain a fusion of old and new ideas.

The movement of the centre of Islam first from Medina to Mecca, and eventually out of Arabia to Baghdad (Kufa) in Iraq, and to Damascus in Syria, from the seventh to the tenth centuries added new elements to the complex amalgam of Islamic historiography. New Islamic and Biblical ancestors (Adam, Noah, Shem or Sam, Ishmael, Abraham, Muhammad) were prescribed to be remembered after the remembrance of Allah. Accordingly, new genealogies and criteria for glory, nobility, and prestige were enunciated for the Faithful; and finally, new Traditions deriving from the life and times of the Prophet Mohammed came into being.

The key technical terms which embody the Islamic idea of history are *'Ilm al-Akhbar,* and *'Ilm al-Tarikh.*

Akhbar *(singular habar),* is a cognate of Akkadian, *habaru,* "to be noisy, to make noise". In Arabic it meant "information (about remarkable events)".[4] The term came to be attached to information concerning Mohammed and other authorities, and used as a synonym for *Hadith,* Traditions.

Tatikh became, by the ninth century, the accepted term for the discipline of history. Its origins apparently go back to the Semitic for "moon (month)", possibly derived from the South Arabian, *tawrikh (tawrih). Tarikh,* then, would have developed from ideas of information for which a lunar time was indicated to the idea of a "date", "era" to "the most important date in the documents of a well-organized, permanent administration", "the year of the 'era' ", and, finally, "history", and "historical work", that is, a work containing dates.[5]

The word *tarikh* has also been identified with the "diary", the earliest examples being those kept by Ibn Bana (105–1079) and Saladin's secretary, Baisani (1135–1200), thus predating European examples by several centuries. The diary was referred to as *tarikh,* book, and by Baisani as *muyawamat.* The association with *tarikh* is confirmed by Ibn Banna's practice of invariably "fixing [the day of] the beginning of the month" in his diary.[5a]

The chronicle or annal became the characteristic form of Islamic historiography which became fully developed in the time of the historian, Tabari in the tenth century. This was the form of historical writing to which the term *tarikh* became attached. There were chronicles or annals devoted to a particular reign, and others of a general type dealing with several reigns over a period of years. Such narratives developed into general histories.

The basic building block of the tradition, however, was the *habar (khabar)*, "a direct continuation of the battle-day narratives"[6], being "the well-rounded description of a single event". A *habar* history was titled with the addition of *dhikr*, "report", *amr*, "affair", or *tarikh*, "story". It was characterized by being "complete in itself", presented in the style of a "vividly told short story", and the insertion of poetry.

The second standard form of historical writing after the chronicle or annal was the Biographical Dictionary. Rulers, saints, scholars and all categories of leaders were featured. The old Arabic traditions of the genealogy and periodisation by generations *tabaqat,* all came into play in the development of the biographical form. However, some depositories of historical information were intended to be legal documents such as the *Fatwa* or legal opinions which became the *Nawazil* of the West African Sudan region, containing "a connected narrative of the problem under examination".[7]

Finally, a characteristic strength of written historiographies, the calendar, was developed early in the history of Muslim historiography. The ancient Arab lunar calendar of twelve months and thirteen months in each third year was changed into a strict twelve month religious calendar by the Prophet Muhammad at his Farewell Pilgrimage:

> "A year is twelve months, as at the time of creation". "Verily twelve months is the number of the months with God, according to God's Book, ever since the day when He created Heaven and Earth".[8]

The caliph 'Umar decreed the beginning of the lunar year, and thence the beginning of the Muslim era from the date the Prophet left Mecca for Medina on *Hijra*, Migration, namely, 16 July, A.D. 622. This year A.D. 622 thus became Year 1 Muharram or AH 1 (Anno Hijrae 1). This institution of an official calendar from the beginning of Islam was clearly a major asset to historiography, reinforcing the idea of *tarikh* as related to chronologically dated events.

From the tenth century, Islamic historiography drew its resources from an ever widening geographical coverage of the world, from Persia (Iran) and Turkey to India, Bangladesh, Pakistan, Southeast Asia and Indonesia eastwards, and westwards, through Africa, to Spain in Europe. This wide geographical expansion, in time, gave rise to regional styles of and contributions to Islamic historiography.

In Africa, the Islamic tradition came into contact with a great variety of regional situations in:

(i) Egypt and Northern Africa, the cradle of ancient traditions

(ii) The Maghrib or Islamic West, the gateway to Spain

(iii) Ethiopia and the Horn of Africa, with an early history of relations with Southern Arabia

(iv) Western Sahara

(v) Western Sudan and

(vi) Central Sudan, with secondary influences from the Maghrib and Egypt

(vii) Eastern Sudan, with its Egyptian and Central Sudanese contacts, and

(viii) East Africa within the Indian Ocean zone of Persian, Arabian, and Indian activities.

The Islamic tradition of historiography then, encountered the oral tradition in many of these regions of Africa for a second time, after its assimilation of the Arab oral tradition in its own formative years. In other regions, it encountered more complex situations or forms of multiple traditions and influences.

It would be best to approach the practice of Islamic historiography in Africa in the context of its regional varieties, situations, and contributions.

4.2 Regional Variations

Several factors have created the varieties in the impact the Islamic tradition has achieved in Africa. An enquiry into four areas would reveal some of the most significant factors:

(i) the internal history of the region which set limits to the extent of Islamisation,
(ii) the pattern of Islamisation,
(iii) the nature and processes of the encounter between the Islamic and internal tradition, and
(iv) the outcome of the encounter and the transformations that occurred in the historiographical tradition within the region.

In North Africa, the Horn, the East African coast, and the Eastern Sudan, Arab populations moved in as immigrants, visitors, or conquerors, and took over as rulers, minorities, or dominating minorities. There were secondary movements from some regions into others, such as the Western, Central and Eastern Sudan belt and the Western Sahara. These immigrants, visitors, or conquerors, converted or influenced the populations of these regions to Islam and to Islamic traditions. Demographic and ideological factors, then, were also significant.

The regions designated for discussion include only those in which Islamic populations have been significant or in which the ideology or practice of Islamic traditions have exercised significant influence. No region of Africa has been isolated for discussion where there is no evidence of an encounter between traditions which has influenced the practice of history in it.

(i) *Egypt*

At the first surge of the Muslim expansion in the seventh century, Egypt was under Christian Byzantine rule from Constantinople, but serving mainly its established role of a supply source of food and funds. In Egypt, a Coptic Monophysite Christian tradition was already the established order. The Coptic peasantry relied on the monasteries which were also agricultural institutions. Local traditions named Saint Mark as founder of the Egyptian Church from the very beginnings of Christianity in the first century, supported by the presence of Jewish communities from the preceding four centuries. From the second century, the Patriarchate of Alexandria played a significant role in the development of the universal Christian Church, with its strong Graeco-Roman heritage, including the production of the Septuagint, and as the nursery of spiritual and intellectual leaders, for example, Clement, Origen, Athanasius (who consecrated Frumentius bishop of the Ethiopian Church), and the monks Antony and Pachomius.[9]

In the history of the expansion of Islam, as in that of Christianity, Egypt featured as one of the early fields of conquest. Its wealth was clearly a compelling attraction. The city of Babylon was seized in 640/1 AD and Alexandria in 641/2 AD. Egypt was thenceforth ruled by orders from Medina (Arabia), Damascus (Syria), and Baghdad (Iraq) under policies varying from conversion of the Copts to Islam, tolerance of religious difference, and the exploitation of gold and grains in taxes. From the ninth century, the local rulers began to demand more and more autonomy, and the centre of authority moved, first to Fustat, and then to Cairo in a new Muslim Egyptian empire.

In the cultural and intellectual domain, the building of the mosque university of al-Azhar in the new city of Cairo in 970 AD was a crucial event in the Islamization of Egypt and its creation into a centre of learning in the Islamic world and the dissemination of Islamic traditions to other parts of Africa.[10]

Papyrus records reveal a gradual change in Egyptian literary output from the use of Greek, and Coptic, in the seventh to Arabic by the ninth century, evidence of the process of Arabization and Islamisation. The early establishment of effective central administration in Egypt also ensured the keeping of archives and the rise of an Islamic historiographical tradition. The work of the earliest Egyptian Islamic historian, Ibn 'Abd al-Hakam, shows the effect of this growing strength of archives from about 700 to 725 AD when a local crop of historians in the new tradition also began to appear.

The papyrus evidence for the development of Egyptian historiography is supplemented by the evidence of archaeology which confirms the continuing influence of the Christian Coptic tradition with which the Islamic tradition interacted. Thus Bishop Sawirus (Severus) b. Muqaffa (died c. 1000 AD), translated the Greek and Coptic histories of the Patriarchate of Alexandria into Arabic. He refuted Eutychius (alias Sa'id b. Batriq) whose history from Adam to contemporary times claimed that the Monophysite, Ya'qubi or

Jacobite Church in Egypt was the one founded by the Apostle Mark. He wrote in Arabic and arranged material "by the reigns of the caliphs".[11] John, Bishop of Nikiou in Lower Egypt wrote a *Chronicle,* a universal history of Egypt culminating in the Muslim conquest. These histories by Christians and Muslims in the era of encounter represent coalescing traditions of historical practice inspite of the difference in the religions placed as the focus of attention.

Ibn 'Abd al-Hakam served as the pioneer model. Few historical works have survived from the Fatimid period, the most notable being Ibn Zulak (died 996), al-Musabbihi (died 1029), al-Quda'i (died 1062), and Ibn al-Sayrafi (died 1147). Of the Copts, Al-Shabushti (died 1008) wrote a detailed history of monasteries.[12]

In the Ayubid period, the historiography reflected the glamour of the crusading leader, Salah al-Din. 'Imad al-Din al-Isfahani (1125–1201), Ibn Shaddad Batal al-Din (died 1234), and Abu Shama of Damascus (died 1268) wrote biographies of Salah al-Din. Two Coptic minority historians, al-Makin (died 1273) and Butrus b. al-Rahib (1270), wrote universal histories from the Creation to the mid-thirteenth century. A biographical dictionary of both Greek and Arab physicians and scientists by 'Ali al-Qifti (1172–1248) recorded the processes of the Graeco-Roman heritage of the Islamic tradition.

In the thirteenth century, the language of even Christian historiography changed from Coptic to Arabic. Indeed, from about the twelfth century, only a few educated clergy knew

Coptic, and even Christian books had to be translated into Arabic to make them accessible to the masses, and even to the majority of the clergy.

The Mamluk period was remarkable for the quantity of historical work and the high quality of some of the work. The subjects ranged from Egyptian history to India, Ethiopia, West Africa, and Asia. The historians included Abu'l-Fida (1273–1332), and al-Maqrizi (1364–1442), adjudged "the most eminent scholar" of the period, Ibn Taghribirdi (1411–69), and Ibn Iyas (1448–1524). It was to this environment of expanding scholarship that Ibn Khaldun (1332–1406) travelled from the Maghrib to live twenty years to work on his monumental *Al-Muqaddima*.

In Egypt then, the Islamic tradition was firmly established by conquering Arabs and immigrants, who eventually converted numbers of the Coptic peasantry to Islam, and Arabised the language even of those who remained Christian Copts. In the outcome, Cairo's al-Azhar was established as a centre of Islamic scholarship in the Islamic world as a whole, and made Egypt a mediator of the Islamic tradition to the rest of Africa.

(ii) **The Maghrib**

The western coastlands of North Africa from the borders of Egypt to Morocco have, from antiquity, had a history within the Mediterranean region, and an inner one facing south and east to the Sahara desert and across it to West Africa, and to

Afroasia. It has, indeed, been a sort of island, with links across the Mediterranean and the Sahara to Europe, Asia, and Africa, and to other islands. In various periods, there have been distinctions between urban centres, mainly on the settled fertile coastal regions, and the unstable highlands and hinterland, grading into the inhospitable desert.

The various Berber communities of the region provided the continuity of the local oral tradition against the external traditions of the Phoenicians of Carthage, the Greeks, and the Romans. The Islamic tradition of the invading Arabs overlaid all of these traditions, taking over directly from the Christian Eastern Roman or Byzantine.

The Punic heritage of Carthage was incorporated into the Berber from its history of a literate civilization in contact with the Greeks, trading and exploring around the Mediterranean and the north-western Atlantic coasts and islands of Africa from about 814–13 BC to 146 BC when it was destroyed by the rising Mediterranean power of Rome. The sole extant written documentation from this period is the brief *Periplus* of Hanno recounting exploration of the West African coast, dated to about 425 BC.[13] Other expeditions by Phoenicians are only noted in Greek and Roman accounts, such as the circumnavigation from the Red Sea commissioned by Pharaoh Necho II (c. 609–593 BC), reported by Herodotus, and the voyage of Himilco noted in the text by the Roman geographer, Avienus, *Ora Maritima*.

The period of rule from Rome lasted from 146 BC to the Vandal invasions of the fifth century AD. The Eastern Empire resumed control from 534 AD to the time of Arab take-over. The Romans who imported "bread and shows" from their African provinces, produced a crop of Afro-Romans or African Romans (Apuleius, Tertulian, Cyprian, Augustine) who made a considerable contribution to the western literary and intellectual tradition. The contribution of St Augustine to the Western Christian historiographical tradition will be outlined later. The Romans are, however, assessed as having achieved only "imperfect Romanization" of the Maghrib since the Roman legacy "disappeared completely", to be replaced by Arabic.[14]

Islamic Maghrib extended from "the near west", *al-Maghrib al-adna*, eastern Maghrib (Libya), through Ifrikiya (Tunisia), central Maghrib, (Algeria), to "the far west", *al-Maghrib al-Aqsa*, Barbary or Morocco. Its conquest by Islam took place in the first century of Islam, the seventh century of the Christian era, along with the conquest of Egypt, but its Arabisation and Islamization took longer to accomplish because of its greater complexity and geographical extent. The populations of the urban centres and coastal plains tended to be Romanised and Christian, while the majority of Berber communities remained traditional and fiercely independent in the interior mountains and desert, and even the Christian communities being divided into hostile sectarian factions. The situation was made even more complex by the nomadic populations of Berbers and immigrant Bedouins from Arabia moving into the Maghrib in the wake of the conquest.

The character of the Maghrib ensured a slow and protracted period of conflict prior to the establishment of settled government and Islamic orthodoxy.

Although the conquering Ukba ibn Nafi had established Kayrawan in 670 AD as a military and Islamic cultural centre, a minority of native Christians still existed in the cities, and by the eleventh century, there were still up to forty seven bishoprics in the Maghrib.[15] The full conquest and Islamisation of the Berbers went on even more slowly. Initial resistance was crushed by the Arab invaders and formal conversion obtained from leaders and rulers in waves of conversion and apostasy with the tide of war until the defeat of the Berber heroine al-Kahina in 703 AD. Thereafter, the Arabs tried policies of peaceful conversion, including the appointment of Islamized Berbers to high command and office. Islamized or not, the Berbers generally remained hostile to Arab domination and rule, and continued the struggle through the adoption of variant religious ideologies within and outside Islam.

Thus the Berbers adopted the democratic ideologies of the Kharijites "the oldest Islamic politico-religious sect" across the Maghrib from Tripolitania through Ifrikiya to southern Morocco. From the eighth to the tenth centuries, the two immamates formed by the Berber Kharijites remained independent of Arab rule.

The Barghawata section of the Masmuda Berbers achieved a Berber form of Islam when in 744-5 AD their prophet Salih ibn Tarif composed a Qoran in the Berber language and issued laws and regulations according to Berber customs. This heresy among the Moroccan Berbers was only subdued by the Almoravids in the eleventh century.

The Almoravid movement (1061–1147) led by the Sanhaja, and the Almohad (1147–1269), founded by Ibn Tumart, a Masmuda, and succeeded by 'Abd al-Mu'rnin, a Zanata, indeed, showed the Berber as the major source of a Maghrib regional variety of Islam, along with the nomadic Arab communities. The other notable factor for the creation of a Maghrib variety of Islam was the influence of Arab immigrants from Spain, mainly into the western Maghrib in centres such as Fez, which formed a counter part to the influence of Kayrawan in the eastern Maghrib. The Malikite school of Sunnite Islam became dominant in the Maghrib, and was exported across the Sahara into the Western and Central Sudan.

The Almoravid and Almohad movements provided the motive force for a local Maghrib tradition in architecture, literature, philosophy (taking off from Ibn Rushd or Averroes of Cordoba, Spain), science, and of historiography, reaching its peak in Ibn Khaldun (1332–1406).

The Arabic historians of the Almoravids were al-Bakri (1067/8 AD), al-Qadi Iyad (1088–1149), al-Zuhri (mid twelfth century), Ibn al-Athir (died 1233), Ibn 'Idhari (1306). The major contemporary accounts on the Almohads were *al-Mujib* by 'Abd al-Wahid al-Marakushi, *Nazm al-juman* by Ibn al-Qattan, and *al-Mann bi'l-imama*, by Ibn Sahib al-Salat.

A number of general histories and chronicles also dealt with both movements : *al Juz'al-talit min Kitab al-Bayan al-Maghrib* by Ibn Idhari, *Juz'min kitab Nazm al-juman* by Ibn al-Qattan, *Kamil fi'l-tarikh* by Ibn al-Athir, *al-Bayan al-Mughrib* by Ibn Idhari al- Karrakushi, *Rawd al-Qirtas* by Ibn Abi Zur'al-Fasi, *Tarikh al-dawlatain* by Zerkeshi, and *Kitab al-'ibar* by Ibn Khaldun. Abu Muhammad 'Abd Allah al-Tijani travelled through most of the Maghrib between 1306 and 1309 to write *Ribla* ("journey").

In his *Kitab al-Ibar*, Ibn Khaldun was "nurtured by his experience in the Maghrib". He contrasted "primitive nomadic life with civilized city life": the one based on *kabila* and *asabiyya* (group consciousness) "founding new empires and continually threatening established states; the latter first blossomed, then withered and finally disappeared beneath the impact of a new nomad force".[16] He concluded that the invasion of the Arab Banu Hilal and the effect of plagues on Maghrib demography had created a "new world". For the period of Maghrib history it covered, it represents "the fundamental documentary source", although it did not follow the rigorous methodology advocated in Ibn Khaldun's *al-Muqadimmah*.

In his *Muqadimmah* , Ibn Khaldun moved beyond the Maghrib to write a philosophy of history representing the maturity of the historiography of Muslim Africa, and the contribution of Islamic historiography as a whole to the pool of world historical theory.

(iii)   ***Ethiopia and the Horn***

Prehistoric archaeology identifies Ethiopia as one of the centres of early human development in Africa. Linguistic studies identify its peoples as speakers of Afroasiatic (Semitic, Cushitic, Omotic) and Nilo-Saharan languages. These classifications indicate the multiple sources of influence in the region from the African continent (mainly Meroe and Egypt) and from Asia (Arabia, Persia/Iran, and possibly India). Egypt became the principal source of Christian and Mediterranean influence but also of Islamic influence. The Falasha Jews of Ethiopia provide evidence of very early Semitic presence, but the Islamic presence eventually became the focus of Asiatic influence in the region. Communities of traditional African religions and cultural practice remained active throughout Ethiopian history as the basic heritage.

The kingdom of Axum, neighbours of Meroe, mentioned in Greek Egyptian sources in the first and sixth centuries AD, in the Ethiopian highlands became the Christian Kingdom and the stable centre of the region. Its foundations were laid in the fourth century in the reign of King Ezana (Abraha) by Bishop Frumentius (Abba Salama/Kesate Berhan) from Egypt.[17] The Ge'ez / Ethiopic script attested from this period became the basis of a Christian literary tradition, and has continued to serve as the liturgical language. These traditions developed into a unifying ideology eventually enshrined in the Ethiopic *Kebra Negast* (Glory of the Kings), of the fourteenth century derived from the thirteenth century Egyptian Arabic text of Abu Salih.[18]

The Islamic presence is grounded in a multitude of traditions of early contact between Ethiopia and Arabia, including: traditions of a letter by Muhammad inviting the Ethiopian *negus negast* (king of kings) to convert to Islam, a migration by a cousin of the Prophet to Ethiopia, a mission by the opponents of Muhammad, and accounts of the activities of Bilal, the Ethiopian follower of the Prophet appointed first *mu'adhdhin* to call the faithful to prayer.[19] These traditions of accord between the Christian kingdom and Islam did not last. Eventually all the coastal regions from Eritrea to Somalia and south-western Ethiopia fell to Islam, forming a ring of Muslim states around the Christian kingdom.

Communities of traditional African religious practice stood as a base against the Christian and Muslim polities. The pre-Christian and pre-Islamic traditions persisted in many parts of the region, neglected, but bearing testimony to the past.

The Christian tradition derived its major external influences from Egypt, including the development of monasteries which became the home of scholars giving lessons in reading, writing, Church music, scriptures, Ge'ez poetry, grammar, and history. Christian Ethiopian historiography gradually developed a Biblical base of ideology including a claim to the possession of "the Ark of the covenant", and a derivation of the Axumite rulers from a union between King Solomon and the Queen of Sheba, and equating the state to Israel. These traditions were embodied in an Arabic manuscript brought by a Coptic priest in the reign of King Gebre-Masqal (Lalibela), in 1225. By the fourteenth century, these claims were enshrined in the Ethiopic *Kebra Negast*. (Glory of the Kings).

The growing strength of the Ethiopian native tradition from the time of Emperor Zera Yakob (1434–68) is exemplified by the philosophy formulated by Zara Yaaqob and his son Waida Haywat, in the reign of Emperor Susenyos (1607–32), comparable in many respects to the contemporary philosophy of Rene Descartes in Europe. According to Sumner, Yaaqob "pursued his studies in the traditional Ethiopian schools until he reached their highest expression in *qane* oral culture, where one is encouraged to develop critical mental habits and exposed to *ge'ez* in all the beauty of its idiomatic purity".[20]

From the first century of Islam, Ethiopia was in contact with its protagonists and antagonists, recorded in Arabic literature and in the identification of Ethiopian words current in Arabia and in the Qoran and *hadith*. The Dahlak Islands provided a middle ground of contact. Arabic and Islamic influences passed from Arabia and the Persian Gulf to Ethiopia and the Red Sea coastlands of the Horn of Africa. The transmission of Islam was carried out in part by Arab migrants to the Horn, but many Islamised Afar, Somali, Galla, and other aristocratic elements also claimed Arab origins and ancestry, inspite of their pride in local identities and roots.[21]

The historiography of the Muslim sultanates is based mainly on Arabic works from Egypt, north Africa and the Muslim East, but a local corpus of chronicles and annals came into being, including: the *Chronological Repertory* of Shoa, and the

History of Walasma.[22] The Egyptian experience of even Christian historians adopting Arabic and Islamic methodology apparently passed into Ethiopian practice as well, since even the *Kebra Negast* had Arabic ancestry.

(iv) **The Western Sahara**

The great sand sea of Africa lies sandwiched between the Arab states of northern Africa and the black African states of the Sahel and Sudan to the south. It stretches across the continent from the Atlantic on the west to the Red Sea and the Indian Ocean on the east. The discussion of this section however, concentrates on the part of the Sahara west of the Nile and the Libyan Desert.

It was, apparently, from about 5000 BC that the Sahara began to "change into desert".[23] Populations of nomadic pastoralists were thus driven south on sedentary populations developing from vegeculture to agriculture. The Sahara thereafter came to represent a barrier between peoples to its north and south, but there are accounts of efforts to bridge it in ancient times. In about 2250 BC Harkhuf sent an expedition from Egypt into the eastern desert, and the Phoenicians after 1100 BC and the Carthaginians after 800 BC, as well as the Greeks after 600 BC could have penetrated it. Indeed, the Sahara was crossed by foot, horse-drawn chariots, and eventually by the camel, "being the transport animal best suited to survive" in the desert, before the jeep, helicopter, and airplane came into use in modern times.

Saharan rock art such as those of Tassili n-Ajjer depict horses drawing chariots in a "flying gallop", and scenes of prehistoric hunters and herders dated to the second half of the first millennium. These scenes disappeared only with the introduction of the camel about the first century BC from Asia, apparently, through Egypt. It spread into Roman north Africa and into the Sahara "only after the beginning of the Christian era"[24] It came into use among the Saharan peoples but became organized into regular caravans for travel and trade between the Maghrib and the Western Sudan only with the establishment of the Arab states after the seventh century AD.

Herodotus began the tradition of reporting on the Sahara from the accounts of Egyptian, north African and Maghribian sources. He reported traditions recording the experiences of mainly two groups, the Nasamonians and Garamantes, living on the edge of the desert. One of his best known accounts concerns the adventures of a group of "wild young" Nasamonians who apparently crossed the desert "in a westerly direction" and were taken prisoner by "some little men of less than middle height", "dwarfs", who took them to a town "all the inhabitants of which were of the same small stature, and all black", and where "a great river with crocodiles in it flowed past the town from west to east"[25] This indicates a crossing of the Sahara from north Africa to the River Niger.

Concerning the Garamantes, Herodotus recorded that they "hunt the Ethiopian hole-men, or troglodytes, in four-horse chariots, for these troglodytes are exceedingly swift of foot".

The "Ethiopians" are, again, apparently, peoples of the sub-Saharan Sudan belt.

Herodotus, then, recorded in detail, accounts of peoples of the Maghrib "nomads living on meat and milk", and does it in his usual method: "I repeat in all this what is said by the Libyans".[26]

The Sahara was occupied by Berber, Libyco-Berber, or Tuareg groups through the Maghrib and north Africa. The modem Haratin are thought to be descendants of the "Ethiopians" reported by Herodotus.[27] The presence of the Saharan writing, *Tifinagh*, related to the Libyan alphabet in the rock art of the Sahara, supports the idea of an essential continuity.

The historiography of the Sahara remained rooted in sources from the Maghrib and Egypt from the Arab Islamic period in the seventh century AD. The quantity of documentation increased gradually through the eleventh and twelfth centuries with the works of al-Bakri and al-Idrisi.[28] The authentic record of the Saharans from antiquity remains the rock art, *Tifinagh* inscriptions, and archaeology.

The Islamization of the Sahara was predicated on the establishment of Arab government in Egypt and the Maghrib. From the eighth century, Islam penetrated the Sahara. The Sahara Berber groups of the Sanhadja: the Masufa, Lamtuna, Djuddala, and others, virtually wrote their own history over the western Islamic world with their leadership of the Almoravid movement from the time of Ibn Yasin from about 1042 AD.

The Almoravid movement conquered the Maghrib from the Sahara, and also initiated a period of active Islamization of the Western Sudan as well.

(v)   **The Western Sudan**

The Western Sudan, extending from the Atlantic coast of Senegal to the borders of modern Nigeria, was inhabited by oral societies at the time of the arrival of Islam mainly from the Maghrib through the Sahara, on the trade caravans. The traders and scholars who followed converged at various centres of trade dictated by the location of the most powerful political authority of the time in control of the trade and security: the Soninke of Ghana until about 1240 AD; the Mandinke of Mali up to about 1468; and the Songhay up to 1591, when the Moroccans invaded.

The early accounts of the states and empires of the Western Sudan are external sources created by Arabs and Berbers from the Maghrib, Egypt, and the Middle East. Some were accounts by travellers and visitors, but others were geographers and scholars deriving their information from those of their compatriots who traded to, visited, or resided in the Western Sudan. There was much bias against the local tradition. Some of the scholars recorded traditions from local sources as well as from North African merchants and business men, and professionals. Ibn Khaldun, for example, recorded accounts of local oral tradition from Western Sudanese Muslims living in Egypt, or on their way to or from pilgrimage.

It was from the period of Songhay ascendancy in the sixteenth century that a Western Sudanese Islamic historiography began to take over the major role of interpreting local history. What, then, did the earlier external historiographers say about the Western Sudan? The predominant tone of condescension towards the local tradition of historiography and culture was best exemplified by Ibn Battuta's description of the *griots* who recited local history to the ruler of Mali around 1352–1353:

"Each of them has enclosed himself within an effigy made of feathers, resembling a [bird called] *shaqshaq* on which is fixed a head made of wood with a red beak as though it were the head of a *shaqshaq* . They stand in front of the sultan in this comical shape and recite their poems. I was told that their poetry was a kind of exhortation in which they say to the Sultan: 'This *banbi* [throne] on which you sit was sat upon by such-and-such a King, and of his good deeds were so-and-so; and such-and-such a king, and of his good deeds were so-and-so; so you do good deeds which will be remembered after you'. Then the chief of the poets mounts the steps of the *banbi* and places his head on the sultan's right shoulder, then upon his left shoulder, talking in their language. Then he descends".[29]

Ibn Battuta confirmed this practice of the oral tradition to be "already old before Islam", and to have continued after the Islamization of Mali. He characterized it as a "comic anecdote".

By the time of this incident in 1352–1353, Islam had been established in the Western Sudan for over three centuries.

The first account of Islamization comes from Al-Bakri (died 1094), who reported the Islamization of Takrur (Futa Toro, Senegal) before 1040 AD:

> "The inhabitants [of Takrur] are Sudan, who were previously, like all the other Sudan, pagans and worshipped *dakakir (dakkur* is their word for idol) until Warjabi B. Rabis became their ruler. He embraced Islam, introduced among them Muslim religious law and compelled them to observe it, thus opening their eyes to the truth. Wadabi died in the year 1040-1 and the people of Takrur are Muslims today".[30]

The two major towns of Sila on the Senegal River were also converted to Islam by Warjabi, but the population of Ghana was not yet converted by 1067-68, but Islam was gradually encroaching, according to al-Bakri:

> "The city of Ghana consists of two towns situated on a plain. One of these towns is inhabited by Muslims, is large and possesses twelve mosques, in one of which they assemble for the Friday prayer. There are salaried imams and muezzins, as well as jurists and scholars".[31]

In "the king's town" traditional religion continued to flourish under the control of persons Al-Bakri termed "sorcerers" anchored on the worship of "idols and the tombs of their kings". However, "the kings interpreters, the officials in charge of his treasury and the majority of his ministers are Muslim".

The king's tolerance of Muslims extended to exempting them from the custom of visitors to his court greeting him by sprinkling dust on their hands. Muslims merely clapped their hands.

In the periods for which Al-Bakri reported, Islam was sold to the people of Ghana on a peaceful platform. Al-Bakri's account of the conversion of the people of a region of Ghana he identified as Malal, became a stereotype in the traditions. According to this account, the king of Malal accepted Islam after a visiting Muslim prayed successfully for rain in the middle of a drought.

This peaceful process came to an end, according to Al-Zuhri, with the irruption of the Almoravids into Ghana in 1076–7:

> "In former times the people of this country professed paganism (kufr) until the year 1076–7 when Yahya b. Abi Bakr the amir of Masufa made his appearance ... Today they are Muslims and have scholars, lawyers, and Koran readers and have become pre-eminent in these fields".[33]

By al-Zuhri's time in the mid-twelfth century, Ghana had apparently become a Muslim nation whose inhabitants travelled to Spain (Andalusia), went on Pilgrimage to Mecca, and spent "large sums on the Holy War".

On the Mali Empire which succeeded Ghana to the hegemony of the Western Sudan, Ibn Khaldun (1332-1406) recorded oral traditions from, among others, *"shaykh* 'Uthman, the faqih of the people of Ghana and one of their chief men, and the most learned, religious, and celebrated of them, whom I met when he came to Egypt, in 1394 in the course of the Pilgrimage with his family ..."[34] According to the account, Mali "outnumbered" and "dominated" the Sudan, conquering "Ghana as far as the Ocean on the west". Concerning religion, "They were Muslims". Barmandana, their first king to make the Pilgrimage "was followed in this practice by the kings after him".

The royal Pilgrimage which made the greatest impression in Egypt was that conducted by Mansa Musa (1312–1337), because of the size of his entourage and the amount of gold he gave away. However, the Pilgrimage expanded Mali's contacts with the Islamic world and deepened the knowledge of the scholars who followed the Mansa. According to Al-Umari (1301–1349):

> "a letter came from the sultan to the court of the Sultan in Cairo. It was written in the Maghribi style of handwriting ... In it he follows his own rules of composition although observing the demands of propriety. It was written by the hand of one of his courtiers who had come on the Pilgrimage".[35]

The Songhay based in Gao and holding sway over the Niger Valley all the way to the border of modern Nigeria, became the last great power in the Western Sudan. Their rulers were Muslim, from the evidence of "royal steles" near Gao.[36] From this period, we have records of a great flowering of learning at centres on the Niger, the most famous of which being Timbuktu, where Islamic scholarship originally brought by Arab and Berber scholars became the property of indigenes of the Western Sudan.

What, then, has been the internal Islamic historiography of the Western Sudan from the sixteenth century? Five categories of local historical writing have been identified: chronicles (particular and general), general histories, biographical dictionaries, and *nawazil* (formal legal opinions).[37]

The two outstanding examples of the **chronicle** were the *Tarikh al-Sudan* (History of the Sudan), written by 'Abd al-Rahman Al-Sa'di (1596–1656) of Timbuktu, *and Tarikh al-Fattash fi akhbar wa-'l-juyush wa-akabir al-nas* (The Chronicle of the Researcher into the History of Countries, Armies, and Principal Personalities), written over a period of years by composite authors. Although of Berber origin, Al-Sa'di's *Tarikh al-Sudan* represents the local scholarship developed at the famous Sankore Mosque at Timbuktu which became the centre of Islamic education in the Western Sudan. Indeed, *Tarikh al-Sudan* has been termed the official history of Timbuktu, recounting the biographies of its principal scholars and of the rulers of the Songhay empire through the period of the Moroccan conquest in 1591.

The *Tarikh al-Fattash,* emended and added to by several authors, was completed by Ibn Mukhtar Qunbulu around 1664 from texts and/or notes from his grandfather Mahmud b. al-Hajj al-Mutawakkil Ka'ti and his uncle Isma'il Ka'ti. The Ka'ti family were of Soninke origin living at Tindirma near Timbuktu, and the *Tarikh al-Fattash* represents the spread of Islamic scholarship among local communities of the Western Sudan. This work, in fact, cites chronicles of an earlier date than even the *Tarikh al-Sudan* such as Al-*Durar al-Hisan fi Akhbar Muluk al-Sudan* (The Good Abundance in the News of the Sudanese Kings) written by Baba Guru al-Hajj Muhammad of the al-Amin Kanu family, immigrants to the Western Sudan from the Central Sudan city of Kano.

The *Tarikh al-Sudan* cites Timbuktu's international scholar, Ahmad Baba (1556–1627) whose outstanding works, *Nail al-Ibtihaj* (The Obtaining of Pleasure) and *Kifayat al-Muhtaj* (The Sufficiency of the Needy), were known throughout the Sudan region, Maghrib, and the Middle East. Though of Sanhaja Berber stock, Ahmad Baba, of the dominant Aqit family, belonged to Timbuktu, at a time when it rivalled the Maghrib in influence, and had direct access to centres of learning in Egypt and the Middle East. Ahmad Baba wrote a total of fifty six works, out of which thirty two have survived. His private library in Timbuktu contained over sixteen hundred books. His *sanad/isnad* (line of transmission of knowledge) led to Mecca, and in Timbuktu to Muhammad Baghayughu, whom Ahmad Baba declared a *mujaddid*, renovator of the faith.[39] Ahmad Baba became, indeed, both "the last of the outstanding Aqits" of Timbuktu, and "the most outstanding student" of Muhammad Baghayughu, whose school, through his family and associates, spread Islamic education through the Western Sudan as the inheritors of the Aqit prestige from the sixteenth century, through the nineteenth century to recent times.[40]

Timbuktu formed a centre from which Islamic literacy was disseminated south and east towards the Atlantic coast of West Africa. The Malinke and Soninke *dyula or* "Wangara", served the same functions here as the Arabs and Berbers, following the trans-Saharan trade into the Sudan. The *dyula* established urban centres along the trade routes which became centres for the transmission of Islam and literacy, throughout the modern republics of Mali, Guinea, Upper Volta, Ivory Coast, and Ghana. In such centres, the *dyula* established Koranic schools from which some graduates proceeded to higher studies under established scholars and teachers to receive a turban, *ishad,* and staff to qualify for appointment as an *imam, qadi,* or *mufti.* Such men formed a professional class of *ulama* in Arabic (singular, *'alim),* or *karamoko* in Malinke, meaning, "one who can read".[41]

These *karamoko* then, served as the agents for the spread of religion and learning and guardians of the Islamic way of life throughout the Western Sudan.

The centres of scholarship were based in the Jenne-Timbuktu axis in the earlier periods, but by the mid-eighteenth century, the *ulama/karamoko* of the regions to the south and east had begun to produce original works of their own, in Arabic and in local languages, especially in Hausa. The collections of Islamic literature in these centres reflect the contacts established throughout the Islamic world from the Maghrib through Egypt to the Middle East. Such centres in the northern region of the Republic of Ghana included Buna, Banda, Wa, Yendi, and Kumasi. The local output of scholarship was also respectable, representing a fusion of traditions from the Wangara-Dyula, Hausa, and local roots. The earliest extant local historical work is *Isnad al-shuyush wa'l-'ulama* or *Kitab Ghunja* (History of Gonja) by al-Hajj Muhammad ibn Mustafa of Gonja, dated AD 1752, written in the chronicle style of the Timbuktu school. Others dating from the late nineteenth century are Mahmud ibn 'Abdallah's *Qissat Salagha Tarikh Ghunja; Tarikh Daghabawi* (History of Dagomba); and *Tarikh ahl Wala* "a history of the kings and *imams* of Wa, compiled in 1922" in Hausa and Arabic versions;[42] many of the Hausa versions of these and other works being accredited to Mallam al-Hasan of Salaga.

The history of Islamic historiography in the Western Sudan clearly shows its accommodation to the local oral tradition from the earliest external Arab and Berber scholars, to the internal Timbuktu school of Berber/Soninke/Malinke scholars, to the historians of diverse local traditions propelled principally by the scholarly tradition of the *dyula*.

(vi)   **The Central Sudan**

The Central Sudan contrasts with other regions in the impact on it of Islamization. Its geographical location and relation to the trans-Saharan trade routes differentiated it from neighbouring regions. It did not receive Arab settlers like the Maghrib and the Eastern Sudan, nor even resident colonies of Arab traders and professionals or travellers to the same extent as the Western Sudan. Its geography gave it sufficient isolation to keep its oral tradition strong enough to be the dominating characteristic of the Islamic historiography in Arabic and local languages. Indeed, a great deal of the earliest Islamic historical expression issued in anonymous transcriptions of the oral tradition. Yet its central position ensured the reception of ideas and influences from the far western Maghrib through the Western Sudan (especially from the Songhay centre of Timbuktu), and from Ifriqiya and the eastern Maghrib down the trade route from Tripoli. Once Islamised, the region had relatively easy access to the Middle East on Pilgrimage.

Kanem-Borno provided the typical case of the history of the Islamisation of the Central Sudan. The earliest account occurs in the *Mahram* of Umme Jilmi (c. 1080 AD), a local document, *mahram* being "letters patent, or grants of privilege, given by various Mais from the earliest times of the Kanem kingdom to certain learned or noble families, which owe their preservation to their contingent material value to the grantees and their descendants".[43] According to this *mahram*, the first ruler to be converted to Islam was Mai Umme (Humai) who authorized the privileges enumerated in the *mahram to* "Mu'alim Muhammad ibn Mani, from whom I learnt the Ku'ran and Risala", and to others.

The *mahram* suggests that Kanem-Borno had been in contact with the Muslim world prior to the 1080s, and all succeeding rulers are reported to have gone on Pilgrimage. Al-Qalqashandi (1355–1418), for example, reported the people to be Muslim, and the ruler to be in correspondence with the Sultan of Egypt, and he specifically disputed the genealogy claimed by the Saifawa/Sefawa ruler:

> "the king mentioned that he was descended from Sayf b. Dhi Yazan. But he did not establish the genealogy, for he said [also] that he was of Quraysh, which is an error, for Sayf b. Dhi Yazan descended from the *tubba's* of the Yemen, who were Himyarites".[44]

Kanem-Borno reached its height in the reign of Mai Dunarna Dibalami in the thirteenth century, and consolidated through the conquests of Mai Idris Alooma (1569–1619), which form the subject of the best known example of local historiography, Ibn Fartuwa's *Tarikh Mai Idris* (History of the First Twelve years of the Reign of Mai Idris Alooma), and *Tarikh Mai Idris wa ghazawatihi* (Kanem Wars of Mai Idris Alooma).[45] Both works were first brought to the attention of Europe by the traveller, Heinrich Barth in 1853. In the first work, Ibn Fartuwa established a relationship with the converter of Borno to Islam, by signing himself "Imam ul Kabir Ahmad ibn Fartua of the tribe of Muhammad Mani". In other sources, he is named Al-Imam Ahmed ibn Fartuwa al-Barnawi; the first chronicler of Kanem-Borno in the Islamic tradition.

Another extant historical work of the seventeenth century exemplifies what became a characteristic historical genre of the Central Sudan, the city chronicle. The book, *An Account of N'gazargamu*, the capital of Borno after the move from Njimi east of Lake Chad, was written by Muhammad Salih ibn Isharku in about 1658.[46]

Palmer's *Sudanese Memoirs* and *History of the First Twelve years of the Reign of Mai Idris Alooma of Bornu* contain examples of several chronicles (Kano, Asben, Mandara, Bagarmi, Ahir), but also a number of categories of historical record of local origin. The *mahram* or "letters patent", Palmer thought, best approximated to "contemporary record". The *diwan* represented a general history or collection of traditions. Indeed, outside the books by Imam ibn Fartuwa and Ibn Isharku, Palmer acknowledged most of his collection to be "anonymous" and to "represent merely oral tradition".[47]

Hausaland followed Kanem-Borno in the Central Sudan for its importance as a centre of Islamic scholarship. The cities of Kano, Katsina, Zazzau (Zaria), and Sokoto were pre-eminent at various times, from about the fifteenth century through the nineteenth century. Hausaland was open to influences from Kanern-Borno, the Eastern Sudan and the Middle East, the Maghrib and Egypt, and to the Western Sudan, especially from the period of Songhay hegemony. From the nineteenth century, the Sokoto Caliphate became itself a centre for the dissemination of Islamic learning and inspiration to its neighbours across West Africa.

The Kano Chronicle, *Tarikh Arbab Hadna al-Bald al-Musamma Kano (*The History of the Lords of the City Called Kano) provides the first documentation of the processes of Islamisation in Hausaland.[48] This remarkable anonymous document records the dynastic history of Kano in great detail down to the nineteenth century, and bears all the marks of oral transmission, and of transcription by the *ulama* of Kano only in the nineteenth century. The chronicle states concerning Islam:

> "The eleventh *sarki* was Yaji, called Ali ... In Yaji's time the Wangarawa came from Melle, bringing the Muhammadan religion. The name of their leader was Abdurahaman Zaite... When they came they commanded the *sarki* to observe the times of prayer. He complied, ... *The sarki* commanded every town in Kano country to observe the times of prayer. so they all did so. A mosque was built beneath the sacred tree facing east, and prayers were made at the five appointed times in it. The *sarki* Garazawa was opposed to prayer ...".

The dates of Yaji's reign from 1349–1385 place these events in the fourteenth century from Mali territory through the agency of Wangarawa who became the functionaries of the Faith and its teachers. The strength of local opposition is also indicated. It would appear that Islam was only firmly established from the fifteenth century in the reign of Muhammad Rumfa (Rimfa), dated 1463–1499. According to the Chronicle:

> "He was a good man, just and learned... In his time the Sherifs came to Kano. They were Abdu Rahaman and his people... Abdu Rahaman lived in Kano and established Islam. He brought with him many books.

> He ordered Rimfa to build a mosque for Friday, and to cut down the sacred tree and build a rninaret on the site. And when he had established the Faith of Islam, and learned men had grown numerous in Kano, and all the country round had accepted the Faith, Abdu Karimi returned to Massar, leaving Sidi Fari as his deputy to carry on his work."[49]

The two accounts of the establishment of Islam from the west in the fourteenth century and from the east in the fifteenth century confirm the multiple routes of influences reaching Hausaland. The visitor to Rumfa has been identified as the scholar Muhammad b. 'Abd al-Karim al-Maghili of Tilemsan (died 1503), who later wrote a *nawazil* on Rumfa's request, on the art of government, *Taj al-din fi ma yajib 'ala al-muluk* (The Obligation of Princes), and eventually settled in Kano.[50]

In Katsina also, al-Maghili is associated with the introduction of Islam, and the traditions name him "Abdulkarimu"[51], again, suggesting a dating in the fifteenth century and early sixteenth century as the period of the spread of Islam through the major cities of Hausaland. By the early eighteenth century, a local historiography had come into being in Arabic. The first history of Katsina, *Kitab ila ma'arifat umara Kashna*, is dated eighteenth century, and *Kitab tartib umara Kashna* is dated in the first decade of the nineteenth century in the period of the Sokoto jihad. These were king-lists in the tradition of the Kano Chronicle, being transcriptions of oral accounts, without the Kano Chronicle's detailed presentation.

An indigenous crop of scholars in the Islamic tradition began to emerge from about the seventeenth century, most of whom were trained in Borno. The historians are represented by Ibn al-Sabbagh (Dan Marina) of Katsina, Muhammad Dan Masani (born in Katsina in 1595), and Muhammad al-Katsinawa (died 1741). There were also a whole group of Borno scholars who migrated into Zazzau, or whose ideas were widely known in Hausaland, such as Muhammad b. 'Abd al-Rahman al-Barnawi (died 1755), al-Tahir b. Ibrahim al-Fallah, alias al-Tahir Fairrama, and Jubril b. 'Umar. Many of the writings of these early scholars are only known through the references in the writings of the jihadists of the nineteenth century following the *mujaddid*, 'Uthman b. Muhammad b. Fudi (born 1754).[52]

'Uthman's jihad which resulted in the foundation of the Sokoto Caliphate in the first decade of the nineteenth century became not only a religious revival but also an intellectual revolution. History was recognized as a means of legitimizing the movement and the new structures it put in place of the Hausa system; and as an instrument for locating the Caliphate within a wider Islamic ideological context.[53] The Shaykh 'Uthman b. Fudi himself wrote a treatise placing his jihad in historical perspective, *Tanbih al-Ikhwan ala Ahwal Bilad al-Sudan*. He was followed by his son, Sultan Muhammad Bello, who wrote a systematic historical account, *Infaq al-Maysur fi Tarikh Bilad al-Takrur*. The Shaykh's brother, Abdullahi b. Fudi, first Emir of Gwandu, wrote, first, an intellectual history of Hausaland, *'Ida al-Nasakh man Akhadhtu min al-Shuyukh* (1812), and second, a general history, *Tazyin al-waraqat* (1813). These works from the centre of the Sokoto Caliphate were crowned by the wide-ranging work of 'Abd al-Qadir b. al-Mustafa (died 1864), *"'Abhbar Hadhihi al-Bilad al-Hausiyya wa al-Sudaniyya* commonly known as *Raudal al-'Afkar* and *Qataa'if al-Jinan ala 'Ahwal Ard al-Sudan".*[54] A Western Sudanese orientation and a connection with the Timbuktu school appear in these nineteenth century historical writings.

How deep, then, were the influences from the east passing through Borno into Hausaland? A linguistic study suggests that in addition to possible early Mali and later Songhay influences from the Western Sudan, the Kanuri of Borno also played a key role in the Islamization of Hausaland.[55] This study concludes that although the Hausa words for "book", 'pen', and 'ink' were derived from Arabic, the word for 'write' was derived from Kanuri, and the word for 'read' had been derived from Arabic, but through Kanuri. Similarly, the names of political titles ending in the suffix *-ma*, were derived from Kanuri. That "a relatively small number of basic nouns having to do with the religious, political, economic and social spheres of Hausa culture are certainly, or in some instances, with high probability, borrowed from Kanuri and bear witness to a long continued and important influence upon the Hausa of their eastern Kanuri-speaking neighbours."[56]

The Hausa tradition of Islamic historiography, however, became a fully integrated product deriving its major resources from the oral tradition. The major documents, even in Arabic, remained rooted in the native tradition. In others, the Arabic script was used to express the oral tradition in the Hausa language. This was the case in the *Song of Bagauda*, "handed down from generation to generation, and added to on the death of each Chief of Kano"; and the *Girgam,* written record, which relates the tradition of the origin of the seven 'legitimate' and seven 'bastard' Hausa states.[57] The historiography of the Hausa, indeed, extended outwards with the expansion of the Sokoto Caliphate, and continued in good health to recent times. Sultan Muhammad Bello, for example, cited a book *Ashar al-Ruba fi Akhbar Yoruba* (The Hilltop Flowers: Accounts of the Yoruba); and as recently as the 1950s, the Emir of Bauchi instructed his imam, Mahmud ibn Muhammad Bello, to compose *Tarikh Umara Bauchi* (History of Bauchi); and a *History of Ilorin,* the Yoruba state incorporated into the Caliphate, also exists.[58]

(vii)   **The Eastern Sudan**

The Eastern Sudan of the Arab geographers comprises the northern and western provinces of the modem Republic of Sudan. It is contiguous with the Western and Central Sudan, south of the Sahara, and north of the rainforest; a belt open to Arab influences from the Maghrib and Egypt. In the case of the modern Republic of Sudan, the southern provinces were largely cut off from these influences by "the water divide (consisting of the sudd, Bahr al-Ghazal and Bahr al-'Arab)",[59] creating a "cultural frontier" that has remained fluid.

The regions south of Egypt along the Nile and bordering Ethiopia were the most fertile and attracted most external attention. It was the home of the Christian kingdoms of Nubia, and later of the Funj (Fundj) Sultanate of Sennar (Sinnar) from the sixteenth century. To the west, the regions of Kordofan and Dar Fur bordered Wadai and Kanem-Borno in the Central Sudan.

Islamization and Arabization proceeded hand in hand in the Eastern Sudan, following the occupation of Egypt in the seventh century. The routes of Arab entry into the region across the Red Sea through Ethiopia and the ports of Suakin (Sawakin) and others, and from the Maghrib were not as important as the route through Egypt. From 641 AD a number of invasions were mounted against Nubia, leading to the destruction of the cathedral at Dongola (Dunkula) in 651-2 and the recognition of the kingdom as *dar al- mu'ahadal aman*, "the abode of pact or guarantee",[60] outside the normal categories of *dar al-Islam*, "the abode of Islam", and *dar al-harb*, "the abode of war". By the end of the fourteenth century, Arabs had penetrated and settled the region as camel nomads *(jamala)*, cattle nomads *(Baqqara/Bakkara)*, gold miners, traders *(djallaba)*, and through inter-marriage with the Beja. All the Christian kingdoms were conquered and/or their rulers converted to Islam.

The first Islamic states in the Nile Valley were the Arab sultanate of 'Abdallabi created from the conquest of the Christian kingdom of Alwa in the late fifteenth century, and the Funj Sultanate of Sennar, whose king Umara Dunqas (Dunkus) established his authority over the 'Abdullahbi at the beginning of the sixteenth century. The Funj are known in Sudanese tradition as *al-Sultana al-Zarka* (the Black Sultanate), suggesting its local, possibly Shilluk, origins. Yet the prestige of Islam and Arabization was already so great that the Funj claimed Umayyad Arab ancestry through an immigrant who married a local princess.

The Fur Sultanate and the Keira (Kayra) Sultanate (1640–1874) on the western borders of the Eastern Sudan were also of local origin, and completed a chain of Islamic states running from the foothills of the Ethiopian Highlands westwards to Futa Toro, Senegal.

The main points of cultural contact with the rest of the Muslim world ran along the trade routes west to east, and south to north. The Sudan Road ran all the way across the Sudan belt from the Western Sudan to Dar Fur, Kordofan, and Sennar. From Sennar, a number of routes ran north into Egypt, or east to the Red Sea. The major bearers of Islam and learning were the sufi, jurists *(faqih; fuqara),* and scholars. Maghribi contacts direct from the north-west or through the Western and Central Sudan established the dominance of the Maliki school. However, the first Sudanese scholar, Mahmud al-'Araki (c.1551), was trained in Cairo, Egypt. On the other hand, teachers of the Eastern Sudan eventually attracted students from as far west as Borno and beyond.

The most significant early historical work of the Eastern Sudan is the *Funj Chronicle:*

> "The earlier part of the *Chronicle,* from the sixteenth century up until the early eighteenth century, consists of a king-list with the accretion of a certain amount of

commentary; the later portion describes in some detail the factional strife in eighteenth-century Sinnar, and some versions also treat the early colonial period".[61]

The *Funj Chronicle*, occupies a position in the Islamic historiography of the Eastern Sudan similar to that occupied by the *Kano Chronicle* in the historiography of Kano.

A second significant historiographical work of the Eastern Sudan is *Tabaqat* of Wad Dayfallah, a biographical dictionary of holy men, collected by a scholar from Halfaya, and covering mainly the territory of the 'Abdallahbi in the period of Funj ascendancy.

A third category of internal historical document are land-charters:

"They offer a wealth of information about the governmental structure, land holding system and legal practices of Sinnar. They assist in establishing a chronology, and give insights into the social history of the eighteenth century."[62]

The *Funj Chronicle* and the *Tabaqat* belong to the Nile Valley, but land-charters occur in the Dar Fur as well. The basic common denominator of the historiography of the region, the bedrock of its historiography, remained the oral tradition, especially in the Dar Fur, and the southern provinces of the Republic of Sudan.

(viii) **Swahili: The East African Coast**

The East African coast and its islands developed a sophisticated culture and society from about the thirteenth century through the influence of Arabs and of Islam. The term Swahili by which the culture came to be known was itself derived from the Arabic *sawahil*, meaning coast, a geographical term akin to Sahel used for the southern shores of the Sahara in West Africa.

In East Africa, however, Swahili became a cultural expression for persons who were Muslim, and spoke a dialect of a language, Ki-Swahili, composed of at least three dialect clusters extending over an area from the coast of Somalia to Mozambique and across the continent to the Congo Basin.[63] The history of Arab trade and of Islam in East and Central Africa through the nineteenth century has meant that Ki-Swahili is spoken as a first language or mother tongue in the islands of Zanzibar, Pemba, Mafia, the Comoros and the immediate coast; as a second language in the modern Republic of Tanzania (where the standard form from Zanzibar has been adopted as a national language), and in parts of Kenya; and used occasionally in Uganda, parts of Kenya, and Zaire; and less often in parts of Rwanda, Burundi and parts of the Congo basin.

Ki-Swahili is established as a Bantu language with a capacity for assimilating elements of other languages with which it came into contact, reflecting the history of the East African coast. Ki-Swahili thus has its largest number of loan words from Arabic, the language of Islam, the distinguishing feature of Swahili culture. It has also incorporated words from Portuguese, Hindi from India, German, and English.

Swahili, therefore, meant a culture and its bearers resulting from the historical process of the contact between Islam and the Bantu peoples of the East African coast, with contributions from possible Shirazi (Persian), Portuguese, and other sources from Asia and Europe. What evidence do we have for all these varying contributions in the melting pot of Swahili culture?

The first documents come from Roman and Greek Alexandria, Egypt, being the accounts of merchants trading in the Red Sea and the Indian Ocean: the first century *Periplus of the Erythraean Sea*, the fifth century *Cosmas Indicopleustes;* and Claudius Ptolemy's fifth century *Geography*.[64] These Graeco-Roman Egyptian sources referred to the East African coast as Azania, and the *Periplus* identified its "last mainland market- town" as Rhapta, "a name derived from the small sewn boats" used by the local people, characterized as "men of the greatest stature, who are pirates", but ruled by chiefs, and trading in ivory and turtle shells. The Azanian coast was held to be under the control of traders from south-west Arabia, who understood the local language and intermarried with the Azanians. The Graeco-Roman contact itself has left no trace on the coast.

The Arab and Islamic influences have left the most permanent mark. A period of immigration from the time of Ptolemy's *Geography* is attested by traditions in Oman, and from the tenth century, accounts of Arab geographers, travellers, and merchants provide more direct information on the progress of Arab settlement and of Islamization of the East African coast, Zanj / Zenj, to the Arabs.[65] According to al-Mas'udi (died c.945 AD), the coast was frequented by ships from the Persian Gulf (Oman and Siraf). The most southerly island of Kanbalu (Qanbalu), possibly Ras Mkumbuu in Pemba, had "a mixed population of Muslims and Zanj idolaters".[66] The geography of the coast trade began with the Berbera coast of Somalia to Zanj, adjoining the country of Sofala, which receded into the legendary land of Waqwaq. According to the geographer al-Idrisi (1100–1166), Unguja, a "principal town" of the coast speaking "the language of Zanzibar" were "mixed" but "actually mostly Muslim".[67] Ibn Battuta (1304–1377) visited the coast in 1331 and provided an early eye-witness account of his visit to Zeila, Mogadishu, Mombasa, and Kilwa Kisiwani. Ibn Battuta referred to the coast and the islands as Swahili, and to the East African mainland as "the Zanj country" into which the sultan of Kilwa raided, the booty being disposed of as prescribed in the Koran. The portion prescribed to be given to the *sharif* was given to sharifian visitors from Iraq and the Hijaz, some of whom Ibn Battuta saw at the Sultan's court.[68]

These and other Arab accounts provide sufficient evidence of the long established trade, settlement, and dominance of Arabs and of the spread of Islam in the islands and coast of East Africa. Since settlement was mainly on the islands, no defensive walls were required, and stone buildings and mosques were constructed. However, the mainland supplied the export commodities, and the pursuit of them eventually led to Arab penetration of the mainland in the nineteenth century, following the establishment of Omani rule over the islands.

The other component of Muslim settlers from the Persian Gulf listed by local traditions were the "Shirazi", Persians from Shiraz, the capital of the region of Fars. The Swahili chronicles, including the Kilwa Chronicle, give prominence to the Shirazi as founders of ruling dynasties. Chittick suggests that these "Shirazi" were not necessarily Persians coming directly from the Gulf, but secondary immigrants who had already become "Swahili" through long residence on the Banadir coast of Somalia, from where they migrated south to the East African coast from the second half of the twelfth century.[69]

We also note evidence of Far Eastern contact with, or knowledge of, the East African coast by Chinese (and Indians?), provided by Chinese accounts of it from the ninth and thirteenth centuries, and the occurrence of Chinaware in the archaeological excavations.[70]

The trade of the East African coast was contested and controlled by the Portuguese in the sixteenth and seventeenth centuries; by the Omani Arabs for most of the eighteenth and nineteenth centuries; by the Germans from the close of the nineteenth; and the British from the period of European colonial rule. All of these historical experiences are reflected in the internal Swahili historiography.

A number of Swahili chronicles have been recovered, written in Arabic, or in Ki-Swahili in Arabic script.[71] The best known local history is the *Kilwa Chronicle put* together around 1520–30 by an unknown author in Arabic, a copy of which was recovered in 1872 and placed in the British Museum. An abbreviated Portuguese version was published in 1552 by de Barros.[72] The fuller Arabic version is generally preferred inspite of itself being abbreviated to some extent in the process of copying from earlier versions, so that the last three chapters listed in the contents are missing. Moreover, the Portuguese was apparently written down from information given orally, so that de Barros was unable to distinguish the names Hasan and Husain.

The anonymous author of the *Kilwa Chronicle* gave it the title: *The Book of Consolation of the History of Kilwa,* made up of an Introduction and ten chapters. The Introduction was designed to be theoretical, "an account of the intellect and the arts of the mind". The first chapter dealt with origins; the foundation of Kilwa by a Persian king of Shiraz and his six sons in seven ships, each of which stopped at a different island port (Mandakha, Shauga, Yanbu, Mombasa, Pemba, Mwa, and Hanzuan). When the sixth ship arrived in Kilwa, there was already a mosque named Kibala, and a Muslim named Muriri wa Bari who assisted the Shirazi to buy the island from its pagan ruler with "many clothes". The second chapter recounts conflict between Kilwa and a people named the Matamandalin. Succeeding chapters chronicle the reigns of different sultans.

A brief account of the provenance of the eight "Swahili histories" reproduced in Freeman-Grenville's *The East African Coast: Select Documents*, reveals something of their nature and range.

The first, *Anonymous : A History of Mombasa, c. 1824*, had been collected by the British Governor of the island and translated from the original Swahili into Arabic from which he translated it into English. A French captain later obtained an Arabic version from which he prepared a French translation. It follows the Islamic tradition of beginning with an invocation and gives a narrative of "the last Shirazi" ruler of Mombasa and "what took place between the Arabs of Oman, the Portuguese and the Swahili". It is a true product of the coastal culture, combining the oral and Islamic traditions of historical narrative.

The second to the sixth histories were reproduced from original Swahili texts published in Berlin in 1907 by C. Velten, an officer in the Gerrnan administration of Tanganyika.[73] He seems to have written down the Mwa Kisiwani account from an oral rendition, and to have obtained the Lindi History in a written form. The Kilwa account states that "the original people who built Kisiwani" were the Mtakata, Mranga, and the Machinga, before the Shirazi arrived. The account was credited to "the elders of Mwa Kisiwani", revealing its provenance in the oral tradition. The other histories also follow the oral narrative style.

The seventh, *The History of Pate* was derived from C.H. Stigand, a British colonial administrator who published it in

1913, from the oral account of Bwana Kitini "a direct descendant of the Pate sultans". Bwana Kitini had, himself, sat at the feet of Muhammad bin Bwana Mkuu, alias Bwana Simba (Lion). Apparently, written versions existed, but the informant insisted on "dictation" in Ki-Swahili. This is by far the longest narrative, and lies wholly within the oral tradition.

The eighth, *The History of Kua, Juani Island, Mafia,* was the most recent, "recited" to Freernan-Grenville by Shaikh Mwinehande bin Juma in 1955. The account makes the Shirazi from Persia the original owners of Kua from whom the Arabs took over control.

In historiography, then, as in language, Swahili has remained within the internal African tradition of oral narration and transmission, but dressed in new Islamic garments.

4.3 Ibn Khaldun: An African Philosopher of History in the Islamic Tradition

The Islamic tradition of historiography has drawn contributions from different cultures of the world. The Turks contributed the tradition of official archives, and the Persian, a universal history in the work of Rashid al-Din Fadl-Allah (1247-1318): Jami'-*al-Tawarikh* (Collection of Histories), written in Persian and translated into Arabic, which the author offered to the world as the first "general history of the peoples of the globe and details of the different races of humanity".[75] The *Muqaddimah* of Abu Zayd Abd al-Rahman Ibn Khaldun

(1332–1406) represents the Maghribi African contribution to Islamic philosophy of history.

Born and bred in Tunis and serving in political offices in Morocco, Spain, and as Malikite judge in Cairo, Egypt, Ibn Khaldun was a north African in every sense. Indeed, the project that led to the writing of the *Muqaddimah* was originally designed to be no more than a traditional history of the Maghrib as a means of gaining insight into the practice of politics. In the course of writing the introduction, he came to the conclusion, first, that history cannot be written from the inside without knowledge of the nature of culture; and second, that a regional history of the Maghrib alone would not answer the wider questions he intended to raise. Accordingly, he expanded the project into one for the writing of three books:

Book I: The Science of Culture
Book II: A Universal History from the Creation centred on the history of the Arabs
Book III: A History of the Maghrib.

The massive *Muqaddimah* (Introduction or Prolegomenon) was, accordingly, merely the first, introductory book of the general project titled *Kitab al-'Ibar wa-diwan al-mubtada'wa-l-khabar fi ayyam al-'Arab wa-l-Ajam wa-l-Barbar wa-man 'asarahun min dhawi as-Sultan al-Akbar* (Book of Lessons and Archive of Early and Subsequent History, Dealing with the Political Events concerning the Arabs, Non-Arabs, and Berbers, and the Supreme Rulers who were Contemporary with Them).[76]

The *Muqaddimah*, the first book, represented Ibn Khaldun's original contribution to historiography, a key to the discipline of history. Designed as an Introduction to the *Kitab al-'Ibar*, it became an independent theoretical work with a life of its own, and the principal memorial to its author, and the outstanding contribution of the Islamic tradition to philosophy of history in general. The presentation betrays its double role. The six chapters delineating the Science of Culture are preceded by an Invocation, Foreword, and Introduction to the general history, as well as an Introduction or Preliminary remarks specific to the *Muqaddimah*.

The Invocation identifies the author, and praises, first, God, creator of men and nations, and second, Muhammad, his family and companions. In the Foreword, Ibn Khaldun briefly defines history, reviews the work of earlier historians, and ends with an outline of the project. He defines history as a discipline with a surface and an inner aspect. The surface aspect is merely narrative of events, its appeal lying in its entertainment and information value. The inner variety is, indeed, a species of philosophy, involving speculation and a search for truth through the investigation of historical processes as well as causes, "the how and why of events". Earlier historians are classified into a few 'authorities', a great many 'reporters' who merely copied the work of the authorities, and others who compiled mere lists of kings. In Ibn Khaldun's assessment, even the 'authorities' were defective. In contrast, his own presentation in the *Muqaddimah was* unique, original, and unusual in its method and in its arrangement of chapters and sections, in its comprehensive and exhaustive treatment of subjects and in its explanation of "how and why things are as they are". Ibn Khaldun acknowledged the project to be based on the history of the Arabs and Berbers of the Maghrib, and yet was "an exhaustive history of the world", and "a vessel for philosophy, a receptacle for historical knowledge".

In the general Introduction, Ibn Khaldun outlines his view of the historical craft as it should be practised, and gives an extended criticism of earlier historians. He praises history as a discipline with many approaches, many aspects, and a distinguished goal. History provides examples from the past for the guidance of present generations. Its practitioners require many sources, great varied knowledge, "a good speculative mind", and thoroughness. A historian cannot depend on the face value of any information in the form in which it has been transmitted from the past, but must work from "the principles resulting from custom, the fundamental facts of politics, the nature of civilization, [and] the conditions governing human social organization".[77] Historians must compare and evaluate materials from antiquity with recent or contemporary materials of a similar category. The application of the underlying principles of history, philosophy, "knowledge of the nature of things", "speculation and historical insight" were essential to the achievement of historical truth. A comparative method is essential because, "The past resembles the future more than one (drop of) water [resembles] another".

It was Ibn Khaldun's realization of the historian's need of knowledge beyond the ordinary that led him to write his monumental *Muqaddimah* as Book I of his universal history and history of the Maghrib to provide the basis of the new science necessary to the historian's achievement of truth. In the book's Introduction or Preliminary Remarks[78] he defines history, lists the reasons why historians had failed to achieve historical truth, and therefore, the necessity for a new science of culture, and sets out the organization of six chapters defining the new science.

What, then, is history? Ibn Khaldun defines its scope very widely to embrace all of "human social organization" or "world civilization", and all areas of human life and society. Historians failed to do a satisfactory job from prejudice and partisanship and inability to deal with traditions and informants, but principally out of ignorance of the nature of civilization, the nature of reality, and of the essence of events and actions. They related absurd and impossible stories because of their ignorance of the basic science necessary to historical understanding.

And why were historians unable to acquire knowledge of this science? Because the science had not been brought into existence. Although similar to Rhetorics and Politics, it was not identical to these disciplines, being, indeed, "an independent science", something "new, extraordinary, and highly useful", "an entirely original science". The object of the new science is human civilization or social organization, its fruit, result, goal or end, "historical information". Ibn Khaldun speculated on the causes of its neglect by previous philosophers, and suggested its limited goal: "the mere verification of historical information".

4.4 Conclusion

What, then, were Ibn Khaldun's ideas of the form and content of the new science? He based its construction on certain qualities that distinguish man from other living things:

(i) the ability to think, resulting in the development of the arts (crafts) and sciences.
(ii) the need for a restraining authority or government
(iii) activities towards making a living, and
(iv) the ability to build civilization in cities and hamlets (sedentary) or in the desert (Bedouin).

These characteristics of man determined the division of the *Muqaddimah* into six chapters dealing with;

(i)   Human Civilization in general
(ii) Desert civilization
(iii) Royal authority or government
(iv) Sedentary civilization
(v)   Crafts and ways of making a living, and
(vi) The sciences.

Chapter I consists of six prefatory discussions.[79] The first defines terms. Man is distinguished by the ability to think, and his natural disposition to work in cooperation and to live in towns and cities in organized societies or civilizations under the restraining influence of a ruler, and the ability to create crafts and sciences. The second preface is a division of the earth into seven zones and sub-zones according to Claudius Ptolemy and the Arabic geographers, "on the strength of observation and continuous tradition". The regions of Africa south of the Maghrib, the Sahara, and the states of the Sudan belt was identified as a region of unknown Negro peoples who "cannot be considered human beings". The third and fourth prefaces treat of the effect of climatic conditions on peoples and civilizations. Negroes, for example, are noted to be black because of the heat of the sun rather than because of descent from an accursed ancestor, Ham. The fifth preface deals with the resources of each zone and the sixth with matters of religion and varieties of perception, namely: the "perception of scholars", the "perception of saints", and the perception of prophets achieved in "the state of revelation". Divination and other forms of supernatural perception are discussed in detail and largely dismissed.

In Chapter II,[80] the nature of desert or Bedouin civilization is expounded, mainly in opposition to sedentary civilization in twenty eight sub-sections. Both Bedouin and sedentary civilization proceed from nature and are governed and determined by a number of factors.

First, ways of making a living. Bedouin civilization is based on subsistence agriculture and animal husbandry, while sedentary peoples live in cities and develop crafts and commerce to accumulate wealth and luxuries. Animal husbandry, the characteristic craft of Bedouin culture is itself categorized by the type of animal raised. Thus Berbers and others who keep cattle and sheep mainly, do not normally need to penetrate deep into the desert, while the Bedouin Arabs who keep camels were obliged to move deep into the desert. Accordingly, Ibn Khaldun uses "Bedouin" and "Arab" as technical terms for desert civilization which is 'prior to" sedentary civilization, the "goal" to which the Bedouin aspired.

Second, while sedentary people tended towards luxuries, pleasures, and indulgences productive of "evil qualities", the Bedouin was concerned only with basic necessities, and therefore, preserved a sense of restraint, and developed fewer vices.

Third, while sedentary peoples became lazy and weak in a life of ease governed by laws and protected by walls and hired militia, the Bedouin remained strong and courageous and self-reliant.

Fourth, the principal source of the vitality of the Bedouin was *asabiyah,* group feeling, defined also as "communal ethos, community sentiment, or social solidarity".[81] Ibn Khaldun developed *asabiyah,* group feeling, as a technical term embracing the qualities springing initially from common descent which underpinned the strength of Bedouin civilization, as well as the qualities of leadership and a dominating spirit in ruling dynasties in sedentary civilization. The greater part of the chapter, therefore, deals with the history and nature of group feeling in Bedouin civilizations, and of the "royal authority" or leadership to which it grows in sedentary civilizations. Thus, group feeling in a single family "decays inevitably" within four successive generations, a generation being forty years in duration. The founding generation possesses all the necessary qualities of leadership, the second receives them through direct contact, the third generation can only make contact with them through "reliance on tradition", and the fourth generation loses contact. Such a dynasty can hardly survive in leadership beyond the fifth or sixth generation. At this point, power is seized by a group with a strong group feeling, such as a Bedouin group from the desert, or a rising family from the border regions.

Chapter III[82] extends the discussion of group feeling, *asabiyah,* in the specific context of leadership in government, in fifty two sub-sections. Group feeling is established as the only means of attaining authority, and its meaning expanded to include "(mutual) affection and willingness to fight and die for each other" among members of the tribe, ruling dynasty, or its allies and subjects. The discussion of the conditions, forms, content and nature of government is pursued in comprehensive detail and exemplified in the history of the Maghrib and the Islamic world.

Chapter IV[83] dealing with the sedentary civilization of towns and cities follows logically from the discussion of "royal authority" or government (instituted through group feeling), since royal dynasties are "prior to" and are "absolutely necessary" to the construction and maintenance of towns and cities. The politics, construction, government, economies, and culture of cities are delineated in detail within the context of Islamic history.

Chapter V[84] on economics begins with an exposition of the principles of a labour theory of value, continuing with the arts and crafts that constitute ways of making a living. Some arts, such as writing, medicine, and singing, are "noble" because of their object, while other crafts, such as agriculture, architecture, and carpentry, are "necessary" to the existence of sedentary civilization, and productive of its wealth and luxury. Agriculture is classified as a primary, natural, and ancient craft practiced by Adam. Man proceeds to the development of the secondary crafts only within sedentary civilization.

Finally, Chapter VI[85] deals with the sciences, "the beginning of human perfection and the end of man's noble superiority". It is set forth in a brief Prefatory Discussion and fifty nine sub-sections. Three degrees of intellect and perception are defined:

(i)   a discerning intellect consisting of perceptions,
(ii) an experimental intellect able to grasp aperceptions, and
(iii) a speculative intellect consisting of both perceptions and aperceptions.

From thought proceeds social organization, action, crafts, and the sciences.

Instruction in the sciences is a craft for making a living, while the sciences sub- divide into two categories: philosophical or intellectual sciences, and traditional or conventional sciences. The intellectual sciences are of four kinds: logic, physics, metaphysics, and the mathematical sciences. The traditional sciences are based on the religious law of the Koran and the Sunnah (traditions), supported by the auxiliary sciences of the Arabic language. The craft of scientific instruction flourished in Baghdad, Basra, and Kufah in the East, but had settled in Cairo, Egypt. Qayrawan in the Maghrib and Cordoba in Spain were early centres, which had given way to the fledgling centre of Tunis.

Of the traditional sciences, that of "prophetic traditions", *hadith*, relates directly to history. It was a very specialized discipline recognizing rules for:

(i)   acceptance or rejection of traditions
(ii)   establishing "chains of transmitters"
(iii)   ranking transmitters
(iv)   defining "the way the transmission took place"
(v)   grading the soundness of traditions into "sound", "good", and "weak" categories
(vi)   evaluating the texts of traditions, leading eventually to the establishment of authoritative collections, Al Bukhari's *Sahih*, being considered of the "highest rank".

Of the intellectual "sciences of philosophy and wisdom", logic represented the legacy of the Greeks. Ibn Khaldun traces its history from Socrates, Plato, and Aristotle to the Muslim masters, al-Farabi, Avicenna, and Averroes, and tries to reconcile it to the Islamic law and theology. The other sciences are elaborated into a comprehensive listing of branches. Physics, for example, is shown to include the sciences of agriculture and medicine. The mathematical sciences elaborated through geometry, arithmetic, music, and astronomy to several esoteric branches. The listing of sciences eventually included such pseudo-sciences as magic and alchemy; and the human sciences of linguistics and literature.

The *Muqaddimah* closes with a one-page Concluding Remark, in which Ibn Khaldun suggests that the long treatise had become something of a diversion from his principal purpose of writing a history. Inspite of its length, the *Muqaddimah* remained merely a preliminary study of "the nature of civilization", and "the problems concerned with it". His treatment of the problems could not be complete, and it was the duty of his successors to "add more problems" and so complete the delineation of the new discipline.

Ibn Khaldun concluded that he completed the first draft manuscript of Book I, the *Muqaddimah* in November 1377 over a period of five months, but continued to revise and correct it in succeeding years, as he continued to compose Book II and Book III, the substantive historical parts of the *Kitab al-'Ibar.*

What, then, was the nature of Ibn Khaldun's contribution? He is generally acknowledged to have created an original summary of Islamic historiography and a new science, identified as Sociology, but clear contributions to most disciplines in the Social Sciences and Philosophy of History are manifest. He established the general law that societies and civilizations are, by nature, mortal, and go through stages or cycles of development. For his critical approach to history and for his cyclical theory and conviction that history provides lessons for political action, Ibn Khaldun has been compared to Thucydides, one of the founders of western historiography.[86]

Ibn Khaldun was an original theoretician, and the *Muqaddimah* has been well received in the west and by modern Muslim scholars. Yet, his great achievement in the area of theory was not fully reflected in the actual practice of history, either in his own time or since, in African or world Islam. Hence the call by modern Islamic scholars for a rewriting of Muslim history.[87]

CHAPTER 5

The Western Tradition

1. *Ikagị / Nyingi di*
    Tortoise is / Parent to his mother.
    Nembe proverb, Nigeria (Alagoa 1986:52-3).

5.1 Definitions and History

The western tradition came into contact with the African oral and internal written traditions at the beginnings of its own development, in the visit of Herodotus to Egypt. It came into closer contact with the African traditions in Egypt and northern Africa in the period of Graeco-Roman dominion over these parts of Africa before being displaced and overlaid by the Islamic tradition. It returned to Africa in the period of western European expansion and became established as a dominating presence all over the continent during the period of imperial and colonial rule from the late nineteenth century.

The tradition has continued to grow in strength in the modem world through its internal processes of renewal as well as through the support provided by the western control of global resources. It now claims a central place as the arbiter of universal standards. Here we discuss only its internal history, its encounter with other traditions operating in Africa, and its local manifestations and practice. We attempt to overcome the problems posed by the size and variety of literature in and on the tradition by taking a route cleared through the forest of interpretations by Collingwood for the periods down to the late nineteenth and early twentieth centuries.[1] For the modern and post-modern eras, we cut a short path through the jungle of comments and movements down to the narrativist philosophy of history brought to birth by Hayden White and propagated by Ankersmit and others.[2]

According to Collingwood, history, in the western tradition may be described in terms of its nature, object, methods, and purpose as:

"(a) a science, or an answering of questions;
(b) concerned with human actions in the past;
(c) pursued by interpretation of evidence; and
(d) for the sake of human self-knowledge".[3]

The western contribution to the growth of historiography is thus characterized as, first, its construction into a critical, scientific discipline able to create a body of knowledge; second, its concentration on human affairs; and third, its methodology of interpretation of diverse forms of documentary evidence. The persistence of various forms of non-scientific history in the west is acknowledged under the category of scissors-and-paste historiography. This historiography, based on the collation of testimonies derived from presumed authoritative sources, could develop into critical and pigeon-hole universal histories, but could not provide a body of knowledge. We adopt Collingwood's definition of scientific history, leaving it open to incorporate other ideas from nature, the social sciences and the humanities.

The western tradition traces its roots to the historiography of ancient Greece and Rome, specifically, to the heritage of Herodotus and Thucydides. Herodotus (born c. 484 BC) in the eastern Greek city of Halicarnassus, derived influences from earlier Greek traditions (Homer, Hecataeus of Miletus) as well as from the East, especially from his visits to Egypt and Persia.[4] His innovation in historiography may be considered possibly more radical than the departure from traditional Greek thought made by Socrates in philosophy. Herodotus took account of change against the tradition of current philosophy which accepted only the unchanging as knowable. He introduced the term *historia,* inquiry, research, and produced a work of humanism in classic prose in the mode of the Homeric epic poems. Inspite of defects of methodology and factual errors, Herodotus achieved the title of "father of history" in the western tradition. Indeed, the charges of fable-spinning brought against him by Graeco-Roman critics have been attributed to his successful use of oral tradition and oral history from Egypt and the East, the very qualities that have endeared him to modern professional historians, sociologists, folklorists, and anthropologists.[5]

Thucydides who began to write before the death of Herodotus followed a different path, and criticized his elder. He sacrificed literary excellence for factual accuracy and relevance, being more interested in laws derivable from the events than in the events and the actors. He was, accordingly, more attuned to contemporary Greek philosophy in seeking the typical, general and unchanging element out of the events he described. He depicted the international political system as ruthless in its pursuit of dominion and state interests regardless of morality and justice. In this and other ways, he has been compared to two independent philosophers of history, the Maghribi Islamic historian, Ibn Khaldun, and to the Italian Renaissance historian, Machiavelli.[6] Thucydides died leaving his work uncompleted, and achieved only limited success in his own time, but became more popular only in first century Rome. His conviction that political laws could be distilled from history for the guidance of political action was passed to Roman historians by Polybius. Thus the greatest of them, Tacitus, used psychological analysis of characters and speeches in the style of Thucydides.

The establishment of Christianity as state religion in the Roman Empire introduced a turning away from the humanism of Herodotus, that history was concerned with "man's deeds, man's purposes, man's successes and failures", and the substantialism of Thucydides, that the historical agent was unchanging, that only his actions changed.[7] The first phase of the Christian legacy was summarized and passed on to Medieval Europe by the African cleric, St Augustine, Bishop of Hippo (354-430 AD) in his book, *De Civitate Dei* (The City of God). According to St. Augustine, the Christian kingdom, being the last of the six ages of the Scriptures, would endue even after the fall of the Roman Empire. He believed in a continuing contention between the City of God and the City of the Damned: a history already predestined by God, in which men could achieve good purposes only through the Grace of God.

The Christian legacy was further developed by the priests and scholars of the Middle Ages. The Graeco-Roman idea of human action based on reason was replaced by the idea of original sin which gave man over to control by desire. Second, the unchanging substances of Greek philosophy were replaced by a world in which everything was subject to change except God. Christian historiography created new concepts of universal history leading back from Creation to a future apocalyptic end. It was a historiography which provided for chronology and periodisation, but no call for rigorous research, some of whose ideas flowed into the Renaissance, and provided targets for the leaders of the Enlightenment.[8]

Renaissance historians returned to a concern for human activity, away from the search for a divine plan. But the man at the centre of history was no longer the rational creature of the Greeks and Romans, but one flawed in nature. Nicolo Machiavelli (1460–1527), indeed, believed in the capacity of history to instruct his Italian prince with ideas comparable to those of Thucydides. By the seventeenth century, Renaissance historians had largely freed themselves from the transcendence of Medieval Christian historiography. Two movements, one stimulated by the ideas of Rene Descartes (1596–1639), the other led by Voltaire (1694–1778), the man who coined the term "philosophy of history", moved European historians further in the same direction.

The philosophy of Descartes, through its extreme scepticism of history, challenged the historians into a movement to counter his negative formulations. Descartes did not recognize history as a discipline capable of creating knowledge, but one productive of escapism and fantasy-building. In the Cartesian historiography that was created by the historians and philosophers of history (Vico, Locke, Berkeley, Hume), new criteria for the pursuit of a critical historiography were constructed.[9]

The philosophers of the Enlightenment considered all earlier ages periods of irrationality controlled by religion and priests, and waged a crusade for the enthronement of a future age of rationality through the agency of enlightened despots. Enlightenment historiography was little interested in past periods, especially in the Middle Ages, although Montesquieu and Gibbon made advances even in this area, and Condorcet in a historiography looking forward to a future age of rationality. The movement widened the scope of historiography into the arts, science, economics and culture in general.

Western historiography was lifted out of the phase of propagandist violence of the Enlightenment by the Romantic movement which rescued from neglect the ages declared irrational, and to establish a view of human nature as subject to change. Jean Jacques Rousseau (1712–1778) posed the will of the people against the idea of the enlightened despot, and proposed the institution of popular education to bring the general will to maturity. The movement achieved respect for the histories of non-western civilizations and even for "savage" societies, and of past ages. Its philosophy of history reached its synthesis in the work of Georg Wilhem Friedrich Hegel (1770–1831). The idea of progress in a universal history of mankind, or philosophy of history, were re-established from Voltaire and Herder, the idea of freedom as a developing cosmic process and of the end of history in the present from Kant and other philosophers of the Enlightenment and Romantic movements. Hegel's theory of the dialectic in which concepts (theses) change into their opposites (antitheses), and develop into new concepts (syntheses), became the basis of the influential materialist dialectic of Karl Marx (1818–1883). Collingwood considers Hegel's *Philosophy of History* defective because of its limitation to political history, since Hegel was more effective in "the history of absolute mind, that is, art, religion, and philosophy", and would have done better in these areas.[10] Hegel's formulation of the idea of the *World Spirit (Weltgeist)* as moving from the Orient through the Greco-Roman world to terminate in Western Europe, ruled Africa and other regions and peoples of the world out as unhistorical and irrelevant.

Marx applied Hegel's dialectic to political and economic history, making economics the base of all developments, all else being mere superstructure. He turned Hegel's three stage movement of freedom: Oriental *one*; Greco-Roman *some*, Western *all*, into a three-stage development of the economic base: primitive communalism, capitalism, socialism. The dialectic of history then was the inevitable, but tortuous, movement (through slave society, feudalism, etc.) of all societies towards the communist utopia through their internal class contradictions. In the capitalist societies created out of feudalism, the class struggle between the exploited proletariat and the exploiting bourgeoisie provided the engine of change.

The historiography of Marxism, therefore, proceeded from the past through the present into a predicted future.

Marxism became an impetus for advances in economic history and a motivating ideology in Eastern Europe, Asia, Africa, and Latin America, but did not greatly influence western historiography in the nineteenth century in the era of positivism.

Positivism, with its base in the methodology of the natural sciences, exercised the dominant influence on historiography. The historians adopted the positivist programme of detailed study of facts, and published, in the main, in monographs, but did not proceed to the positivist requirement of formulating general covering laws. Nineteenth century historians were confident in their grasp of research techniques, and in the prestige conferred on historical processes by Darwin's *The Origin of Species* (1859). The leaders of this great movement of scientific history, such as Leopold von Ranke (1795–1886), established the canons of exact critical documentary research to discover particular facts to investigate "what really happened" in the past *(wie es eigentlich gewesen)*, but could not produce syntheses or philosophies of history to explain the course of history.[11] The advances in positivist historiography spread from Germany to France, England, and the United States of America.

Western historiography has moved rapidly in theory and practice in the twentieth century. The confidence gained in the positivist enterprise led to attitudes which insisted on the primacy of historical processes, and to historicism, extended in meaning by Popper to include Marxism and similar theories which held that "change can be foreseen because it is ruled by an unchanging law".[12] The idealist view of Collingwood that historians achieve knowledge of the past through rethinking the thoughts and re-enacting the actions of historical agents in their own minds; Hempel's positivist theories of historical explanation through covering laws; as well as Walsh's colligatory concepts remain contested.[13]

French historians attempted another route of escape from the constraints of positivism under the banner of the journal, *Annales d'Histoire Economique et Sociale,* founded in 1929 by Lucien Febvre (1878–1956) and Marc Bloch (1886–1944). The *Annales* school came to represent a historiography marking the end of positivism, linked to other disciplines, opposed to a history of events, and promoting economic and cultural history in place of political history, the serious study of modes of feeling in place of traditional biographies. From 1946, the movement came under the leadership of Fernand Braudel (1902–1985), and the journal took the title, *Annales, Economies, Societes, Civilization.* Braudel's book, *La Mediterranee et le Monde Mediterraneen a la Epoque de Philippe II,* published in 1949 established the major principles of the *Annales* school, put on display at the International Congress of the Historical Sciences in Paris, in 1950.

Braudel's revolutionary book set out and illustrated his ideas of slow historical changes engendered by geography and environment, the *longue duree,* long duration or long term; the "gentle rhythms" of social history, the *conjuncture,* conjuncture; and the history of events, of "men in particular", *l'histoire evenementiele.* Braudel's system has been termed a "dialectic of time-spans" moving through "a geographic time, a social time, and an individual time".[14]

A New History is exemplified in France by the work of Emmanuel Le Roy Ladurie, insisting on the use of statistics and computer programmes.[15] Claims to the inauguration of New History have come from other parts of Europe and from the United States of America, using combinations of Social Science and oral historical techniques.[16]

However, the most serious current philosophical challenge is the claim of the narrativist philosophy of history - to have superseded all forms of epistemological philosophies of history practised in the western tradition up to the present.[17] The modern agenda for narrativity drawn up in Hayden White's *Metahistory: The Historical Imagination in Nineteenth Century Europe* (1973) gives autonomy to the historical text, or narrative, meaning, all forms of historical writing, the end product of the historian's labours, which it identifies as literary, metaphorical, and allegorical in nature. Four forms or plot types are distinguished: Romance, Comedy, Tragedy, and Satire, corresponding to four tropes or genres: Metaphor, Metonymy, Synecdoche, and Irony.

Ankersmit has stressed the primacy of narrativity and proposed technical terms: *narratio,* for the autonomous historical text, with its own internal narrative logic; *narrative substances*, being the complete image of the historical work, composed of narrative sentences. Ricoeur has achieved a sophisticated reconciliation of narrativity to other philosophical movements of the twentieth century through the consideration of different configurations of time, in a work that promises to become influential, *Time and Narrative*.[18]

Narrativity has not received the unqualified acceptance of the western historical tradition. Yet it has the potential for uniting historians and historiographies and philosophies of history. *Metahistory*, for example, already brings together historians (Michelet, Ranke, Tocqueville, Burkhardt) and philosophers (Hegel, Marx, Nietzsche, Croce). Narrativity also has the potential to accommodate the African oral tradition and other non-western traditions of historiography: and thus achieve the claim of the tortoise to be parent even to those who brought him into being.

5.2 Conditions of Encounter with African Traditions

The conditions of contact between Africa and the west have changed through a number of identifiable periods: the earliest periods of encounter between Egypt and northern Africa and the Greek and Roman west, the participation of these same African regions and of Ethiopia in the experience of early Christendom, the period of European expansion from the fifteenth century down and up the coasts of west, central, southern and eastern Africa, leading to the European colonization of most of Africa in the nineteenth century. Indeed, the intensity of contact in the colonial period has led to a simplified periodization based on it, namely, pre-colonial, colonial, and post-colonial. In such a simplified periodisation, we have to recognize the enormous time-span of the "pre-colonial", the fact that Egypt and northern Africa had encountered earlier Hellenic and Roman "colonial" periods of western contact, and finally, the recent characterization of the post-colonial period as "neo-colonial" because of the degree of continued western dominance over Africa and so many non-western nations of the world.

For the earliest recorded periods of antiquity, the historiography of Herodotus, the "father" of western historiography (c.484–c.430 BC), of Manetho, the Egyptian historian (c. 285–246 BC), and of St. Augustine (354–430 AD), the Berber bishop of Hippo, provide convenient guideposts.[19]

Herodotus visited Egypt in the Twenty Seventh Dynasty (525–444 BC) in the First Persian Period at a time ancient Egypt had already passed its prime but ancient Greece was yet to attain the height of its development. In historiography, Herodotus acknowledged Egyptian methods of keeping records, calendric time and chronology superior to those of the Greeks of his own time. According to Herodotus, another Greek historian, Hecataeus of Miletus, had previously visited Egypt, and had been similarly convinced of the inferiority of Greek methods of determining genealogies. We may note the uniqueness of this period in the history of the encounter between Africa and the west. It was a period in which the west approached Egypt with respect, expecting to learn from the long traditions of written and oral historiography practised in it.

By 332 BC, Alexander the Great had conquered Egypt, and Manetho the priest operated within a "colonial" situation, writing his *Aegyptiaca*, History of Egypt, in Greek for the rulers and the few Egyptian elite accepted into the ranks of the privileged citizenship of Alexandria, "the greatest emporium of the inhabited world".[20] Manetho's history, therefore, represented a synthesis of ancient Egyptian historiographical practice in the idiom of the Greek western tradition. It may, indeed, be characterized as a fore-runner of African historiography of the colonial and post-colonial era from the late nineteenth century. In Egypt, the ancient traditions underwent subjection to Hellenic (332–30 BC), Roman (30BC–395AD), and Byzantine (395–640 AD) subjection, before falling under the current Arab domination. Coptic Christianity became the last receptacle for the combined heritage of ancient Egyptian and Graeco-Roman western traditions, elements of which were transferred to Ethiopia to establish the base of traditions of that Christian kingdom.

For the rest of northern Africa, St. Augustine embodies the high point of acculturation to the Graeco-Roman Christian heritage of philosophy and learning, so that he could live and work in his home town of Thagaste (Souk-Ahras, Algeda) or serve in Rome or Milan as a Professor of Rhetorics. He was, in spirit, a member of that universal society of the City of God which knew no distinction of race or nationality. Yet the final step of his conversion to Christianity was precipitated by his reading of the life of St Antony, the monk of the Egyptian desert, in a garden in Milan in 386 AD, twelve years after being converted to philosophy by his reading of Cicero. He wrote *De*

Civitate Dei (The City of God) in defence of Christianity against its detractors, but ended with an original summation of early Christian historiography, complete with the doctrine or original sin, the grace of God, and predestination. In his *Confessions,* St Augustine made further original contributions in the philosophy of time:

"Augustine's philosophy of time seems to be an original expression of the relaxed relative view of it in the African oral tradition in the context of the western preoccupation with its exact measurement. Augustine makes an effort to pin lime down, but discovers it to be always moving, always in the process of passing 'towards non-being'. If we were to measure time, the only possible unit to consider would be lime passing in the present, yet, 'the present has no space' between a past and a future whose reality is only attested to by memory and prophecy.

"Augustine saw the mind as the key to an understanding of time or of our accounts of the past, or prophecies or predictions of the future. Historical accounts of the past are images recovered from the mind where they had been 'implanted ... like footprints as they passed through the senses'; and even prophecies and predictions of the future are only possible 'from present things, which already exist and are seen'. Accordingly, the past, present and future are merely 'the present of things past, the present of things present, and the present of things future'. And it is the mind alone that synthesizes time: 'Time is nothing more than distension ... of the mind itself'.

"The result is, apparently, instability and indeterminacy. Augustine found the balance in God and the idea of eternity. God precedes all times, created all times, and with Him 'today does not give way to tomorrow, nor does it succeed yesterday'. 'In the eternal nothing can pass away but the whole is present'.[21]

The European Middle Ages were periods of relative isolation of most of Africa except for Mediterranean north Africa, whose Islamic expansion passed from the Maghrib into Spain, and continued in a variety of relationships with the west: peaceful and warlike (as in the Crusades). Ibn Khaldun, the notable product of this African-Andalusian heritage, reports that the major area of the continuation of the Graeco-Roman intellectual tradition in the Islamic tradition was in philosophy and the sciences where early translations of the Greek masters were made into Arabic and provided the basis of advances and contributions. In historiography, Ibn Khaldun was left to work from within the Islamic tradition from his experience of Maghribian history. As with the rest of Africa, the period of the establishment of the hegemony of the western tradition came in the wake of the expansion of Europe from the fifteenth century, culminating in the period of imperialist colonial conquests in the late nineteenth century.

The first impulses for the expansion of Europe were sparked off by the direct pressure of Islam, in part, as an extension of the Crusades, to unflank the enemy, to seize the sources of his wealth and power, or to link up with some imagined Christian ally. Thus Prince Henry of Portugal was set on his path of navigating the seas around Africa by the capture of Ceuta from Morocco in 1415, and by about 1715, the outlines of European hegemony over the Old and the New World were already broadly etched.[22] In Africa, the Atlantic and Indian Ocean coasts of West, Central, Southern, and Eastern Africa were under European mercantile exploitation for slaves, ivory, gold, spices. The major focus of the expansion, however, quickly shifted to India, the Far East, and the New World of the Americas and the West Indies for the exploitation of spices, gold, silver, tobacco, sugar, cotton, furs, and fisheries. Africa, however, remained a crucial link through the supply of slave labour to American plantations and as a half-way station to the East. The continent, accordingly, contributed, through its part in the triangular mercantilist system of the Atlantic (Europe-Africa-America), towards oiling the engines of the Industrial Revolution of the eighteenth century leading to the growth of nineteenth century capitalism, and to its culmination in expansionist imperialism of the late nineteenth century.[23]

The forced migration of large numbers of Africans to the New World provided a potential for new configurations of the African historical tradition in relationships with the western tradition. However, this potential was long delayed in realization because of the conditions of slavery in the West Indies and North American plantations. It was only from about the late nineteenth century and early twentieth century that various movements with historical roots came into being among New World Africans (Back to Africa, Pan Africanism etc.). In Africa itself, the slave trade did not provide conducive conditions for dialogue between the African and western traditions. The trade did not attract a good press, and its processes did not require penetration of the continent or close intercourse between the parties. Only coastal establishments were maintained. Accordingly, European intellectual and missionary interest in Africa was, apparently, less than was shown in the preliterate cultures of the Americas or on the previously literate cultures of India, Indonesia, Japan and China before the middle of the eighteenth century.[24]

Inspite of the unfavourable conditions, over four hundred books and articles were published in the Weest by 1800 and another three hundred by 1865 on West and West Central Africa. The figures for southern Africa were about the same up to 1865, but higher for the rest of the nineteenth century. Lower numbers of publications were made for Central Africa before 1800. The quantity of published material for East Africa was lower than for West Africa before 1865, but levelled up from about that date. The quality of the output was, however, uneven, and often unreliable. No detailed recordings of local traditions were published, as was done in the Americas and Asia. The paradigm of social Darwinism provided the framework for most of these writings, and did not improve the quality of the ethnographic monographs produced in this period. Various official reports, including the Portuguese Angolan chronicles, *catalogo dos governadores de Angola*, came into being from the sixteenth century. All of these documents were prepared at Luanda and similar coastal locations by the visiting European agents and partly Europeanized coastal populations, and did not make contact with the African oral tradition. Clearly, the violence and suspicion engendered by the slave trade created a gap between the visitors and the local community, which was maintained by the language barrier.

In the Kongo kingdom, a local literate class developed in contact with the Portuguese in the sixteenth century, but in West Africa, the beginnings of a written historical expression appeared only in the late eighteenth century, including the statements of former slaves residing outside the continent (Equiano, Capitein, Sancho, Cugoano, Anton Wilhem Amo Afer).[25]

The violence of the era of the slave trade was transformed into new forms in the heart of Africa in the era of colonialism. The new situation took shape after the European nations settled their differences and agreed terms to moderate their scramble for the partition of Africa at the Berlin Conference of 1885. The process of dividing Africa between the European nations was completed in the first two decades of the twentieth century, leaving only Liberia and Ethiopia as independent African nations, but only until their eventual domination by America and Italy before World War II took the next sixty to seventy years for some thirty new nation states to emerge from the colonial experience in the 1960s.

The European colonial system was established through ruthless destruction of primary resistance of African states, kingdoms and empires at various stages of development throughout the continent. Some were occupied by European settler populations, thus producing more complex problems of exploitation and adjustment to colonial domination for the local populations. In most cases, large monopoly capitalist enterprises operated to exploit mineral and agricultural resources of the continent, for which the colonial governments opened ports, railroads, and provided other basic infrastructures for the development of the economy. The colonial system was, in its essential elements, an authoritarian, violent instrument for keeping the conquered population under control, and, therefore, created conditions which separated "natives" from whites, conditions not conducive to a dialogue between the African and Western traditions.

Colonial conquest and a great deal of the colonial experience was traumatic for African populations. In the situation of disorientation, some moved towards Christian conversion and the formal education offered in Christian mission schools, seen as the key to the technology of the conquerors. Accordingly, African pressure forced colonial governments to open more schools than the objectives of colonial policy would have warranted, and many African communities extended the process by constructing independent and Muslim schools.[26] The contradictions which resulted from such initiatives by African peasants, workers, and intelligentsia, and the pressures of the international situation after World War II, eventually transformed the colonial states into new independent African states from the 1960s.

The historiography spurned in the West by the colonial situation varied from theories of primitives without history, to theories of Hamitic motivation for African historical development; to efforts to preserve the local tradition (Islamic written or oral), to efforts for the creation of anti-colonialist histories on the **part** of the African politicians and intellectuals. African efforts to document historical traditions were often supported by missionary agents, and to some extent, by colonial anthropologists. However, the colonial situation was more productive of confrontation than of equal creative dialogue.

In what ways, then, did the colonial regimes actively propagate the European tradition of historiography? First, in the curricula of the primary and secondary schools, and second, in the new western-type universities of Khartoum, Makerere, Ibadan, Legon, and their successors from the 1950s. The colonial government and missionary primary and secondary schools taught almost exclusively, the history of the 'mother country' and the history of her colonial conquests and achievements. It was only in a small minority of cases that the history of the local community was taught by a few enterprising teachers.[27] The new universities introduced African history curricula from the 1950s, served as the nurturing seedbed for a new historiography of decolonization in support of the nationalist struggle for independence, and for the creation of teachers, teaching aids, and curricula for instruction at the lower levels of education.

The post-colonial period did not immediately constitute conditions suitable for the practice of a historiography independent of the western tradition. The African scholars in the new universities were, themselves, trained in metropolitan universities in Europe and America, mostly in the scientific historiography of the nineteenth century. Further, the initial upsurge of optimism for the creation of new schools of nationalist historiography was soon overtaken by the weight of neo-colonialist pressures on the new states, and by the incompetence or venality of some of the new political leadership.[28] In the situation of the growing dependence of the new states on the west in this period of late or multi-national capitalism[29], African historians face depressing psychological challenges: from alienation in colonialism to hope and even euphoria during the process of decolonisation, to disillusion. Marxist approaches which provided an efficient counter ideology in the heyday of world socialism has fallen under a cloud in the period after the collapse of the Soviet Union. Current conditions, then, represent a challenge to African historians for the creation of new historiographies from the varied traditions practiced on the continent.

5.3   Western Representations of African History

Western representations of Africans from antiquity have derived from ignorance, prejudice, ethnocentrism, cultural chauvinism and arrogance, and eventually, from racism. As ignorance was replaced by knowledge, some humane and professional analysts and visitors gained in objectivity and progressively changed from a representation of the African as object to subject of his own history. However, prejudice in its changing forms has persisted through the colonial period into the present.

The fantastic accounts of black peoples outside the regions of their immediate knowledge reproduced from popular myths by the Greek, Herodotus, and by the North African Arab, Ibn Khaldun, illustrate the universality of ethnocentric error and prejudice deriving from ignorance. The accounts of both historians become humane and generous as they begin to discuss groups and individuals of whatever race or colour, from direct evidence. There were, then, cases of error subject to correction through better knowledge. In other cases, however, ethnocentrism and racism were ingrained articles of faith rationalized on what were conceived to be scientific or philosophical grounds. The conditions of the slave trade, colonialism, and neo-colonialism in Africa provided the environment, and the facts of colour and technological difference provided justifications for various conceptions of European superiority and of African inferiority.

Representations based on race were made on concepts drawn from biology, physical and social anthropology, from Christian scripture, colour of skin, from the theory of evolution, and from language and general cultural differences. From these were constructed categories separating civilized from savage and barbarous races on historical grounds. First, history itself was defined as synonymous with alphabetism, the possession of the skills of writing, so that societies or epochs without literacy became ahistorical or prehistoric. Second, on the basis of certain indices of civilization, such as state formation, contact with the west, possession of the wheel, stone buildings, or of other cultural items, societies were adjudged admissible or inadmissible into the territory of history.

Curtin has drawn out the complex web of influences from which British images of Africa were constructed between 1780 and 1850.[30] The period of gradual wind-down of the slave trade and of the rise of "legitimate trade" promised closer relations with African communities, yet the image of Africa as the "dark continent" persisted into the 1850s. British interest was largely focused on West Africa, the core area of the slave trade, but began to include South Africa from the 1820s, and East and Central Africa from the 1850s, and the Congo from the 1870s. The period of the scramble for African territory in the 1880s and 1890s marked the high point of consolidation of British and European images of Africa.

European biologists and theorists constructed a Great Chain of Being in which Africans stood at the bottom and Europeans at the top. Whether they believed in a single origin of humanity, monogenesis, or in multiple origins, polygenesis, the prevalent view placed the Caucasian or white race above all others, and the African or black at the bottom. The Bible provided the source for views which equated the African with a cursed Ham, inferior to the presumed descendants of Shem and Japhet. Even liberal men of letters could not go beyond ideas of a "noble savage" in the representation of the African, and anti-slavery humanitarians remained trapped in the meshes of the prevalent racial categories. And from 1859, even the ideas of natural selection in Darwin's *Origin of Species* could not liberate European representations of the African from racial determinism. Race and language came to be equated, and while the death of the American Indians from European contact was accepted as evidence of inferiority, the survival of the African in the New World marked him out as the "natural enemy" of the European, especially in the context of high European mortality in West Africa, identified as "The White Man's Grave".[31] In the racist environment then, closer contact did not remove error, but compounded it, adding new dimensions of rationalization to existing racist images.

Thus the rationalization of a racist representation of African history reached its most advanced stage in Seligman's *Races of Africa* first published in 1930.[32] Seligrnan identified two white races—Hamites and Semites—and three black races—Negroes, Khoisan (Bushrnen and Hottentots), and Negrillos (Pygmies), in Africa, distinguished by language and an assorted bag of characteristics. In this racial scheme, the Hamites, cursed by earlier Biblical accounts, become "Europeans" belonging to "the same great branch of mankind as the whites", and assigned a civilizing mission in Africa:

> "Apart from relatively late Semitic influence ... the civilizations of Africa are the civilizations of the Hamites, its history the record of these peoples and of their interactions with the two other African stocks, the Negro and the Bushman".[33]

The Hamitic myth / hypothesis which proposed an external, usually white, origin for every evidence of civilization in Africa remained active in European representations of African history formulated in increasingly sophisticated and subtle forms until overtaken by the work of many scholars of many lands from the 1960s.

We may note the progression of subtlety of formulation of the ideas of Eurocentric historiography, alphabetism, contact with the west, civilization as qualification for entry into history in the positions of Hegel (1830), Professor A.P. Newton (1923), and of Professor Hugh Trevor-Roper (1963).[34]

Summarizing the dominant ideas of Africa in his time derived from missionary and travellers' accounts, Hegel dismissed Africa in less than nine pages of the introduction to his World history, to be free to proceed with the histories of Asia and Europe. "Africa proper", for Hegel, meant only Africa south of the Sahara, north Africa being considered by him as part of Europe, and the Nile Valley he subsumed under Asia. "Africa proper", also identified as Negro, was characterized by a number of sweeping generalizations, as:

1. "the land of childhood, which, lying beyond the day of self-conscious history, is enveloped in the dark mantle of Night. Its isolated character originates, not merely from its tropical nature, but essentially in its geographical condition".

2. "...want of self-control distinguishes the character of the Negroes. This condition is capable of no development or culture, and as we see them at this day, such have they always been."

3. "At this point we leave Africa, not to mention it again. For it is no historical part of the world; it has no movement or development to exhibit. Historical

> movements in it—that is in its northern part—belong to the Asiatic and European World... What we properly understood by Africa, is the Unhistorical, Undeveloped Spirit, still involved in the conditions of mere nature, and which had to be presented here only as on the threshold of the World's History".[35]

Newton and Trevor-Roper represent twentieth century refinements of nineteenth century European positions in the nature, sources, and methods of history. Accordingly, to Newton, Africa had "no history before the coming of Europeans. History only begins when men take to writing". Since there was no writing, Africa before European contact was not the concern of historians, but of archaeologists, linguists, and anthropologists.[36] Hugh Trevor-Roper similarly saw African history to be "only the history of the Europeans in Africa". The rest was "darkness" for historians, although "interesting to sociologists and anthropologists". Historians are interested in "purposive movement", which was absent in Africa, and in learning about significant developments in world history, which, in the last five hundred years, resided in Europe. A fully Eurocentric historiography is, accordingly, enunciated, in the context of which, African history could only be characterized as "the unrewarding gyrations of barbarous tribes in picturesque but irrelevant corners of the globe".[37]

Western historiography of Africa has not remained uniformly negative, Eurocentric, or racist. Some travellers and visitors sought to represent African reality objectively as they perceived it.[38] James Bruce on the Nile, Bowdich and Dupuis on Asante, Heinrich Barth in North and Central Africa, and Gustav Nachtigal on the Sahara and Sudan exemplify comparatively objective reporters. The denial of African history on the score of absence of writing or of written documents was already tackled by Leo Frobenius (1873-1938), the German ethnographer, whose inspired amateur studies impressed Senghor, one of the founders of the movement for African cultural nationalism, *negritude;* by the empathy his work achieved with African culture.[39] Yet this form of European appreciation of the African oral tradition and history seemed to confirm the doubts of the Eurocentrics that African history could not be the concern of professional historians. It was, accordingly, only from the 1960s, following Jan Vansina's seminal work, *Oral Tradition: A study of Historical Methodology* (1961/1965), that professional historians could effectively push African history with assurance into the domain of history in general, pressing into service the resources and insights of the linguists, archaeologists, and anthropologists in the process.[40]

At the close of the twentieth century then, ethnocentrism and racism are on the retreat in the European construction of African history by professional Africanist historians, inspite of their continuing pessimism about specific aspects of the African oral tradition. However, western school textbooks, radio, television, and popular press images of the African and of his/her past linger decades behind the advance of scholarship.[41] The formal acceptance of African history as a legitimate academic discipline was symbolized in Britain by the establishment of *The Journal of African History* in 1960 and the launching of the eight-volume *Cambridge History of Africa* from 1974, matched by the establishment of institutions for the study of African history in many nations of Europe, the Soviet Union, the United States, Canada, Australia, and New Zealand. There was brisk movement from the period of the birth of new African nation states in the 1960s which has begun to slacken in the period of the decline of many of these states in recent decades. However, the eight-volume United Nations Educational Scientific and Cultural Organisation (Unesco) *General History of Africa* has provided an international seal to the recognition of African history as deserving a place in World History.

The new western historians of Africa included former colonial administrators in Africa (such as Sir Harry Johnston, Maurice Delafosse, Sir Richard Palmer, Yves Urvoy), some of whom probably took time to shed all the prejudices from the colonial period. Some of these and others from research or academic positions in the colonies joined the academic departments created in metropolitan universities (Raymond Mauny, Yves Person, Thomas Hodgkin, Roland Oliver, John Fage), and others moved from imperial or commonwealth history to the history of African peoples and problems (e.g. Philip Curtin). From these positions, they became the teachers of some of the new generation of African historians who studied their craft in the west, leading to a continuing growth of the western tradition inside Africa. The tradition of gifted amateur historians (Frobenius) continued to blossom in Basil Davidson, whose *Black Africa Rediscovered* (1959) achieved instant acceptance in Africa. Marxist historical materialism disseminated from the

Soviet Union, its satellites, and from socialist circles in Western Europe, initially appeared, from its criticism of the colonial system and capitalist exploitation, to represent an alternative paradigm to the dominant western tradition, inspite of its western origins. After decades of exchanges across the seas for conferences, study visits, or for temporary to tenure academic appointments in western universities, African historians have now reached the point where they can discriminate between traditions of historiography, and make conscious choices.

5.4   African Practice of the Western Tradition

The long historical perspective provides a basis for balanced judgment. Movement in the encounter between the western and the African oral tradition has gone full circle. The Egyptian priests whom Herodotus and other Greek historians met in the fifth century before the Christian era had no need to learn a foreign tradition. They enjoyed the advantage of prestige and had perfected methods for the preservation of past knowledge for the guidance and edification of present generations. Scholars moved from the west to Africa to see what they could learn. By the time of Manetho in the third century, it had become necessary for the Egyptian priesthood to adopt the western practice of constructing formal accounts of the past, not necessarily to western prescriptions, but in an effort to exhibit Egyptian civilization for the instruction of a western and local readership in a changing colonial world.

In the last decade of the twentieth century of the Christian era, African historians are fully dominated by the western tradition. Western scholars continue to visit, not to learn the craft, but to teach it; and African historians are carried in a flood of migration to the west as part of an international brain drain out of the Third World. In historiography, the history of the encounter between Africa and the west in the past few centuries comprises several phases: a pre-colonial and early colonial period in which a small minority of African intellectuals tried to appropriate western skills for the recording of the African oral tradition; a colonial period of nationalist polemics against western racist and Eurocentric misrepresentations of African history; a post colonial period of professional academic historical writing to decolonise African history; and recent searches for new alternatives to the dominant western paradigms.[42]

The effort to master skills from the west for African uses embraced inventions of new scripts and adaptations of western alphabets to write the histories of African communities in African languages, as well as the use of western languages and scripts. European missionaries and colonial authorities supported such efforts. The most successful exponents of this historiography were Sir Apolo Kagwa (1865–1927) for the kingdom of Buganda, and Nyakatura (1895–1979) for Bunyoro-Kitara in Uganda, East Africa; Jacob Egharevba for the Benin Empire, Rev Sarnuel Johnson (1846–1901) for the Yoruba, and Akiga Sai (1898–1959) for the Tiv of Nigeria; the Rev Carl Reindorf (1834–1917) of Ghana; and Plaatje (1877–1932) of South Africa.[43] All were motivated by the determination, in the words of Akiga Sai, to ensure that their compatriots "should know the things of the fathers as well as those of the present generation". These historians served as a bridge between the oral tradition and the western tradition, combining dynastic political history with records of custom and culture. Theirs was not a historiography of confrontation, simply one utilizing a new to preserve knowledge of an old tradition.

The historiography of remembrance of times past, and, eventually, of confrontation and containment, received significant input from Africans in the Diaspora. Curtin presents a sample of narratives in the first category, including those of Philip Quaque of Cape Coast (1741–1816) who became the first African ordained in the Church of England; John Wright of the Egba, "the first African ordained as a Methodist clergy" in 1848; and Samuel Ajayi Crowther (1806–1891), "the first African to become an Anglican bishop".[44]

The second category of combative historiography comprised a cosmopolitan crew from the West Indies and North America and Africa: adherents of Marcus Garvey's back-to-Africa movement, and Pan African ideologues such as W.E.B. Dubois, George Padmore, and Kwame Nkrumah. African students in Europe or North America combined to form associations and met in formal congresses. Casely-Hayford of the British Gold Coast colony formed the Congress of British West Africa in 1919; and the cultural component of the Pan Africanist movement was formed by Francophones in France: Senghor of Senegal, Leon Damas of Guyana, and Aime

Cesaire of Martinique. In 1947 Alioune Diop institutionalized the movement in Paris in the journal *Presence Africaine*.[45]

The historiography of the early nationalist period was polemical in character, intended to assert what western historiography denied. It was written by political activists who were not necessarily historians. They produced what has been termed 'drum and trumpet' history to recount the achievements of African kingdoms and empires: Ghana, Mali, Songhai, and Zimbabwe in an effort to contain colonial propaganda.[46] One answer to the dismissal of the black African as without a history of civilization was to claim ancient Egypt as black African, or black African peoples as derived from or related to the ancient Egyptians. All earlier efforts in this direction, such as those by the Rev Lucas of Nigeria, have been eclipsed by the prolific output of the Senegalese writer, Cheikh Anta Diop (died 1986).[47]

The 1960s ushered in a period of professional academic historians based in university departments of history run by western historians or by Africans trained in western universities. Western style national associations of historians were established, along with professional journals. The historians responded to the political appeal of Kwame Nkrumah's assertion of an African personality, and to the debate among the creative writers and artists over Senghor's celebration of *negritude*, and its denigration by Nigeria's Wole Soyinka and Cameroun's Mongo Beti, but did not get directly involved or directly reflect these movements in their writing. Rather, their major concern remained the correction of western misrepresentations of African history in a project for the decolonisation of African history. The correction of misrepresentations through recovery of African history from the inside, was followed by calls for engagement in the political process of nation-building. Interdisciplinary research and the oral tradition were cited as the appropriate techniques and sources for the recovery of the authentic past. From the 1970s, alternative radical paradigms related to Marxism brought in an agenda stressing economic history and a broadening of perspectives to include the ruled as well as the rulers, the poor as well as the privileged, entered the agenda. In the 1980s reassessments and critical reviews of earlier prescriptions became necessary, and in the 1990s, a climate of disillusion has set in under the crushing conditions of the collapse of the political systems and economies of many African nations.

The national schools of historiography have developed at varying rates, deriving inspiration from Britain, in the case of former British colonies and South Africa, or from France, in the case of the Francophone states, or from other European nations or from North America. The Dar es Salaam school of Tanzania has been the most articulate and critical of the directions taken by African historiography, and some of its members have suggested a number of forms of historical practice that have come into being among professional academic historians. Temu and Swai (1981) have noted two opposed schools of historiography:

(i) a "nationalist school" comprised of "nihilist and imperial historians", applying an "idealist problematic", and

(ii) a "new school", disparaged by the dominant school as "radical pessimists", who claim to be Marxist in approach.[48]

An expatriate member of the Dar es Salaam history department identifies three phases or traditions of historiographical development:

(i) a bourgeois historiography, idealist in its methodology and colonialist in its political outlook,

(ii) a "bourgeois nationalist" historiography, petty bourgeois in character and transitional in method and outlook, and

(iii) a phase moving in the direction of a Marxist historiography: proletarian in class character, materialist in methodology, and socialist in political outlook.[49]

A brief survey of the development of professional historiography in the academies of Nigeria, Senegal, Zaire, South Africa, and East Africa would shed some light on the degree to which practice of the western tradition has matured and dominated the African tradition.

(i) *Nigeria*

The establishment of departments of history at the universities at Ibadan in Nigeria and Legon in Ghana from 1948 accelerated the pace at which western historiography was developed in Anglophone West Africa. K.O. Dike and S.O. Biobaku in Nigeria, and Adu Boahen and others in Ghana established curricula for training students in African history, and national professional associations and journals to provide bases for historical research. *The Journal of the Historical Society of Nigeria* began publication in 1956, and ten years later, *Tarikh* , a journal for school teachers and students was launched. At the Silver Jubilee celebration of the Society in 1980, its most ambitious project, the collaborative synthesis, *Groundwork of Nigerian History* was issued.[50]

The works which provided the models for the Ibadan School were Dike's *Trade and Politics in the Niger Delta, 1830-1885* (1956), and Biobaku's *The Egba and Their Neighbours. 1842-1872* (1957).[51] Both scholars proceeded to set up teams of scholars in several disciplines to undertake research into the history of the Benin kingdom and of the Yoruba people respectively, giving priority to the use of oral and non-written sources.

Dike (1917-1983), contributed to the theory, practice, and the building of institutions for the practice of the discipline in Nigeria.[52] Dike addressed himself to the theory of African historiography in a relatively few papers only, but always in a powerful and authoritative manner, and in influential international fora.[53] His first and basic statement of principles which also laid down an agenda for research in African history, was made while he was still a graduate student of Kings College London, in answer to Dame Margery Perham's repetition of the view that Africa was "without writing and so without history".[54] Dike showed, first, that the evidence cited for the incapacity of man in tropical Africa, such as the absence of the wheel, were things largely irrelevant to the environment, and that the use of selected cultural items for the characterization of whole cultures was a misapplication of the methods of cultural anthropology. Second, that the charge of no writing, no history, could not hold for Africa, since Africa not only possessed considerable Arabic and European sources, but had a secure base of documentation in the oral tradition and the ethnographic record. For Dike, history was crucial to the struggle for independence and self-government: "For young and emergent nations there is no study as important as that of history". Scientific historical research was essential to dispel doubts of African capacity and to develop self knowledge and the self confidence of African leaders and peoples. Later statements expanded his advocacy of the oral tradition and his understanding of its dynamic nature, especially, among the Aro of Eastern Nigeria.

Dike's practice was encapsulated in his revised doctoral dissertation, *Trade and Politics in the Niger Delta,* which became an instant international success as marking a new beginning in African historiography. He achieved a masterly synthesis of European documents and of local traditions to present local rulers and peoples as equal, indeed, leading, actors in their own history in a time of intense interactions with the west. He was, however, quickly sucked into administrative positions, and his collaborative work on the Aro was only published in 1990 after his death.[55] His legacy in Nigerian historiography has endured also in the institutions he initiated and built: the Historical Society of Nigeria, the National Archives of Nigeria, and the Ibadan Institute of African Studies, among others.

Biobaku, the other pioneer in Nigerian historiography spent more time in administration than in academics and made his mark mainly in "his advocacy of the use of oral tradition, his inter-disciplinary approach to historical problems, his controversial theory of the Egyptian origin of the Yoruba".[56] Like Dike, Biobaku's work endures in the inspiration and opportunities provided by his Yoruba Research Scheme to younger scholars to transcend his ideas and realize some of his dreams.

The Ibadan School pioneered by Dike, Biobaku and sustained by Ajayi expanded throughout Nigeria with the expansion of the university system in Nigeria. Each new university department of history tried to establish its identity, but the Zaria department was most successful in differentiating itself from Ibadan through its research into Islamic history under Abdullahi Smith, and by the radicalism of Yusuf Bala Usman and his colleagues, which attracted some of the radicals from the Dar es Salaam school as well, including Temu and Swai. However, the advocacy of a radical scholarship has not yet yielded a harvest of radical historiography in Nigeria.

Already, with Ajayi, the Ibadan School has a leader attached to a historiography for self-government, development, and the solution of national problems: one fully accepted into the western historical establishment.[57] The Nigerian national school must be one of the closest to maturity in the practice of the western tradition in Africa, but has not yet reached the point of self-critical evaluation and self-correction for sustained forward movement.

(ii) **Senegal**

Negritude, the movement of African cultural nationalism preoccupied Leopold Sedar Senghor, President of Senegal, and most of the intellectual leadership at independence. History remained the virtual preserve of the *griots* and of popular local historians. Professional practice at the University of Dakar was firmly under the control of French scholars, former colonial administrators, and the academic establishment in Paris. Accordingly, it was only in 1966 that the first African historian, S.M. Cissoko, joined the department of history, and in 1980 that the Association des Historiens du Senegal was formed. The development of western historical practice, however, blossomed rapidly because of the advanced development of infrastructures in Dakar, such as the *Bulletin de l'Institut Fondamental de l'Afrique Noire,* Samir Amin's Institut Africain de Development et de Planification with its international clientele, and a fine archives institution. Accordingly, it was not long before a recognizable Dakar school of historiography emerged, playing a key role in the Association des Historiens Africains and in its journal, *Afrika Zamani,* published in Yaounde, Cameroun.

There was an early effort to decolonize African history with concentration in the colonial period in the areas of politics and religion, especially for the Wolof geographical region of the Senegal River basin, resistance to colonialism, the "harmony" and "balance" of precolonial society. A second perspective of Senegalese history adopted a dialectical view and the methods of historical materialism, representing the history of "an ordinary region of humanity, where exploitation exists as it does everywhere else". On another level, two forms of historiography have been identified; first, a "colonial tradition of hagiography" dealing with the "civilizing mission" of the French, and a second, "nationalist historiographic tradition" derived from the oral tradition, and from the nationalist struggle.[59]

Senegalese historians have followed the tradition of Francophone West African historians (such as Joseph Ki-Zerbo of Burkina Faso/Upper Volta), in their active participation in partisan politics. Thus the first two Senegalese Doctors of Philosophy in History, Abdoulaye Ly and Cheikh Anta Diop, became leaders of opposition political parties, a position only recently matched by the Ghanaian historian, Professor A.A. Boahen, in Anglophone West Africa. Cheikh Anta Diop only joined the Dakar department of history in 1982, before his death on 7 February 1986. While still a student in Paris, Diop had espoused the doctrine of the black origins of Egyptian, and therefore, of Greek, and western civilization, a position he defended in research, writing and public lectures and symposia through Africa, the Caribbean, the Americas, and Europe. According to *Presence Africaine,* he thus became a "heretic", "anathema", and "a paranoid Black" to the west, and to Africans, "a protector standing guard at the gate" of "the black man's identity".[60]

In the 1990s, Senegal has supplied its quota of historians working on all aspects of the national history and society, as well as migrants to western academia in Europe and the Americas.

(iii) *Zaire*

Western academic historical research began with the Department of history Lovanium University in Kinshasa in 1965. In 1970, "all university teaching and research history focused on Lumumbashi, and there rapidly developed a Lubumbashi school whose graduates and general orientations dominated—virtually monopolized—historical thinking and research in the country".[61] The history department was complemented by the creation of Centre d'Etudes et de Reserches Documentaires sur l'Afrique Centrale (CERDAC) under the influence of T. Obenga's orientations towards ancient Egyptian connections and relationships, and the Societe des Historiens Zairos in 1974 as part of the "nationalist reassessment inspired by the policy of authenticity", and by 1976, the department of history was "almost entirely Zaireanised".[62]

Zairean historians have been influenced in their writing by political currents in Zaire and by the general imperatives of nation building. They launched a series of journals: one for the international professional audience, and another for a national readership; and made efforts to create a network of archives. The circumstances of crises in which the state came into being and in which it has continued since independence have combined to institute a form of historiography termed *histoire immediate,* defined as "a means of understanding, drawing simultaneously on history, sociology and anthropology".[63] The method is described as being attuned to reflect the concerns of exploited, alienated, oppressed, and marginalised classes in times of crises; to historians interested in change; and to the production of "total" history through oral documentation.

As in other African schools, the Lumumbashi school has been influenced by some of its western teachers, notably, by Jewsiewicki and Vellut, to adopt an approach "intermediary between radical and liberal paradigms", drawing from "the *Annales school,* Anglo-Saxon, and neo-Marxist approaches".[64] The greater proficiency in the use of written than in oral sources has been one factor dictating concentration on the colonial period of Zairean history, but recently greater diversification into pre-colonial, cultural, social, demographic, political and other areas mark the Lumumbashi school as a dynamic and promising one.

(iv) **Southern Africa**

Southern Africa is taken here to comprise the republics of South Africa, Namibia, Botswana, Lesotho, Swaziland, Angola, Mozambique, Zimbabwe, and Zambia, on the basis of the unity of their historical experiences: "early Bantu movements and settlement, the nineteenth century Mfecane revolution ... the mineral revolution and its aftermath, European imperialism and the African response to colonialism (including African efforts at ending white domination)".[65] The proceedings of the Unesco meeting of experts at Gaborone, Botswana, in 1977, and published as *The historiography of southern Africa,* as one of the documents for the preparation of a *General History of Africa,* provide a convenient source for basic information on the state of African historiography in the region.

The history departments of the University of Botswana and Swaziland did not have a strong local historiography. Plans were afoot for research in local oral tradition at both Gaborone, Botswana, and Kwaluseni, Swaziland; and the few African scholars on the staff were yet to defend their doctoral dissertations. The Vice Rector, Dr Phinias Makhuratne, a non-historian, stated that Botswana and Swazi historiography up to 1977 was one written "from a foreign—or white—point of view", confirming the brief official report of current research, that "J.S. Matsebula's amateur work, *History of Swaziland,* remains the only work for use in Swaziland at all levels" of education.[66]

The History Department of the National University of Lesotho at Roma, had an expatriate head, but also three qualified African historians who ran a journal, *Mohlomi, Journal of Southern African Historical Studies.*[67] In contrast, the expatriate head of the department at Chancellor College, Zomba, Malawi "inherited an all-African department", with plans for textbooks of Malawian history and other research initiatives.[68] Although "expatriate dominated", the history department of the University of Zambia, Lusaka, pursued a vigorous programme of research in collaboration with the department of African Studies and the Institute of African Studies.[69] No reports were submitted from Namibia, Zimbabwe, Angola, and Mozambique, apparently with the same tale of external domination of their historiography.[70]

The historiography of the republic of South Africa contains several sub-historiographies: African, Afrikaner Nationalist or Boer, English-speaking or British, and Asian and Coloured.[71] We follow Chanaiwa's typology of traditions: imperial, missionary, colonialist, and liberal-revisionist, out of which the African historiography struggles to emerge.[72]

The **imperialist** tradition treated the history of South Africa as part of the history of the British Empire, important mainly for its strategic location on the Cape sea route to India. **Afrikaner** nationalist historiography considered imperial historians as negrophiles, but they generally treated Africans as merely "part of the environmental factors", and idealized "civilizing mission" and "imperial trusteeship". **Missionary** historians were the first white group to "record and study African history, culture and language" and so provide data for the traditions. But the missionary tradition was often limited by sensationalism for propaganda, self-righteousness, and lack of rigour, and by the use of such derogatory terms for African peoples as "heathen" affected by the "curse of Ham". The **colonialist** tradition reflects the settler factor and the history of maintaining the domination of a minority over the majority. Colonialist historiography embraced English-speaking and Afrikaner historiographies which differed over attitudes to the

British Empire, but agreed on many other subjects. Colonialist historiography was a history of the whites in South Africa, centred on racial struggle in which the Africans were deprived of "history, cultural heritage and humanity".

White colonialist historiography changed, through the late nineteenth century to recent times, into the **liberal revisionist** tradition. This tradition adopted a universalist attitude, but continued to display aspects of the earlier traditions. It was still Eurocentric, and applied European social science theories to explain "native" African history in the European 'civilizing process".

Chanaiwa outlines the changes in **the African tradition** through the periods 1800-1950, and from 1950 to 1977. The African tradition in the period 1800 -1950 derived its inspiration from the white missionary tradition. The writers were Christians educated in mission schools, and alienated from African culture. They were often Christian clergy who admired white power, wealth, and technology, accepted colonialism as a part of life, and aspired to change their people through "Christianity, education and industrial schools". The group of African writers in this period included Tengo Jabavu (1859–1921), Tiyo Soga (1829–1871), first African United Presbyterian minister to be ordained in the United Kingdom, and Waiter B. Rubusana (1858–1916), a Congregationalist minister and first African member of the Cape Provincial Council. They translated English religious literature into African languages, but also published "African history, customs and proverbs". Some of the musical compositions of this period became classics, such as Enoch Sontoga's *Nkosi Sikeleli*

I-Africa (God Bless Africa). Inspite of their failure to record African history in depth, the works of this early group reflected "the social and intellectual history of nineteenth century southern Africa".

The African intellectuals of the second period came to grips with the historiography of the colonial situation, being part of and observers of the "Black Problem" of the colonialist tradition. The historiography was marked by racial consciousness and "near-presentness". Examples of the genre include Solomon Tshekiso Plaatje, *Native Life in South Africa, Before and Since the European War and the Boer Rebellion* (1916); Davidson Don Tengo Jabavu, *The Black Problem* (1920); *Criticism of the Native Bills* (1935), and *Native Disabilities in South Africa* (1935). Others recorded African traditions and customs, autobiographies, and the biographies of African heroes, e.g. John Henderson Soga, *The South -Eastern Bantu (1930): Ama-Xosa: Life and Customs:* Azariele Sekese, *Mekhoa le Maele aa Basotho* (Customs and Proverbs of the Basuto); Thomas Mokopu Mofolo, *Moeti oa Bochabela* (The Traveller to the East), *Chaka*.

These African writers were motivated by the slogan "it takes a native to know a native", and worked to transmit information to future African researchers. Before the Second World War, they were concerned principally with "the origins, nature, and effects of colonial laws", but later, with "nationalism, historical consciousness, and a liberation ideology".

Chanaiwa characterized African historians within contemporary South African historiography as hamstrung by lack of funding, white liberal-revisionist paternalism, and lack of communication among scholars and between the different traditions. Recent analyses of South African historiography confirm "the continued absence of an African contribution" and of "a black voice" in South African historiography.[73] The new Mandella era provides the ingredients for a revolution in historiography to match the promise of harmony in the political domain.

(v) **East Africa**

The University of Nairobi provided the base for the Historical Association of Kenya in 1966, the proceedings of its first 1967 annual conference constituting its *Hadithi 1*, (from Arabic *Hadith*, Swahili, *Hadithi*, meaning story, account, report, history, legend) published in 1968.[74] The Nairobi school was founded by Professor Bethwell Alan Ogot, whose work in the reconstruction of the history of the Luo almost solely from oral traditions has been noted as an "epoch-making feat in the heart of Imperial London" where he had studied.[75] Ogot functioned as pioneer and midwife of historical writing and publication in Kenya and the East African region, including *Zamani: A Survey of East African History* (edited with J.A. Kieran) in 1968, eventually serving as President of the International Scientific Committee for the drafting of a *General History of Africa*.

Ogot outlined his philosophy of African history in his first Presidential address to the 1967 annual conference of the Historical Association of Kenya. First, he considered African history "an integral part of the study of mankind", which could not be ignored or passed over in any world history. Second, he judged some attempts to construct a Marxist historiography of Africa according to prescribed stages of development to be efforts to "impose a foreign and artificial rhythm of life upon African history". The radical call to concentrate on current problems was well and good, but African interest in ancient kingdoms and empires had also "acquired a significance" beyond measurement in material terms. Third, it was wrong to focus the study of African history on centralized states since such a historiography would tell only "half of the story" of ancient Africa. Accordingly, the proper approach to the study of African history lay in the analysis of:

(i) "how the different historical entities in the continent have evolved", and
(ii) "what have been the definable phases of growth", taking account of "the influence of ecological factors".[76]

The history department of the University of Dar es Salaam, Tanzania, established in 1964, has not been dominated by a single name as in the case of the Nairobi school. Its founder, Terence Ranger, moved it out of colonial historiography, but the local leadership of the succeeding nationalist historiography lay with Isaria Kimambo, whose history of Tanzania (edited jointly with Arnold Temu, 1969), has been termed the "crowning achievement" of the nationalist tradition.[77] Kimambo laid emphasis on the reconstruction of the pre-colonial history of the various ethnic groups of

Tanzania, through the collection of their oral traditions, which he did for the Pare, and advocated a movement away from politcal history to economic history "at regional or district level", and to "local agrarian research".[78]

The second period in the development of the Dar es Salaam school, termed "petty bourgeois" transitional, was marked by radical criticism of the "bourgeois" nationalist historiography of the preceding period. It is identified with Walter Rodney's seminal work *How Europe Underdeveloped Africa* (1972) and by Temu and Swai's extended critique of nationalist historiography, *Historians and Africanist History* (1981), dedicated to Rodney.[79] At the national level, the new historiography was related to the ideas generated by the Arusha Declaration of 1967 for *ujamaa,* African socialism, and economic nationalism or self-reliance. At the international level, it was inspired by the work of Frantz Fanon, and the theories of the "development of underdevelopment" current in Latin America. Rodney's perspective moved attention away from the African nationalists in the anti-colonial struggle and the "determinant role of local struggle" to their "virtual powerlessness" and the "continuing exploitation of Africa ... by metropolitan capital" (in Rodney's words, "the international capitalist system").[80] Rodney thus made an immediate contribution to the creation of African historical knowledge. In contrast, Temu and Swai presented a detailed critique of the older nationalist historiography, which they accused of idealizing history and of "taking things as they present themselves rather than as they really are".[81]

The advocacy of a "rigorously materialist" historiography by Bernstein (sociologist) and Depelchin (a historian), has been criticized within the Dar es Salaam school by Wamba and from without by Law, as representing the residual idealism of Althusser rather than the pure historical materialist ideas of Marx.[82]

The Dar es Salaam school, then, continues to function as a seedbed of ideas and debate extending beyond the East African region to the rest of Africa and even back to the western community of "Africanist" historians, from where some of the radical ideas originated.

5.5 'Africanist' Historiography

Africanist historians have recently been distinguished from African historians, and defined as historians of Africa from outside the continent, essentially, from the west; inspite of an earlier definition of *Africanist* as meaning a specific form of historiography practiced by Africans and non-Africans alike.[83]

In this second view, Africanist historiography was distinguished from a colonial school, and from a radical school. The colonial school had been "discredited", and the radicals were described as "pessimists" following a "Fanonesque analysis" leading to the conclusion that Africa was "powerless until the whole pattern of the world has been changed by revolution". In contrast, African historiography emphasized "African activity, African adaptation, African choice, African initiative". It was precisely this "Africanist" historiography that Temu and Swai (1981) set out to criticize in defence of the radical school.

In the 1990s, we can no longer espouse one school against another as the sole bearer of light. African history can derive benefit from multiple methodologies and schools as it has from the insights of multiple disciplines. Similarly, African historiography has already gained from the contributions of historians working from "outside" as from scholars working "inside" Africa: inspite of charges of "theoretical sterility" against African scholars, and of "a cult of theory" against the west. In a consideration of the contribution of the western historiographical tradition to African history, the representations from within and without Africa need to be brought together. Accordingly, Africanist historiography is defined as that historiography of Africa which, through study marked by empathy, attempts to produce historical knowledge of the continent and of its relations with other continents. It is a definition that recognizes the common western provenance of all the various schools and of the historiography practised by the African academic historians struggling to create an autonomous African interpretation.

The process of the instruction of Africanist historians in the western tradition was carried out in the 1960s through a number of international conferences, congresses, and symposia. These meetings generally succeeded in placing oral traditions and interdisciplinary research at the centre of the agenda. Anthropology, previously assigned sole custody of African history, remained an active participant in the prescription of field methodology and the interpretation of oral data, inspite of residual suspicion of its role as an agent of colonialism and purveyor of racist ideas among African intellectuals. Archaeology and Linguistics took over the major roles of extending our perspectives of the African past. New scientific techniques for deriving chronology, determining histories of migrations, contacts, and ancient relationships between peoples promised great possibilities.

The internal African input has not matched the promise and the opportunity. Efforts by Ki-Zerbo and others to promote an Association of African Historians transcending the national societies and schools, did not get beyond the publication of a few numbers of *Afrika Zamani* in Yaounde, Cameroun, from 1974. The Association remained restricted to Francophone West Africa.

The crowning achievement of Africanist historiography must be the project for a *General History of Africa*, sponsored by the United Nations Educational Scientific and Cultural Organization (Unesco). A truly gigantic international enterprise, its scientific committee had an African president, and the eight volume editors were also all Africans:

Volume I: Methodology and African Prehistory by Joseph Ki-Zerbo of Burkina Fasso
Volume II: Ancient Civilizations of Africa, by O. Mokhtar of Egypt
Volume III: Africa from the Seventh to the Eleventh Century, by M. El Fasi of Morocco.

Volume IV: Africa from the Twelfth to the Sixteenth Century, by D.T. Niane of Guinea

Volume V: Africa from the Sixteenth to the Eighteenth Century, by B.A. Ogot of Kenya

Volume VI: Africa in the Nineteenth Century until 1880, by J.F.A. Ajayi of Nigeria

Volume VII: Africa under Colonial Domination, 1880-11935, by A.A. Boahen of Ghana

Volume VIII: Africa since 1935, by A.A. Mazrui of Uganda.

The Unesco *General History of Africa* is fully comparable with the *Cambridge History of Africa* from which it is most obviously distinguished by the greater will to speak from an African focus, and, as far as practicable, in an African voice.

What, then, is new in this "cult of theory", driven by a passion for innovation, fashions and fads in an apparently endlessly changing kaleidoscope of approaches, perspectives, paradigms, and epistemologies? The radical critique, drawing from the Marxist storehouse of ideas gave birth to forms of historiography identified under the political economy rubric as:

(i) a market economy approach represented by A.G. Hopkins

(ii) a dependency group represented by Samir Amin and Immanuel Wallerstein from studies of West African societies but later domiciled in Dar es Salaam, and

(iii) a mode of production analysis promoted mainly by French scholars.[84]

These movements of perspective reveal some of the ways in which Africans have made contributions, consumed ideas, failed to take part in exchange of ideas or to put ideas into practice through lack of opportunities, financial or infrastructural support.

The special number of the *Canadian Journal of African Studies* to review the functions of mode of production analysis in African history generally found it virtually drained of useful life within about a decade of its operation.[85] Much effort had been expended on attempts to discover in Africa the modes of production models propounded by Marx for Europe and Asia, or to describe new typologies for Africa (e.g. African mode of production, and lineage mode of production), and the articulation of various modes of production, although it had been creatively used in actual historical practice in southern Africa. Here again the conclusion was that mode of production had become "a piece of massive conceptual overkill" derived from a flawed Althusserian systematization of Marx, who had been "more historically and empirically flexible".[86]

This over-simplified account of the mode of production debate leads to the conclusion that while the western "cult of theory" does generate innovation, it also has its limitations and weaknesses. It clearly needs to be modernized by the realities of the concrete African situation in which African historians operate, especially in the light of the questions Jewsiewicki and Newbury pose in the title of their book, *African Historiographies: What History for Which Africa?* Practitioners of the western tradition continuously suggest new "relevant" subjects and approaches, but do not always relate them to audiences. That is, the additional question of, "Which Africans?" is rarely asked and therefore a communication gap remains between the preferred productions of the western tradition and the African populations which should ideally be the beneficiaries of the output.[87] Some African critics of the west have gone even further to deny the value of "talkative" Marxism if it does not directly address the "genuine audience—the African people", and does not draw from Africa's own value reservoir of untapped intellectual resources", and issue in practice, as in the case of Fanon and Cabral.[88]

Finally, how closely do the frequent changes advocated in theory in Africanist historiography reflect changes in western historiography itself? Indeed, how closely does western Africanist practice reflect changes in western philosophy of history? Some time lag must be admitted, and even a resistance to new theory on the part of historians in general. Has Africanist historiography, for example, yet examined the relevance of the narrativist philosophy of history as one which takes account of different ways of doing history?

CHAPTER 6

Conclusion:
Historiography in Transition

Even a bird with a long neck/ Cannot see the future.
Kanuri proverb, Nigeria (Ojoade 1978: 174).

6.1   African Traditions

We 'decomposed' African historiography into the four constituent traditions of the oral, internal written, the Islamic, and the western written traditions. It is time to 'recompose' or reconstitute them into an entity. The oral and internal written traditions, we discovered to be closely related one to the other, in Ancient Egypt as in more recent cases, and to be as fully integrated as two traditions could possibly be. The Islamic and western external traditions also, as they increasingly domesticated within the African communities, achieved varying degrees of absorption into the oral tradition, and varying degrees of accommodation to the oral tradition. In the African context, therefore, we accord the oral tradition a primary role as the basic form of historical practice to which each of the other forms must seek accommodation. At the same time, we note a tendency on the part of the external written traditions to denigrate the oral tradition as a retrograde or primitive form of historical practice. The western tradition has been most overtly critical of the oral tradition, inspite of its own roots. There is, however, a certain ambivalence to the oral tradition in the theories of Levi-Strauss and of other western thinkers.[1]

First, in Levi-Strauss, his "savage mind", being "mind in its untamed state", as opposed to "mind cultivated or domesticated", is conceived as operating "systems of classification" which, being embedded in a "totemic void", were antipathetic to history.[2] In some instances, however, such as in certain Polynesian mythologies, savage societies reached a critical point, "where diachrony irrevocably prevails over synchrony"[3], but this did not make them historical societies. Thus, although all societies exist in "history and change", "primitive societies" "want to deny it", adopting a "timeless model" of the past.[4] Yet Levi-Strauss accords certain concrete objects in primitive societies the status of archives or of "pure historicity", and "totemic myths" the status of "pure history".[5]

Second, Levi-Strauss saw in the orality or state of being "without a system of writing" of 'primitive' societies, a negative characterization, behind which lay "a positive reality".[6] Indeed, he considered "modern societies" more deserving to be characterized in negative terms, since in them, experiences were "largely the result of a process of indirect reconstruction, through written documents" where the link to the past was no longer through "an oral tradition which implies direct contact with others (storytellers, priests, wise men or elders), but by books amassed in libraries, books from which we endeavour—with extreme difficulty—to form a picture of their authors". Accordingly, Levi-Srauss characterized "the tremendous revolution brought about by the invention of writing" as one which deprived humanity of "something fundamental", rendering communication "somewhat 'unauthentic' ".

Derrida's reconstruction casts doubt on the value to be placed on the efforts of Levi-Strauss, as of Rousseau, to accord a positive character to speech and the oral tradition over writing.[7] In each case, he represents the attempt to discover a "lost primordial unity of speech before writing" as "a romantic illusion", since there was no "innocent" original form or "authenticity". Derrida classifies such efforts as logocentric projects in which speech is equated with nature and writing with culture, a supplement to nature, and an expression of western guilt, of nostalgia, and as a form of ethnocentrism.

Deconstruction, therefore, returns us to the position that the western tradition is basically opposed to the oral tradition, even where it is outwardly receptive to it. However, we can accept the effort to discover a positive value in the oral tradition as an opening that may be utilized towards the creation of a total African historiography integrating all the traditions, oral and written, of internal or external origin, practised on the continent.

6.2   Alienation and Identity

It is difficult to ignore the compelling case made by Frantz Fanon concerning the alienating effects of the colonial experience on Africans and other members of the Third World.[8] The unequal and negative aspects of contact with the west, and its work of devaluing even African pre-colonial history were forcefully re-stated and extended through the earliest periods of European activity in Africa by Walter Rodney.[9] And recently the West African philosopher, I.D. Keita, concluded that 'alienation' remained the most appropriate term to describe the 'African problematic' in contemporary post-colonial Africa characterised as it is by "great disappointment" over unfulfilled dreams.[10]

In what ways then do we see Keita's "modernizing African" become psychologically alienated in his practice of history? We may observe the African moving away from the oral tradition through education in the western tradition, so that he needs re-education in his own oral tradition and be admonished to return to it to regain identity, achieve communication with his primary mass public in the urban slums and rural communities.[11] Indeed, we discover that African intellectuals cannot achieve their desire to "prove to whitemen, at all costs, the richness of their thoughts, the equal value of their intellect", until they come fully to terms with the oral tradition and adopt it as the grounds on which to relate to the western tradition.[12]

The practice of the oral tradition within African rural communities escapes the extremes of psychological alienation suffered by the "modernizing" practitioners of the western tradition in the African academic community. The oral tradition was able to relate to the western tradition within its own self-identity to freely adopt and integrate elements from outside. It is this position of change within a stable system that we understand Jan Vansina to identify as tradition in his recent seminal work *Paths in the Rainforests and* which we expect the new African historiography to achieve.

6.3 Tradition

Vansina's book confirms in practice the validity of the concept of tradition. A millennium of change in the ancestral political tradition brought into the vast African Equatorial Rainforests by western Bantu immigrants is delineated to the time of its collapse through conquest of its heirs by the bearers of the Christian European tradition. Here we need only consider the general fivefold properties of traditions identified by Vansina.[13]

First, the definition of traditions as "fundamental continuities" composed of "a concrete set of basic cognitive patterns and concepts". In our study the African oral tradition from its record in the Egyptian written tradition down to its practice in the living oral societies of sub-Saharan Africa constitute the dominant historical tradition on the continent. In Chapter 2, an effort has been made to discover some of the basic philosophical concepts that emanate from a body of the oral tradition. All succeeding chapters explore the historical development of forms of the tradition innovating and achieving varying degrees of accommodation with other traditions.

Second, that "traditions are processes". This expression of the reality of change within a continuity expresses the spirit of this study in which the forms of the traditions of historiography across Africa are described in historical perspective in processes of interaction and change.

Third, that traditions contain within them both "continuity and change". That traditions contain a centre of continuity in their "basic ideas about ultimate reality", but retain a capacity to make "choices" and to choose "options for the future and leave other options open". In the context of this nature of traditions, this study requires African historians to make choices in their current historiographical situation, to choose the oral tradition as base for building new historiographies with contributions from the western and Islamic traditions as superstructure.

Fourth, the recognition that the "specific definition of a tradition is partly in the mind of the beholder", that is, that a subjective element may be allowed the scholar delimiting and defining traditions. Indeed, the delimitations set out in this study as between African and external traditions, and between forms of the African oral tradition over parts of the continent must admit this subjective element. They are presented, principally, as categories capable of pointing up basic forms and conceptions of the tradition in transition.

Fifth, the observation that "traditions need autonomy" in order to survive and thrive. That the Bantu tradition in Equatorial Africa, for example, collapsed "when its bearers were conquered after 40 years of war and lost their independence of action with their self-determination".[14] According to Vansina, the challenge of a competing aggressive tradition alone cannot overwhelm and destroy another tradition, since the challenged tradition has the capacity to "accept, reject, or modify innovation". This capacity only disappears with the loss of liberty to choose which results from loss of independence. Loss of political independence may, however, leave a minimum space of choice, so that, as in the case of the

Maghrib, where freedom of worship and education in the Islamic tradition was permitted, "the core of the tradition can be kept and transmitted". In this case, the Islamic tradition persisted through European colonialism to independence, and the Berber African tradition continues to seek its proper space within which to grow.

We observe the death of a historical tradition in the case of the millennia old tradition of ancient Egypt. Greek domination put the ancient tradition into crisis, resulting in the work of Manetho in the context of Greek respect of the Egyptian priestly class and its traditions. But the succeeding Roman and Christian traditions permitted only the survival of the Christian Coptic tradition which must be acknowledged something new and different from the ancestral tradition, and continues an attenuated existence within the current Islamic polity.

Our advocacy of a creative new historiography derived from the African oral tradition and the aggressive external but virtually internalised Islamic and western traditions, is based on the conviction that the core of the oral tradition has remained alive through the challenges of colonialism and neo-colonialism. That it is still possible to exercise a degree of choice. Indeed, in Vansina's view also, even where a tradition collapses and dies, it is not automatically replaced by the challenging tradition, but by "a new tradition based on parts of the old cognitive views, views derived from elsewhere, and novel views originating with a single person at first, and later gradually accepted by that person's community".[15]

6.4 The Narrative Tradition

The African oral tradition of historiography is basically a narrative tradition performed in a variety of media in contexts of aesthetic and emotional engagement. Indeed, the narrative literary qualities of the oral tradition have been among the most serious objections raised against it by practitioners of the modernist, scientific, epistemological, and positivist western tradition emerging from the late nineteenth century. In contrast, some cultural movements and historiographical schools of a post-modernist orientation have been more favourably disposed to oral historiography, and have even been noted as marked by a "commitment to the return to narrative".[16]

In its ardent crusade against positivism, and in its commitment to explore new sources and areas of research, the French *Annales* school may be counted one such school, more open to the oral tradition than the orthodox western tradition. Note, for example, Braudel's 1946 call for a rebirth of "history on a grand scale", and his affirmation that "history need not simply be condemned to the study of well-walled gardens".[17]

This alignment of oral tradition with the *Annales* school deliberately flies in the face of the assessment made by Clarence-Smith, which declared oral traditions worthless and buried by the work of Braudel and the *Annales* school, and even goes beyond Vansina's refutation of Clarence-Smith.[18]

Vansina identified Clarence-Smith's arguments against oral tradition to be based on Foucault's theory of "signs", not on the views or work of Braudel or of the *Annales* school.

It is only in recent times, however, that a narrativist philosophy of history has been formally opposed to an epistemological philosophy, a postmodernist to a modernist.[19] Thus, for Hayden White for example, the narrative form:

> "far from being merely a form of discourse that can be filled with different contents, real or imaginary as the case may be, already possesses a content prior to any given actualization of it in speech or writing".[20]

The African oral narrative tradition, then, need not fall victim to the assaults of some apostles of the orthodox western tradition who may still seek to insinuate doubts in the minds of the practitioners of the oral tradition. The oral tradition has, in its centuries of development, already achieved varying degrees of accommodation with the Islamic tradition in the different regions of Africa in which it has operated; from the Maghrib through the Sahara to the Western, Central, and Eastern Sudan, the Horn of Africa, to the East African coast. The degrees of accommodation and integration confirm the view that historical traditions exercise powers of choice and possess options in their relations with other traditions.

The emerging western philosophy of narrativity provides support for the view that the African oral tradition will eventually meet with elements within the western tradition also, to which it can relate positively.

6.5 Transition

What, then, is the future of the African oral tradition and of African historiography? Even a bird with a long neck cannot foresee the outcome, of the dialectic relationship between the Africa oral tradition, the Islamic tradition, and the dominating western tradition.

The transition into a new African historiography cannot be achieved through an aping of the western or of any other tradition, only through innovation from the firm base of the oral tradition. In the eloquent words of Frantz Fanon:

> "we must invent and we must make discoveries", "we must turn over a new leaf, we must work out new concepts, and try to set afoot a new man".[21]

In this case, we must create a new African historiography.

REFERENCES

Chapter 1: Introduction: Terms of Discourse

[1] Leslie C. Aiello, "The fossil evidence for Modem human origins in Africa: a revised view", *American Anthropologist,* Vol. 95, No. 1, 1993, 73-96.

[2] James Henry Breasted, *The Dawn of Conscience.* New York, 1933/1968, pp. 9- 1 0; Cheikh Anta Diop, *Civilization or Barbarism: An authentic Anthropology.* New York, 1991.

[3] Joseph H. Greenberg, *The Languages of Africa,* Bloomington, 1963, pp. 42-65.

[4] Martin Bernal, *Black Athena: The Afroasiatic Roots of Classical Civilization, New* Brunswick, 1987/1991; Diop, *Civilization or Barbarism.*

[5] M. Guthrie, "Bantu origins: a tentative new hypothesis", *Journal of African Languages,* 1, 1962, 9-2 1; J.H. Greenberg, "Linguistic evidence regarding Bantu origins", *Journal of African History,* 13, 1972, 189-216; Jan Vansina, "Bantu in the crystal ball", *History in Africa,* Vol. 6, 1979, 287-333, Vol. 7, 1980, 293-325.

Chapter 2: The Oral Tradition

[1] Ruth Finnegan, *Oral Literature in Africa,* Oxford University Press, 1970; Isidore Okpewho, *The Epic in Africa,* Columbia University Press, 1979; Okpewho (ed.), *The Oral Performance in Africa,* Ibadan, Spectrum Books, 1990.

[2] Jan Vansina, *Oral Tradition,* 1961/65.

3. Jan Vansina, *Oral Tradition as History,* 1985; J.C. Miller (ed.), *The African Past Speaks, 1980.*
4. Paul Thompson, *The voice of the past: Oral History.* Oxford University Press, 1978, 1988.
5. Jan Vansina, "The use of ethnographic data as sources for history", in T.O. Ranger (ed.), *Emerging Themes of African History.* London, 1968, 97-124; E.J. Alagoa, "The ethnographic dimension of oral tradition", *Kiabara,* 4, 2, 1981, 7-24.
6. E.J. Alagoa, "The encounter between African and western historiography before 1800", *Storia delta Storiografia,* 19, 1991, 74-78.
7. Herodotus. *The Histories, Book* II, p. 166, A. de Selincourt and A.R. Burn (trans.), 1954-1972.
8. Herodotus, Book II, p. 186.
9. A. Momigliano. "The place of Herodotus in the History of Historiography", *History,* XLIII, 1958, 1-13.
10. W.G. Waddell. *The Aegyptiaca of Manetho, 1971,* XI.
11. Waddell, 1971, 195, 77.
12. Ward. "The present status of Egyptian chronology", *Bull. Am. Schools of Oriental Research.* No. 288, 1992, p. 54.
13. H.R. Hall. "The Eclipse of Egypt", *The Cambridge Ancient History, Vol.* III, 1970, 251-269.
14. E.J. Alagoa, "Oral tradition and oral history in Africa", in Toyin Falola (ed.), *African Historiography: Essays in honour of Jacob Ajayi,* Longman, 1993, 4-13.

15 E.J. Alagoa, "An African philosophy of history in the oral tradition", in Robert Harms, Joseph C. Miller, David S. Newbury and Michele D. Wagner (eds.), *Paths towards the past: African historical essays in honor of Jan Vansina*. Atlanta, GA: African Studies Association Press, 1994, 15-25.

16 Y.Y. Mudimbe, *The Invention of Africa*, 1988, 160-16 1.

17 P.O. Bodurin (ed.), *Philosophy in Africa;* Appiah, *In My Father's House. 1992.*

18 R.G. Collingwood, *The Idea of History*, 1946; W.H. Walsh, *An introduction to Philosophy of History*, 1951; P. Gardiner (ed.), *The Philosophy of History*, 1974.

19 F.R. Ankersmit, *Narrative Logic: a Semantic Analysis of the Historian's Language*, 1983.

20 Mudimbe, *The invention of Africa, 1988,186.*

21 E.J. Alagoa, "Nembe: The city idea in the Eastern Niger Delta", *Cahiers d'Etudes Africaine*, XI, 42, 1971, 327-331.

22 Robin Horton, *The gods as guests, 1960.*

23 Nigel Barley, *Foreheads of the Dead.* 1988.

24 E.D.W. Opuogulaya, *The Culture of the Wakirike.* 1975.

25 E.J. Alagoa, "Idu: a creator festival at Okpoma (Brass) in the Niger Delta", *Africa*, 34, 1, 1964,1-8.

26 Robin Horton, "The Ekine Society", *Africa*, 33, 2, 1963, 44-114; E.J. Alagoa, "Delta masquerades", *Nigeria Magazine*, 93, 1967, 145- 1 55.

27 Jan Vansina, *Oral Tradition*, 1961/65; *Oral Tradition as History*, 1985.

28   E.J. Alagoa, "Riddles in Nembe", *Oduma*, 2, 1975, 17-21.
29   E.J. Alagoa, "Songs as historical data", *Research Review*, 5, 1, 1968, 1-16.
30   E.J. Alagoa, "Ijo drumlore", *African Notes*, 6, 2, 1971, 61-7 1; "Ama-teme-suo kule", in Tunde Okanlawon (ed.), *Comparative Literature*, 1988, 102-104.
31   E.J. Alagoa, "The use of oral literary data for history: examples from the Niger Delta- proverbs", *Journal of American Folklore*, 81, 321, 1968, 235-242; *Nembe proverbs*, 1986.
32   E.J. Alagoa, *Nembe proverbs*, 1986, 76-77.
33   Alagoa, 1986, 88-89.
34   S.A. Ekwulo, *Ikwerre Proverbs*, 1975, 2-3.
35   Ekwulo, 1975, 4-5.
36   Ekwulo, 1975, 28-29.
37   J.O. Ojoade, "Some Itsekiri proverbs", *Nigerian Field*, 1980, 93.
38   J.O. Ojoade, "Proverbs as a mirror of Birom life and thought", in E. Isichei (ed.), *The History of Plateau State of Nigeria*, 1982, 87.
39   J.O. Ojoade, "Some Kuteb aphorisms", *Nigerian Field*, 1982, 56.
40   Ekwulo, 1975, 6-7, 16-17.
41   Ojoade, "Proverbial evidences of African legal customs", *International Folklore Review*, 6, 1988, 3 1.
42   Ojoade, 1988, 3 1.
43   Ojoade, 1988, 3 1.
44   Alagoa, 1986,18-19.
45   Ekwulo, 1975, 6-7.

46. Ekwulo, 1975, 24-25.
47. Kwasi Wiredu, "The Concept of Truth in the Akan Language", in Bodurin (ed.), 1985, 43-54.
48. Ekwulo, 1975, 28-29.
49. E.J. Alagoa, *The Python's Eye*, 1981, 33.
50. Ekwulo, 1975, 36-37.
51. Alagoa, 1986, 62-63.
52. Ekwulo, 1975, 2-3.
53. J.O. Ojoade, "God in Nigerian proverbs", *Nigerian Field*, 1978, 174.
54. Ojoade, 1978, 176.
55. John Ryan, *The Confessions of St. Augustine*, 1960, 293.
56. Alagoa, 1986, 10-11.
57. Alagoa, *The Python's Eye*, 1981, 14.
58. Ekwulo, 1975, 22-23.
59. Ekwulo, 1975, 2-3.
60. Ekwulo, 1975, 4-5.
61. Alagoa, 1986, 46-47.
62. Alagoa, 1986, 60-61.
63. Alagoa, 1986, 104-105.
64. Alagoa, 1986, 72-73.
65. Alagoa, 1986, 116-117.
66. Alagoa, *The Python's Eye*, 1981, 11-12.
67. Ekwulo, 1975, 34-35.
68. J.F.Ade Ajayi & E.J. Alagoa, "Black Africa: The historian's perspective", *Daedalus*, 103, 2, 1974, 125-134; "Sub-Saharan Africa", in *International Handbook of Historical Studies*, edited by G.G. Iggers & U.T. Parker, Westport, 1979, 403-418.

69   E.J. Alagoa (ed.), *Oral Tradition and Oral History in Africa and the Diaspora: Theory and Practice.* Lagos, 1990.

70   Alex Haley, *Roots.* New York, Doubleday, 1976.

Chapter 3: The Internal Written Tradition

1   Alan Gardiner, *Egypt of the Pharoahs,* Oxford University Press, 196 1, Chapter XIV, "Prehistory", p. 392.

2   The form and dates of the dynasties and pharaohs follow Stephen Quirke, *Who were the Pharaohs? A history of their names with a list of cartouches,* New York, 1990.

3   Alan Gardiner, *Egypt of the Pharaohs,* pp. 33-37.

4   John H. Taylor, *Egypt and Nubia,* Cambridge, MA, 1991, p.5.

5   W. V. Davies, *Reading the Past.. Egyptian Hieroglyphs, pp.* 10 ff., 37-40, 57-62. The distribution of Dynasties into Periods follows the pattern at p. 8.

6   W.V. Davies, *Egyptian Hieroglyphs,* p. 27.

7   J. Cerny, *Paper and Books in Ancient Egypt.* Chicago, 1952, p. 4.

8   Donald B. Redford, *Pharaohnic King-lists, Annals and Day-Books.* 1986. The discussion of this section follows Ludlow Bull, "Ancient Egypt", in John Oberman (ed.), *The Idea of History in the Ancient Near East,* 1955, pp. 3-33.

9   Ludlow Bull, "Ancient Egypt", p.27.

10. Cf. H.& H.A. Frankfort, "Myth and Reality" in H.& H.A.Frankfort, John A. Wilson, Thorkild Jacobsen, William Irwin, *The Intellectual Adventure of Ancient Man: An Essay on Speculative Thought in the Ancient Near East*, Chicago, 1946, pp. 3-27.
11. Ludlow Bull, "Ancient Egypt", p. 23.
12. Ludlow Bull, "Ancient Egypt", p. 24.
13. Bull, "Ancient Egypt", p. 24.
14. Bull, "Ancient Egypt", footnote 32, p. 25.
15. John A. Wilson, "Egypt: the nature of the universe" in H.& H.A, Frankfort et al, *The Intellectual Adventure of Ancient Man*, pp. 31-6 1.
16. John A. Wilson, "Egypt: the nature of the universe", p. 52.
17. Herodotus, *The Histories*, translated by A. de Selincourt & A.R. Burn, Harmondsworth, 1954-1972, Pt. 11, p. 186.
18. Herodotus, 11, p. 130.
19. The discussion under this section will be derived from the following sources: Richard A. Parker, *The Calendars of Ancient Egypt*, Chicago, 1950; W.M. O'Neil, *Time and the Calendars*, Manchester, 1975; William A. Ward, "The present status of Egyptian Chronology", *Bulletin of the American Schools of Oriental Research*, No. 288, 1992, 53- 66.
20. Parker, The Calendars of Ancient Egypt, p.31.
21. Bull, *"Ancient Egypt", pp. 26-28.*
22. Donald B. Redford, *Pharaohnic King-lists, Annals and Day-Books, 1986.*
23. Redford, *Pharaonic King-lists*, p. 203.

24 Redford, *Pharaonic King-lists*, p. 67.
25 Redford, *Pharaonic King-lists*, p. 78.
26 Redford, *Pharaonic King-lists*, p. 83-84.
27 See Redford, *Pharaonic King-lists*, for examples of day-books.
28 E.J. Alagoa, "The encounter between African and Western historiography before 1800", *Storia della Storiografia*, 19, 1991, pp. 78-80.
29 W.G. Waddell, *Manetho*, 1971, pp. ix, xi-xii.
30 According to Redford, *Pharaonic King-lists*, pp. 206-229.
31 Waddell, *Manetho*, p. vii. The history of the Aegyptiaca follows Richard Laqueur (1928).
32 The texts are taken from the following collections: Adolf Erman, *The Ancient Egyptians: A Source book of their writings*, New York, 1927/1966; and William Kelly Simpson (ed.), *The Literature of Ancient Egypt.. An Anthology of Stories, Instructions, and Poetry*, New Haven & London, 1973.
33 Simpson (ed.), *The Literature of Ancient Egypt*, p. 306.
34 W.K. Simpson in Erman, *The Ancient Egyptians*, Pp. xvi-xvii.
35 Simpson (ed.), *The Literature of Ancient Egypt*, p. 160.
36 Simpson (ed.), *The Literature of Ancient Egypt*, pp. 162, 173, 174.
37 Simpson (ed.), *The Literature of Ancient Egypt*, p. 336, from *The Satire on the Trades / The Instruction of Dua-Khety*, *The Instruction of Duauf* in Erman, *The Ancient Egyptians*, pp. 67-72.

38 Simpson (ed.), *The Literature of Ancient Egypt*, p. 182. *The Teaching for Merikare, The Instruction for King Kerikare* (Erman), p. 75.

39 Simpson (ed.), *The Literature of Ancient Egypt*, p. 183.

40 Simpson (ed.), *The Literature of Ancient Egypt*, pp. 191, 190. 41. Simpson (ed.), *The Literature of Ancient Egypt* p. 190.

42 Simpson (ed.), *The Literature of Ancient Egypt*, pp. 185, 186.

43 Simpson (ed.), *The Literature of Ancient Egypt*, p. 245, 263.

44 Simpson (ed.), *The Literature of Ancient Egypt* p.,207.

45 Simpson (ed.), *The Literature of Ancient Egypt*, "The Admonitions of an Egyptian sage", pp. 218, 226.

46 Simpson (ed.), *The Literature of Ancient Egypt*. "The Lamentations of Khakheperresonbe" p. 231.

47 The following examples come from Redford, *Pharaonic King-lists*, pp. 257-294.

48 See R.G. Collingwood, *The Idea of History*, 1946; Ludlow Bull, "Ancient Egypt", 1955, pp. 32-33; Herbert Butterfield, *The Origins of History*, 1981, pp. 47-60; Redford, *Pharaonic King Lists*, pp. xvi-xxi; John A. Wilson, "Egypt", in *The Intellectual Adventure of Ancient Man*, edited by H. & H.A. Frankfort, 1946, pp. 119.

49 Cf. C.B. Kiebel, "Memory sticks and other mnemonic devices", *The Nigerian Field*, vol. 55, Parts 3-45 Oct. 1990, 91-98 for examples from Nigeria. See I.J. Gelb, A *Study of Writing*, 1963, Table titled "Origin of the alphabet".

50 John H. Taylor, *Egypt and Nubia*, 1991, pp. 50-51; Albertine Gaur, *A History of Writing*, 1987, p. 65; Jean Leclant, "'The present situation in deciphering of Meroitic script", 1974, pp. 107-119.

51 A. Gaur, A *History of Writing*, pp. 72, 91.

52 A. Gaur, A *History of Writing*, p. 100; Cf. I.J. Gelb, *A Study of Writing*, p. 149.

53 A. Gaur, A *History of Writing*, pp. 122-123; W.V. Davies, *Egyptian Hieroglyphs*, pp. 25-27.

54 I.J. Gelb, A *Study of Writing*, p. 209; I.M. Lewis, "The Gadabuursi Somali Script", *Bulletin of the School of Oriental and African Studies*, Vol. 21, 1958, 134-156.

55 Fafima Massequoi Fahnbulleh, "The Seminar on Standardization of the Vaj Script", *University of Liberia Journal*, January 1963, p. 11-37.

56 I.J. Gelb, *A Study of Writing*, p. 208. The following scripts are also cited here.

57 Gelb, A *Study of Writing*, p. 208-209; Gaur, A *History of Writing*, p. 13 1.

58 Kathleen Hau, "Evidence of the use of pre-Portuguese written characters by the Bini?", *Bull. de l'IFAN*, Vol. 2 1, ser B, Nos. 1-2, 1959, 109-154.; "A royal title on a Palace Tusk from Benin ((Southern Nigeria)", *Bull. de l'IFAN*, Vol. 26, ser B, Nos. 1-2, 1964, 21-39; "The ancient writing of Southern Nigeria". *Bull. de l'IFAN*, Vol. 29, ser B, Nos. 1-2, 1967, 150-189; "Pre-Islamic writing in West Africa", *Bull. de l'IFAN*, ser B, No. 1, Vol. 35, 1973, 1-45.

59   J.K. Macgregor, "Some Notes on Nsibidi", *Journ. Royal Anthropological Institute*, Vol. 39, 1909, 209-219; E. Dayrell, "Some Nsibidi signs", *Man*, Vol. 10, 1910, 113-115; E. Dayrell, "Further Notes on Nsibidi Signs", *JRAI*, Vol. 41, 1911, 521-540; E.J Alagoa, "Peoples of the Cross River Valley and the Eastern Niger Delta", in O. Ikime (ed.), *Groundwork of Nigerian History*, 1980, pp. 62-63.

60   R.F.G. Adarns, "Oberi Okaime: A new African language and script", *Africa*, 1947; K. Hau, "Oberi Okaime script, Texts and Counting System", *Bull. de l'IFAN*, Vol. 23, ser B, Nos. 1-2, 1961, 291-308.

61   Gelb, A *Study of* Writing, p. 231.

62   Jack Goody (ed.), *Literacy in Traditional Societies*, 1968, see African cases in (i) Ivor Wilks, "The transmission of Islamic learning in the Western Sudan", pp. 162-197. (ii) Jack Goody, "Restricted literacy in Northern Ghana", pp. 198-264; (iii) I.M. Lewis, "Literacy in a nomadic society: the Somali case", pp. 265-276; (iv) Maurice Bloch, "Astrology and Writing in Madagascar", pp. 277-297.

Chapter 4: The Islamic Tradition

1   Julian Oberman, "Early Islam" in R.C. Dentan (ed.) *The Idea of History in the Ancient Near East*, 1955, pp. 264,281, 306; P.M. Holt, "Introduction" to *The Cambridge History of Islam*, Vol. 2B, edited by P.M .Holt, et al, 1970, p. xv.

2   Oberman, "Early Islam", p. 241.

3   Oberman, "Early Islam", p. 280.
4   Franz Rosenthal, A *History of Muslim Historiography*, Leiden, 1968, p. 11.
5   Rosenthal, A *History of Muslim Historiography*, pp. 12-14.
5a George Makdisi, "The Diary in Islamic Historiography: Some Notes", *History and Theory*, Vol. 25, No 2, 1986, 173-185.
6   Rosenthal, A *History of Muslim Historiography*, pp. 66-71.
7   I.U.A. Musa, "The rise of Muslim Sudanic Historiography in *Bilad as-Sudan:: a* tentative analysis", Zaria, 1978, p. 13.
8   G.S.P. Freeman-Grenville, *The Muslim and Christian Calendars*, 1963, p.1, citing Quran, Sura IX, verse 36. All succeeding quotations come from Freeman-Grenville.
9   W.H.C. Frend, "The Christian period in Mediterranean Africa c. AD 200-700" in J.D. Fage (ed.) *The Cambridge History of Africa, vol. 2, from c. 500 B. C. to AD 1050*, Cambridge, 1978, pp. 410-489.
10 T. Bianquis, "Egypt from the Arab conquest until the end of the Fatimid State" (1171) in M. El Fasi and I. Hrbek (eds.), *Unesco General History of Africa, Vol. III.. Africa from the seventh to the eleventh century*, Paris, 1985, pp. 163-193.
11 Michael Brett, "The Arab conquest and the rise of Islam in North Africa", in J.D. Fage (ed.), *The Cambridge History of Africa, Vol. 2*, p.495

12 For the following section, see Ivan Urbek, "Egypt, Nubia and the Eastern Deserts", in Roland Oliver (ed.), *The Cambridge History of Africa, Vol. 3, from c. 1050 to c. 1610*, Cambridge, 1977, pp. 22-23, 38-39, 63-67, 95-97.

13 Donald Harden, *The Phoenicians*, Penguin Books, 1980, pp. 163-168 for Hanno's account.

14 I.M.Barton, *Africa in the Roman Empire*, Accra, 1972, pp. 34, 59; J.A. Ilevbare, *Carthage, Rome, and the Berbers*, Ibadan, 1980, p. XVII, 17 1.

15 M. El Fasi and 1, Hrbek, "Stages in the development of Islam and its dissemination in Africa", *Unesco General history of Africa, III*, pp. 61-67 for "The Maghrib".

16 R. Idris, "Society in the Maghrib after the disappearance of the Almohads", in *Unesco General History of Africa, IV*, 1984, p. 115.

17 T.T. Mekouria, "The Horn of Africa", in *Unesco General History of Africa. III*, pp. 558-574.

18 Taddesse Tamrat, "Ethiopia, the Red Sea and the Horn", in *The Cambridge History of Africa, vol. 3, from c. 1050 to c. 1600*, 1977, pp. 99-182.

19 E. Ceruili, "Ethiopia's relations with the Muslim world", in *Unesco General History of Africa, III*, 1988, pp. 575-585.

20 Claude Sumner, "Ethiopia: Land of Diverse Expressions of Philosophy, Birthplace of Modern Thought", in *African Philosophy*, edited by Claude Sumner, Addis Ababa, 1980, pp. 393-400.

21. Herbert S. Lewis, "The origins of the Galla and Somali", *Journal of African History*, 7, 1, 1966, 27-46; 1. M. Lewis, "The Somali conquest of the Horn of Africa", *Journ. Afr. Hist*, 1, 2, 1960, 213-229.
22. E. Ceruili, "Ethiopia's relations with the Muslim world", 1988, pp. 577-585.
23. Raymond Mauny, "Trans-Saharan contacts and the Iron Age in West Africa", *Cambridge History of Africa, Vol. 2, from c. 500 BC to AD 1050*, pp. 272-341.
24. Mauny, "Trans-Saharan contacts", p. 288ff.
25. *Herodotus: The Histories*, translated by Audrey de Selincourt, revised by A.R. Burn, Penguin Books, 1952/1972, Book 2, p. 141; for other references see Book 4, pp. 329-334.
26. *Herodotus*, Book 4, p. 333.
27. P. Salama, "The Sahara in classical antiquity", *General History of Africa. II. Ancient Civilizations of Africa*, edited by G. Mokhtar, Unesco, 198 1, pp. 5 13-532.
28. T. Lewicki, "The role of the Sahara and Saharians in relations between north and south", *Unesco General History of Africa, III*, pp. 276-313.
29. N. Levtzion & J.F.P. Hopkins, *Corpus of early Arabic Sources for West African History*, Cambridge, 1981, pp. 293, 297.
30. Levtzion & Hopkins, *Corpus of early Arabic sources*, p. 77, Abu 'Ubayd 'Abd Allah b. 'Abd al-'Aziz al-Bakr, *Kitab al-masalik wa-'l-mamalik* (The Book of Routes and Realms).
31. Levtzion & Hopkins, *Corpus of early Arabic sources*, pp. 79-80, al-Bakr, *Kitab al- masalik wa-'l-mamalik*.

32. Levtzion & Hopkins, *Corpus of early Arabic sources.* p.82.
33. Levtzion & Hopkins, *Corpus of early Arabic sources*, p. 98. Abu Allah Muhammad b. Abi Bakr al-Zuhri, *Kitab al-Ja'rafiyya* (Book of Geography).
34. Levtzion & Hopkins, *Corpus of early Arabic sources*, p. 333. Abu Zayd 'Abd al-Rahman Ibn Khaldun, *Kitab al-'ibar wa-diwan al-mubtada'wa-'l-khabar fi ayyam al-'arab wa-'l-ajam wa-'l-Bilabarbar,* (The Book of Examples and the Register of subject and Predicate [or, of the Origin and History], on the Days of the Arabs, the Persians an the Berbers).
35. Levtzion & Hopkins, *Corpus of early Arabic sources,* p. 27 1, Shihab al-Din Abu 'l-'Abbas Ahmad b. Yaha b. Fadl Allah al-'Adawi *alias* Ibn Fadl Allah al-'Umari, *Masalik al-absar fi mamalik al-amsar.* (Pathways of Vision in the Realms of the Metropolises).
36. J. Spencer Trimingham, A *History of Islam in West Africa,* London, 1962, p. 89.
37. I.U.A. Musa, "The Rise of Muslim Sudanic Historiography in *Bilad as-Sudan: a* tentative analysis", Paper presented at the 23rd Congress of the Historical Society of Nigeria, held at Ahrnadu Bello University, Zaria, 4th - 8th April 1978.
38. Elias N. Saad, *Social History of Timbuktu: The role of Muslim Scholars and Notables, 1400-1900,* London, 1983; E.J. Alagoa, "al-Sa'di'Abd al-Rahman", Lucian Boia (ed.), *Great Historians from Antiquity to 1800: An International Dictionary,* New York: Greenwood Press, 1989, p. 3.

39 E.J. Alagoa, "Ahmad Baba", *Great Historians from Antiquity to 1800,* p. 2 for other references.

40 E.N. Saad, *Social History of Timbuktu,* p. 62; Ivor Wilks, "The transmission of Islamic learning in the Western Sudan", in Jack Goody (ed.), *Literacy in Traditional Societies,* Cambridge, 1968, pp. 162-197; Thomas Hodgkin, "The Islamic Literary Tradition in Ghana", in I.M. Lewis (ed.), *Islam in Tropical Africa,* London, 1966, pp. 44 462.

41 Ivor Wilks, "The transmission of Islamic learning ", p. 167.

42 T. Hodgkin, "The Islamic Literary Tradition", p. 450-452; Jack Goody, "Restricted Literacy in Northern Ghana", in J. Goody, (ed.), *Literacy in Traditional Societies,* pp. 24 261.

43 H.R. Palmer, *Sudanese Memoirs,* Vol. 3, pp. 1, 3-5.

44 Levtzion & Hopkins, *Corpus of early Arabic sources,* pp. 344-345. Abu'l-'Abbas Ahmad al-Qalqashandi, *Subh al--a'shaft sinaat al-insha,* (The Dawn of the Night-blind on the Art of Letter-writing) completed 1412 AD.

45 H.R.Palmer (ed. & tran.), *History of the First Twelve years of the Reign of Mai Idris Alooma of Bornu, 1571-1583, by his Imam, Ahmad Ibn Fartua,* Lagos, 1926, London 1970; H.R. Palmer, "Kanem Wars of Mai Idris Alooma", Vol. *I, Sudanese Memoirs,* Lagos 1928, London, 1967; E.J. Alagoa, "Ibn Fartuwa, Ahmad", in Lucian Boia (ed.), *Great Historians from Antiquity to 1800: An International Dictionary,* 1989, 5.

46 Thomas Hodgkin (ed.), *Nigerian perspectives: An historical anthology,* London, 1960. pp. 134-5, citing H.R. Palmer, "Two Sudanese Manuscripts of the seventeenth century", *Bulletin of the School of Oriental and African Studies,* Vol. 3, 1929, pp. 545-7.

47 H.R. Palmer, *Sudanese Memoirs,* Vol. 1, preface; Vol. 11, pp. 6-17; Vol. In, pp. 1-2; Hodgkin (ed.), *Nigerian Perspectives,* p. 70 fn. 4.

48 H.R.Palmer, "Kano Chronicle", *Journal of the Royal Anthropological Institute,* Vol. 38, 1908, pp. 63-98; *Sudanese Memoirs,* Vol. 3, pp. 97-132. The following citations come from the *Memoirs.*

49 H.R. Palmer, "Kano Chronicle", *Sudanese Memoirs,* Vol. 3, p. 111.

50 Abdullahi Smith, "The early history of the Central Sudan", in J.F. Ade Ajayi & Michael Crowder (eds.) *History of West Africa, Vol. 1',* Second Edition, 1976, p. 192 fn. 143.

51 Yusufu Bala Usman, *The Transformation of Katsina: (1400-1883),* Zaria, 198 1, pp. 21-22,71-76.

52 Ahmed Mohammed Kani, "The rise and influence of scholars in Hausaland before *1804", Kano Studies,* New Series, 1981, pp. 47-69.

53 Ahmed M. Kani, "Aspects of historiographical developments in the Sokoto Caliphate up to 1860", Paper presented at the Congress of the Historical Society of Nigeria held at Sokoto, May 1991, 10 pp.

54 Ahmed M. Kani, "Aspects ... p. 5. See also M. Hiskett (tr.), Abdullahi b. Fudi, *Tazyi al-waraqat,* Ibadan, 1963.

55 Joseph H. Greenberg, "Linguistic evidence for the influence of the Kanuri on the Hausa", *Journal of African History,* Vol. 1, No 2, 1960, 205-212.

56 Greenberg, "Linguistic evidence..", p. 212.

57 M. Hiskett, "The 'Song of Bagauda': A Hausa King List and Homily in Verse", *Bulletin of the School of Oriental and African Studies,* I: Vol. 27, 1964, 540-567; II: Vol. 28, 1965, 112-135; III: Vol. 28, 1965, 363-385; H.R. Palmer, *Sudanese Memoirs,* Vol. 3, 132-4 for the *Girgam.*

58 O.S.A. Isma'il, "Some reflections on the literature of the *Jihad* and the Caliphate" in Y.B. Usman (ed.), *Studies in the History of the Sokoto Caliphate,* Zaria, 1979, pp. 165- 180.

59 Y.B. Hasan & B.A.Ogot, "The Sudan, 1500-1800", in B.A. Ogot (ed.), *General History of Africa Vol V: Africa from the sixteenth century to the eighteenth century,* Unesco, 1992, p.170.

60 Yusuf Fadl Hasan, "The penetration of Islam into the Eastern Sudan", in I.M. Lewis *(ed.), Islam in Tropical Africa,* London, 1966, p. 146.

61 R.S. O'Fahey & J.L. Spaulding, *Kingdoms of the Sudan,* London, 1974, p. 9.

62 O'Fahey & Spaulding, *Kingdoms of the Sudan,* p. 9.

63 Wilfred Whiteley, *Swahili : The rise of a National Language,* London, 1973, 1974, 1975, pp. 3-9.

64 G.S.P. Freeman-Grenville, The *East African Coast: Select Documents from the first to the earlier nineteenth century,* Oxford, 1962, 1-7.

65. Neville Chittick, "Kilwa and the Arab settlement of the East African coast", *Journal of African History*, Vol. 4, No 2, 1963, 179-190; "The Coast before the arrival of the Portuguese", in B.A. Ogot (ed.), *Zamani: a Survey of East African History*, Nairobi, 1968, 1973, pp. 98-114.

66. G.S.P. Freeman-Grenville, *The East African Coast*, Abu-'l-Hasan 'Ali b. al-Husayn al Mas'udi, *muruj al-dhahab wa-maadin al-jawhar* (The Meadows of Gold and the Mines of Jewels).

67. G. S.P. Freeman-Grenville, *The East African Coast*, pp. 19-20. Abu 'Abd Allah Muhammad al sharif al-Idrisi, *Nuzhat al-mushtaq fi ikhtiraq al-afaq* (The pleasure of Him who longs to cross the horizons).

68. Freeman-Grenville, *The East African Coast*, pp. 27-32. Shams al-Din Abu 'Abd Allah Muhammad Ibn Battuta, *Rihla* (Journey).

69. Neville Chittick, "The 'Shirazi' colonization of East Africa", *Journal of African History*, Vol. 6, No 3, 1965, 263-273.

70. Freeman-Grenville, *The East African Coast*, pp. 8, 21-22; Chittick, "The 'Shirazi' colonization", pp. 246, 268.

71. G.S.P. Freeman-Grenville, *The East African Coast*, pp. 34-49: Anonymous: an Arabic History of Kilwa Kisiwani c. 1520; pp. 213-304: **Histories of Mombasa, Kilwa** Kisiwani, Lindi, Sudi, Dar es-Salaam, Bagamoyo, Pate, and Kua.

72. Freeman-Grenville, *The East African Coast,* "Anonymous: An Arabic History of Kilwa Kisiwani c. 1520", pp. 34-49; J. de Barros, *Da Asia,* Lisbon, 1552, pp. 89-93.

73. C. Velten, *Prosa und poesie der Suaheli,* Berlin, 1907, pp. 243-52, 265-72, 279-84, 289-305. Histories of Kilwa Kivinje, Mikindani, Kionga, Pangani, and Kisaki were not used by Freeman-Grenville as being of 'lesser historical value".

74. C.H. Stigand, *The Land of Zinj,* 1913, pp. 29-1,02. Three other versions are cited by Freeman-Grenville.

75. J.J. Saunders, "Rashid al-Din, the first Universal Historian", *History Today,* Vol. XXI, No 7, 197 1, p. 47 1.

76. Franz Rosenthal (tr.), *Ibn Khaldun. The Muqaddimah; An Introduction to History,* 3 vols., 1958, 1967, Vol. 1, p. 13, fn. 28; Muhsin Mahdi, *Ibn Khaldun's Philosophy of History,* Chicago, 1964, 1971, p. 63, translates the title as "The Book of the *'Ibar,* the Record of the Origins and Events of the Days of the Arabs, Persians and Berbers, and those of their Contemporaries who were Possessors of Great Power"; Levtzion & Hopkins, *Corpus of early Arabic Sources,* p. 317 renders it "The Book of Examples and the Register of subject and Predicate [or of the Origin and History], on the Days of the Arabs, the Persians and the Berbers".

77. F. Rosenthal, *Ibn Khaldun,* Vo.l 1, "Introduction", pp. 15-68.

78. Rosenthal, *Ibn Khaldun, Vol.* 1, "Preliminary Remarks", pp. 71-85.

79 Rosenthal, *Ibn Khaldun, Vol.* 1, "Chapter 1: Human civilization in general", pp. 87-245.
80 Rosenthal, *Ibn Khaldun, Vol.* 1, pp. 249-3 10.
81 M. Mahdi, *Ibn Khaldun's Philosophy of History,* pp. 196, 263. *Asabiyah was* previously used principally in the sense of dominating other groups.
82 Rosenthal, *Ibn Khaldun, Vol.* 1, pp. 313-48 1; Vol. 11, pp. 3-23 1.
83 Rosenthal, *Ibn Khaldun, Vol.* 11, pp. 235-307. 84. Rosenthal, *Ibn Khaldun, Vol.* 11, pp. 311-407.
85 Rosenthal, *Ibn Khaldun, Vol.* 11, pp. 411-463; Vol. HI, pp. 3-481.
86 Lenn Evan Goodman, "Ibn Khaldun and Thucydides", *Journal of the American Oriental Society,* Vol. 92, No 2, 1972, 250-270.
87 Ziauddin Sardar, *The Future of Muslim Civilization,* London: Croom Helm, 1979, chapter 8: "The future is in the past", pp. 167-188.

Chapter 5:   The Western Tradition

1 R.G. Collingwood, *The Idea of History,* London: Oxford University Press, 1946, 1956, 1977.
2 F.R. Ankersmit, *Narrative Logic: A Semantic Analysis of the Historian's Language.* The Hague/Boston/London, 1983; "Historiography and Postmodernism", *History and Theory,* Vol. 28, No 2, 1989, 137-153; Hayden White, *Metahistory: The Historical Imagination in Nineteenth Century Europe,* Baltimore, 1973, and other writings.

3   Collingwood, *The Idea of History*, 10-11.
4   J.B. Bury, *The Ancient Greek Historians*, New York: Dover Publications Inc., 1958, pp. 36-74.
5   Amaldo Momigliano, "The place of Herodotus in the History of Historiography", *History*, XLVIII, 1958, 1-13.
6   Lenn Evan Goodman, "Ibn Khaldun and Thucydides", *Journ. Am. Oriental Soc.*, 92, 2, 1972, 250-270; J.B. Bury, *The Ancient Greek Historians*, p. 143-144.
7   Collingwood, *The Idea of History*, p. 41.
8   Collingwood, *The Idea of History*, pp. 46-85.
9   Collingwood, *The Idea of History*, pp. 59-76; Descartes, A *Discourse on the First Philosophy, Principles of Philosophy*. Translated by John Yeitch, London: Everyman Library, 1977, pp. 6-7.
10 Collingwood, *The Idea of history*, pp. 113-122; G.W.F. Hegel, *The Philosophy of History*, New York: Dover Publishers, Inc., 1956.
11 Collingwood, *The Idea of History*, pp. 126-133.
12 Karl R. Popper, *The Poverty of Historicism*, New York: Harper & Row, 1964, p.161; cf. Melyin Rader, *Marx's Interpretation of History*, New York: Oxford University Press, 1979, pp. 86-88; *History and Theory*, Beiheft 14, 1975: "Essays on historicism".
13 Collingwood, *The Idea of History*, pp. 282-302; Carl G. Hempel, "Reason and Covering Law in Historical Explanation", in *The Philosophy of History*, edited by Patrick Gardiner, Oxford, 1974, pp. 90-105; W.H. Walsh, "Colligatory Concepts in History", in Gardiner (ed.), *The Philosophy of History*, pp. 127-144.

14. Fernand Braudel, *On History*. (Translated by Sarah Matthews), London: Weidenfeld & Nicolson, 1969, 1980; *The Mediterranean and the Mediterranean World in the Age of Philip II*, 2 volumes, (Translated by Sian Reynolds), London: Fontana/Collins, 1969, 1975, 1981.

15. Jean Glenisson, "France", in G.G. Iggers and H.T. Parker (eds.), *International Handbook of Historical Studies*, Westport: 1979, pp. 175-192; E. U Roy Ladurie, *Montaillou: Cathars and Catholics in a French Village 1294-1324*, Penguin, *The Territory of the Historian*, (Translated by Ben & Sian Reynolds), 1979; Traian Stoianivich, *French Historical Method.. The 'Annales' Paradigm*, Ithaca, 1976.

16. Theodore K. Rabb & Robert 1. Rotberg (eds.), *The New History, The 1980s and Beyond: Studies in Interdisciplinary History*. Princeton: Princeton University Press, 1982.

17. F.R. Ankersmit, "The Dilemma of Contemporary Anglo-Saxon Philosophy of History", *History and Theory*, 25, Beiheft 25, 1986, 1-27; "Hstoriography and Postmordernism", *History and Theory*, 28, 2, 1989, 137-153; *History and Theory*, Beiheft 19,1980: "*Metahistory:* Six Critiques".

18. F.R. Ankersmit, *Narrative Logic*, 1983; Paul Ricoeur, *Time and Narrative*, 3 volumes (Translated by Kathleen McLaughlin and David Pellauer), 1983, 1990.

19. E.J. Alagoa, "The Encounter between African and Western Historiography before 1800", *Storia della Storiografia*, 19, 1991, 73-87.

20   A.F. Shore, "Christian and Coptic Egypt", in J.R. Harris (ed.), *The Legacy of Egypt,* Oxford, 197 1, p. 390.

21   E.J. Alagoa, "The Encounter between African and Western historiography before 1800", p. 82.

22   J.H. Parry, *The establishment of the European Hegemony, 1415-1715,* New York: Harper & Row, 1966.

23   Eric R. Wolf, *Europe and the People without History,* Berkeley, 1982.

24   B. Heintz and Adam Jones (eds.), "European Sources for sub-Saharan Africa before 1900: Use and Abuse", *Paideuma,* Vol. 33, 1987.

25   D. Forde (ed.), *Eftk Traders of Old Calabar,* London, 1956; P.D. Curtin (ed.), *Africa Remembered: Narratives by West Africans from the Era of the Slave Trade,* Madison & Ibadan, 1967; Thea Buttner, "Aspects and Roots of African historiography: The Encounter or Dialogue with Western historical writing and thinking", *Storia della Storiografia, Vol.* 19,1991, 111-116.

26   Frantz Fanon, *The Wretched of the Earth,* New York, 1966, 1978; *Black Skin, White Masks,* New York, 1967, 1982; Walter Rodney, *How Europe Underdeveloped Africa,* London, 1972, 1976, 1978; Philip D. Curtin, "The Black Experience of Colonialism and Imperialism", in Sidney W. Mintz (ed.), *Slavery, Colonialism and Racism,* New York, 1974, pp. 17-29; J.F. Ade Ajayi and E.J. Alagoa, "Black Africa: The Historians' Perspective", in Mintz (ed.), *Slavery, Colonialism and Racism,* pp. 125-134.

27 E.J. Alagoa (Ed.), *The Teaching of History in African Universities*, Accra, Association of African Universities, 1977.

28 Bogumil Jewsiewicki and David Newbury (eds.), *African Historiographies*, Part IV "Africa from within: National Historiographies", pp. 179-235: Ethiopia by Robert S. Love; Nigeria by E.J. Alagoa and Paul E. Lovejoy; Senegal by Mohamed Mbodj, Mamadou Diouf, and Martin A. Klein; Zaire by Mumbanza Mwa Bawele and Sabakinu Kivilu.

29 Martin Jay and Jane Flax, Forum on *Postmordernism, or, The Cultural Logic of Late Capitalism,* by Fredric Jameson, in *History and Theory,* Vol. 32, No 3, 1993, 296-3 10.

30 Philip D. Curtin, *The Image of Africa: British Ideas and Action, 1780-1850*, Madison, 1964.

31 Curtin, *The Image of Africa,* pp. 363-387: "The Racists and their opponents".

32 C.G. Seligman, *Races of Africa*, New York: Oxford University Press, Fourth Edition 1966. (First published 1930, Second Edition 1939, Third Edition 1957).

33 Seligman, *Races of Africa,* p. 61. See Edith R. Sanders, "Hamitic hypothesis, its origin and functions in time perspective", *Journal of African History,* 10,4 (1969), 521-532.

34 G.W. F. Hegel, *The Philosophy of History,* New York, 1956; A.P. Newton, "Africa and historical research", *Journal of the African Society,* 22 (1922-3); Hugh Trevor-Roper, "The Rise of Christian Europe", *The Listener,* 28 November, 1963, pp. 871-1065.

35 Hegel, *The Philosophy of History,* pp. 91, 98, 99.
36 Newton, "Africa and historical research", p. 267.
37 Trevor-Roper, "The rise of Christian Europe", p. 871.
38 J.D.Fage, "The development of African historiography", *General History of Africa I: Methodology and African Prehistory,* J. Ki-Zerbo (ed.), Unesco, 1981, pp. 25-42; P.D. Curtin, "Recent trends in African historiography and their contribution to history in general", *General History of Africa I,* pp. 54-7 1; Adam Jones, *Raw, Medium, Well Done,* Madison, 1987.
39 E.J. Alagoa, "Frobenius, Leo", in Lucian Boia (ed.), *Great Historians of the Modern Age,* New York, 1991, pp. 2-4.
40 P.D. Curtin, "Recent trends", and Jan. Vansina, *Oral Tradition as History,* Madison, *1985; Paths in the Rainforests: Towards a History of Political Tradition in Equatorial Africa,* Madison, 1990; *Living with Africa,* Madison, 1994.
41 Roy Preiswerk and Dominique Perrot, *Ethnocentrism and History: Africa, Asia and Indian America in Western Textbooks,* New York, 1978; C.C. Wrigley, "Historicism in Africa: Slavery and State formation", *African Affairs,* Vol. 70, No 279, 1971, 113-124.
42 See J.F. Ade Ajayi and E.J. Alagoa, "Black Africa: The Historians' perspective", in Sydney W. Mintz (ed.), *Slavery, Colonialism, and Racism,* New York, 1974, pp. 125-134; J.F. Ade Ajayi, "Historical Education in Nigeria", *Journal of the Historical Society of Nigeria,* Vol. 8, No 1, 1975, 3-8; J.F. Ade Ajayi and E.J. Alagoa, "Sub-Saharan Africa". in G.G. Iggers and H.T. Parker

(eds.), *International Handbook of Historical Studies: Contemporary Research and Theory,* Westport, 1979, pp. 403-418; E.J. Alagoa, "Towards a history of African historiography", in Lucian Boia (ed.) *Etudes d'Historiographie,* Bucharest, 1985, pp. 53-64.

43   Rev Sarnuel Johnson, *The History of the Yorubas,* Lagos, 1921, 1937, 1956, 1957, 1960; Sir Apolo Kagwa, *Basekabaka be Buganda* (The Kings of Buganda), 1901, 1912, 1927; John William Nyakatura, *Abakama ba Bunyoro-Kitara* (The Kings of Bunyoro-Kitara), 1947; Solomon Tshekisho Plaattje, *Mhudi: An epic of South African Native Life a hundred Years Ago,* 1930; Rev Carl Christian Reindorf, *The history of the Gold Coast and Asante,* 1895, 1966; Akiga Sai, *Akiga's Story: The Tiv Tribe as seen by one of its members,* 1939, 1965; J.U. Egharevba, A *Short History of Benin,* 1934, 1960. For accounts of the life and work of these historians, except Egharevba, see E.J. Alagoa, in Lucian Boia (ed.), *Great Historians of the Modem Age: An International Dictionary, New* York, 1991, pp. 4-1 1.

44   P.D. Curtin (ed) *Africa Remembered: Narratives by West Africans,* Madison and Ibadan, 1967, p. 8.

45   Joseph E. Harris, *Africans and their history,* New York, 1972, pp. 183 ff.

46   E.W. Blyden, *West Africa before Europe,* London, 1905; J.C. Casely-Hayford, *Ethiopia Unbound: Studies in Racial Emancipation,* London 1911; J.C. de Graft Johnson, *African Glory,* New York, 1954; *African Empires of the Past,* Paris: Presence Africaine, 1957.

[47] J.0. Lucas, *The Religion of the Yorubas,* Lagos, 1948; *Religions in West Africa and Ancient Egypt,* Apapa, 1970; Cheikh Anta Diop, *Nations negres et Culture,* Paris: Presence Africaine, 1954; *L'Unite culturelle de l'Afrique Noire, 1959; L'Afrique Noire precoloniale, 1960; Anteriorite des civilisations negres. Mythe ou verite historique?* 1967; etc.

[48] Arnold Temu and B. Swai, *Historians and Africanist History: A Critique,* London, 1981, XI.

[49] Henry Slater, "Dar es Salaam and the post nationalist historiography of Africa", in B. Jewsiewicki and D. Newbury (eds.), *African Historiographies,* 1986, pp. 250-25 1.

[50] Obaro Ikime (ed.), *Groundwork of Nigerian History,* Ibadan: Heinemann for Historical Society of Nigeria, 1980.

[51] K. 0. Dike, *Trade and politics in the Niger Delta, 1830-1885; an introduction to the economic and political history of Nigeria,* Oxford, 1956; S.O. Biobaku, *The Egba and their neighbours 1842-1872,* Oxford, 1957; J.D. Omer-Cooper, "The contribution of the University of Ibadan to the spread of the study and teaching of African history within Africa", *Journal of the Historical Society of Nigeria,* Vol. 10, No 3, 1980, 23-3 1; E.J. Alagoa, "Nigerian academic historians", in B. Jewsiewicki and D. Newbury (eds.), *African Historiographies,* 1986, 189-196; Paul E. Lovejoy, "Nigeria: The Ibadan School and its critics", Jewsiewicki and Newbury (eds.), 1986, pp. 197-205.

[52] E.J. Alagoa, "Of Days, Bread, and Mushrooms: The Historian as Hero", First Dike Memorial Lecture of the Historical Society of Nigeria, Nsukka, May 1985; "Dike, Kenneth Onwuka" in Lucia Boia (ed.), *Great Historians of the Modern Age,* 1991, pp. 1-2; Chieka Ifemesia (ed.), *Issues in African Studies and National Education: Selected Works of Kenneth Onwuka Dike,* Awka: Kenneth Onwuka Dike Centre, 1988.

[53] K.O. Dike, "African History and Self-Government", *West Africa,* February -March 1953, pp. 177-178, 225-226, 251; "The Study of African History" in Lalage Bown and Michael Crowder (eds.) *The Proceedings of the First International Congress of Africanists,* Longman, 1964, 55-67; (with J.F. Ade Ajayi;) "African historiography", *International Encyclopaedia of the Social Sciences,* Vol. 6, 1968, 394-400; (with F.I. Ekejiuba) "Change and persistence in Aro oral history", *Journal of African Studies,* Vol. 3, No 3, 1975, 277-296; "The study of African History: The present position", Paper presented at the Third International Congress of Africanists, Addis Ababa, 1973, in Ifemesia, 1988, 92-101; "African history twenty-five years ago and today", *Journal of the Historical Society of Nigeria, Vol.* 1 0, No 3, 1980, 13-22.

[54] Dike, "African history and self-government", 1953; M. Perham, "The British Problem in Africa", *Foreign Affairs,* 1951.

[55] K.O. Dike and Felicia Ekejiuba, *The Aro of south-eastern Nigeria 1650-1980: A study of socio-economic formation and transformation in Nigeria,* Ibadan: University Press Ltd., 1990.

[56] A.B. Aderibigbe, "Biobaku: The scholar and his works", in G.O. Olusanya (ed.), *Studies in Yoruba History and Culture: Essays in Honour of Professor S. 0. Biobaku,* Ibadan, 1983, p.20.

[57] Toyin Falola (ed.), *African historiography: Essays in Honour of Jacob Ade Ajayi,* Longman, 1993; J.F. Ade Ajayi, "Historical Education in Nigeria", *Journal of the Historical Society of Nigeria,* Vol. 8, No 1, 1975, 3-8.

[58] Martin Klein, "The development of Senegalese historiography", pp. 215-223; Mohamed Mbodj and Mamadou Diouf, "Senegalese Historiography: Present Practice and Future perspectives", pp. 207-214, in Jewsiewicki and Newbury, (eds.), *African Historiographies,* 1986.

[59] Mbodj and Diouf, "Senegalese Historiography", pp. 208-209.

[60] Society of African Culture, "The death of Cheikh Anta Diop", *Presence Africaine,* No 136, 4th Quarter, 1985, pp. 8-9.

[61] Mumbaza Mwa Bawele and Sabakinu Kivilu, "Historical Research in Zaire: Present status and Future perspectives", B. Jewsiewickie and D Newbury (eds.), *African Historiographies,* 1986, p. 225.

[62] Bawele and Kivilu, "Historical Research in Zaire", p. 226.

63 Benoit Verhaegen, "The method of histoire immediate: its application to Africa", Jewsiewicki and Newbury (eds.), *African Historiographies*, 1986, p. 227.

64 Bawele and Kivilu, "Historical Research in Zaire", p. 230.

65 Balam Nyeko, "The importance of southern African history in the school curriculum: a synthesis", Unesco, *The Historiography of Southern Africa*, 1980, p. 57.

66 N.M. Bhebe, "History research in Swaziland", Unesco, *The Historiography of Southern Africa*, 1980, p. 73. See p.85 for the Vice Rector's remarks.

67 Elleck K. Mashingaidze, "The promotion of the study of history at the National University of Lesotho", Unesco, *The Historiography of Southern Africa*, 1980, pp. 66-70. The author was D. Phil (York), the other African members of the department were S.I. Mudenge, PhD (London), and L.B.J. Machobane, MEd (Tuskegee) amd MA (LeHigh).

68 J.B. Webster, "History research in Malawi", Unesco, *The historiography of southern Africa* 1980, pp. 71-72. The department had the scholars O.J. Kalinga and Kings Phiri.

69 B.S. Krishnamurthy, "History research at the University of Zambia", Unesco, *The historiography of southern Africa*, 1980, pp. 8 1-82. The expatriates included Dr. Leroy Vail and Dr. Clarence Smith.

70 Gerald Bender and Allen Isaacman, "The changing historiography of Angola and Mozambique", in Christopher Fyfe (ed.), *African Studies Since 1945: A Tribute to Basil Davidson*, London, 1976, 220-248.

71. L.M. Thompson, "Afrikaner Nationalist Historiography and the Policy of Apartheid", *Historians in Tropical Africa,* Salisbury, 1962, pp. 371-386.

72. David Chanaiwa, "Historiographical traditions of southern Africa", Unesco, *The historiography of Southern Africa,* 1980, pp. 25-44.

73. Shula Marks, "The historiography of South Africa: Recent developments", in B. Jewsiewicki and D. Newbury (eds.), *African Historiographies,* 1986, p. 170.

74. Bethwell A. Ogot, "Preface", *Hadith 1,* 1968, pp. v. Compare *Tarikh* for the teachers' journal of the Historical Society of Nigeria.

75. A.B Aderibigbe, "Biobaku: The Scholar and his works", G.O. Olusanya (ed.), *Studies in Yoruba History and Culture,* 1983, p. 9; B.A. Ogot, A *History of the Southern Luo,* Nairobi, 1967.

76. B.A. Ogot, "Some approaches to African history", *Hadith 1,* 1968, 1-9.

77. Henry Slater, "Dar es Salaam and the post nationalist historiography of Africa", B. Jewsiewicki and D. Newbury (eds.), A*frican Historiographies,* 1986, p. 253; I.N. Kimambo and A.J. Temu (eds.), A *History of Tanzania,* 1969.

78. A.J. Temu and B. Swai, "Old and New themes of African history since the 1960s: the Case of Tanzanian Historiography", in E.J. Alagoa (ed.), *The Teaching of History in African Universities,* 1977, p-92, citing I.N. Kimambo, "Historical Research in Tanzania", Dar es Salaam, 1968.

[79] Walter Rodney, *How Europe Underdeveloped Africa*, London, 1972, 1976, 1978; Arnold Temu and B. Swai, *Historians and Africanist History*, London, 198 1.

[80] Henry Slater, "Dar es Salaam and the postnationalist historiography of Africa", p. 255; Rodney, *How Europe Underdeveloped Africa*, p. 7.

[81] A. Temu and B. Swai, *Historians and Africanist History*, p. 52.

[82] H. Bernstein and J. Depelchin, "The Object of African History: a Materialist Perspective", *History in Africa*, Vol. 5, 1978, 1-9; Vol. 6, 1979, 17-43; H. Slater, "Dar es Salaam...", p.257-58, citing Wamba dia Wamba, "Brief theoretical comments on the quest for materialist history: concerning the article, 'The object of African History'", Dar es Salaam, 1980; Robin Law, "For Marx but with reservations about Althusser: a comment on Bernstein and Depelchin", *History in Africa*, Vol. 8, 1981, 247-25 1.

[83] Ndaywell E Nziem, "African historians and Africanist historians", B. Jewsiewicki and D. Newbury (eds.), *African Historiographies*, 1986, 20-27; T.O. Ranger (ed.), *Emerging Themes of African History*, 1968, "Introduction", p. XXI.

[84] Ralph A. Austen, "'Africanist' historiography and its critics: can there be an autonomous African history?", Toyin Falola (ed), *African Historiography*, 1993, pp. 208- 211.

[85] Vol. 19, No 1, *1985, Canadian Journal of African Studies*, pp. 174.

86   Gavin Kitching, "Suggestions for a fresh start on an exhausted debate", *Canadian Journal of African Studies,* Vol. 19, No 1, 1985, p. 118..

87   E.J. Alagoa, "Communicating African History", *Storia della Storiografia, 15,* 1989, 75-89.

88   Ayi Kwei Armah, "Masks and Marx: The Marxist Ethos vis-à-vis African Revolutionary Theory and Praxis", *Presence Africaine,* No 131, 1984, 60-65. One might add Waiter Rodney to the list of practical revolutionaries.

Chapter 6: Conclusion: Historiography in Transition

1   Claude Levi-Srauss, *The Savage Mind,* Chicago, 1966.

2   Levi-Strauss, 1966, p. 232.

3   Levi-Strauss, 1966, p. 233.

4   Levi-Strauss, 1966, p. 234, 236.

5   Levi-Strauss, 1966, p. 242.

6   Levi-Strauss, *Structural Anthropology,* pp. 265-6. See Terence Hawkes, *Structuralism and Semiotics,* Methuen & Co. Ltd., 1977, pp. 49-50.

7   Madan Sarup, *Post-Structuralism and Postmodernism,* 1988, pp. 41-45.

8   Frantz Fanon, *The Wretched of the Earth,* 1961; *Black Skin, White Masks,* 1982.

9   Walter Rodney, *How Europe Underdeveloped Africa,* 1972.

10   I.D. Keita, "Alienation, Philosophy and the African Problematic", *Kiabara, Vol. 5, No.* 2,1982,115-123.

[11] Jewsiewicki & Newbury (eds.), *African Historiographies. What History for Which Africa*, "Introduction", pp. 9-17; E.J. Alagoa, "Communicating African History", *Storia della Storiografia*, 15, 1989, 75-89.

[12] Frantz Fanon, *Black Skin, White Masks*, p. 10; E.J. Alagoa, "African Oral Tradition from Within and Without", in E.J. Alagoa (eds.), *Oral Tradition and Oral History in Africa and the Diaspora: Theory and Practice*, 1991, p 2-8.

[13] Jan Vansina, *Paths in the Rainforests: Toward a History of Political Tradition in Equatorial Africa*, 1990, pp. 257-260.

[14] Vansina, *Paths in the Rainforests*, p. 25 1.

[15] Vansina, *Paths in the Rainforests*, p. 260.

[16] Hayden White, *The Content of the Form: Narrative Discourse and Historical Representation.* 1989, Preface, p. xi.

[17] Fernand Braudel, *On History*, 1980, pp. 4-5.

[18] W.G. Clarence-Smith, "For Braudel: a note on the 'Ecole des Annales' and the Historiography of Africa", *History in Africa* 4(1977), pp. 275-281; Jan Vansina, "For oral tradition (But not against Braudel)", *History in Africa*, 5(1978), pp. 351-56.

[19] F.R. Ankersmit, "The Dilemma of Contemporary Anglo-Saxon Philosophy of History", *History & Theory*, Vol. 25, *Beiheft* 25, 1986, 1-27; "Historiography and Postmodernisrn", *History & Theory*, Vol. 28, No. 2, 1989, 137-153.

[20] Hayden White, *The Content of the Form*, p. xi.

[21] Frantz Fanon, *The Wretched of the Earth*, 1978, pp. 315-316.

BIBLIOGRAPHY

Adams, R.F.G. "Oberi Okaime: a new African language and script", *Africa*, 1947.

Aderibigbe, A.B. "Biobaku: the scholar and his works", G.O. Olusanya, (editor), *studies in Yoruba History and Culture*, 1983, 4-25.

Aiello, Leslie C. "The fossil evidence for modern human origins in Africa: a revised view", *American Anthropologist*, Vol. 95, No 1, 1993, 73-96.

Ajayi, J.F. Ade, "Historical education in Nigeria", *Journal of the Historical Society of Nigeria*, Vol. 8, No 1, 1975, 3-8.

Ajayi, J.F. Ade & E.J. Alagoa, "Black Africa: The historian's perspective", *Daedalus*, Vol. 103, No 2, 1974, 125-134.

Ajayi, J. F. Ade & E.J. Alagoa, "Sub-Saharan Africa", *International Handbook of Historical Studies; Contemporary Research and Theory*, edited by G.G. Iggers & H.T. Parker, Westport, 1979, 403-418.

Alagoa, E.J. "Ama-teme-suo Kule", in *Comparative Literature and Foreign languages in Africa today: Collection of essays in honour of Wilfried F. Feuser*, edited by Tunde Okanlawon. Port Harcourt, 1988, 102-104.

Alagoa, E.J. "Delta Masquerades", *Nigeria Magazine*, No 93, 1967, 145-155.

Alagoa, E.J. "Idu: a creator festival at Okpoma (Brass) in the Niger Delta", *Africa*, Vol. 34, No 1, 1964, 1-8.

Alagoa, E.J. "Ijo drumlore", *African Notes* (Ibadan), Vol. 6, No 2, 1971, 61-71.

Alagoa, E.J. "Riddles in Nembe", *Oduma*, (Port Harcourt), Vol. 2, 1975, 17-21.

Alagoa, E.J. "Nembe: the city idea in the Eastern Niger Delta", *Cahiers d'etudes Africaines,* Vol. XI, No 42, 1971, 327-331.

Alagoa, E.J. "The Nigerian community of academic historians", in *African Historiographies,* edited by B. Jewsiewicki & D. Newbury, 1986, 189-196.

Alagoa, E.J. *Noin Nengia, Bere Nengia: Nembe n'akabu / More Days, More Wisdom: Nembe Proverb.* Port Harcourt: Delta Series no 5, University of Port Harcourt Press, 1986.

Alagoa, E.J. Of Days, Bread and Mushrooms: The Historian as Hero. First Dike Memorial Lecture, *in "Dike Remembered, African Reflections on History: Dike Memorial Lectures, 1985-1995".* Port Harcourt: The University of Port Harcourt Press for the Historical Society of Nigeria, 1998.

Alagoa, E.J. *Oral Tradition and Oral History in Africa and the Diaspora: Theory and Practice.* Lagos: Centre for Black and African Arts and Civilization for Nigerian Association for Oral History and Tradition, 1990.

Alagoa, E.J. "Songs as historical data: examples from the Niger Delta", *Research Review* (Legon), Vol. 5, No 1, 1968, 1-16.

Alagoa, E.J. "The encounter between African and western historiography before 1800", *Storia della Storiografia,* 19, 1991, 73-87.

Alagoa, E.J. *The python's eye: The past in the living present.* Port Harcourt: University of Port Harcourt Press, 1981.

Alagoa, E.J. "The use of oral literary data for history: examples from the Niger Delta - proverbs", *Journal of American Folklore,* Vol. 8 1, No 321, 1968, 235-242.

Alagoa, E.J. *Okpu: Ancestral Houses in Nembe and European Antiquities on the Brass and Nun Rivers of the Niger Delta.* Port Harcourt: Onyoma Research Publications, 2001.

Ankersmit, F.R. "Historiography and Postmodernism", *History and Theory,* Vol. 28, No 2,1989,137-153.

Ankersmit, F.R. *Narrative Logic: A semantic analysis of the historian's language.* The Hague: Martinus Nijhoff Publishers, 1983.

Ankersmit, F.R. "The dilemma of contemporary Anglo-Saxon philosophy of history", *History and Theory,* Vol. 25, Beiheft 25, 1986, 1-27.

Appiah, Kwame Anthony, *In my father's house: Africa in the Philosophy of Culture,* Oxford University Press, 1992.

Armah, Ayi Kwei, "Masks and Marx: The Marxist Ethos vis-a-vis African revolutionary theory and Praxis", *Presence Africaine,* No 131, 1984, 35-65.

Barley, Nigel. *Foreheads of the dead: An anthropological view of Kalabari ancestral screens.* London, 1988.

Barros, J. de (1 552-1613). *Da Asia.* Lisbon: Vol. 1 1552.

Barton, I.M. *Africa in the Roman Empire.* Accra: Ghana Universities press, 1972.

Bawele, Mumbaza Mwa & Sabakinu Kivilu. "Historical research in Zaire: Present status and future perspectives", in B. Jewsiewicki & D. Newbury, (eds.), *African Historiographies,* 1986, 224-234.

Bender, Gerald & Allen Isaacman. "The changing historiography of Angola and Mozambique", in Christopher Fyfe (ed.), *African studies since 1945: a tribute to Basil Davidson,* London: Longman, 1976, 220-248.

Bennett, N.R. "The Arab Impact", in B.A.Ogot (ed.), *Zamani: a survey of East African History,* Nairobi, 1968, 210-228.

Bernal, Martin. *Black Athena: The Afroasiatic Roots of Classical Civilization. Vol. 1: The Fabrication of ancient Greece 1785-1985.* Vol. II: The *Archaeological and Documentary Evidence.* New Brunswick, NJ: Rutgers University Press, 1987/1991.

Bernstein, Henry & Jacques Depelchin. "The object of African History- a materialist perspective ", *History in Africa,* Vol. 5, 1978, 1-19, Vol. 6, 1979, 17-43.

Bianquis, T. "Egypt from the Arab conquest until the end of the Fatimid state (1171) " in M. El Fasi & 1. Irbek (eds.), *Unesco General History of Africa, III. Africa from the seventh to the eleventh century.* 1988, 163-193.

Biobaku, S.O. "Myths and Oral History", *Odu: Journal of Yoruba and Related Studies, 1,* January 1955, 12-17.

Biobaku, S.O. *The Origin of the Yoruba.* Lagos: Federal Information Service, 1955.

Biobaku, S.O. "The Yoruba Historical Research Scheme", *Journal of the Historical Society of Nigeria, 1,* December 1956, 59-60.

Biobaku, S.O. "The problem of traditional history with special reference to Yoruba traditions", *Journal of the Historical Society of Nigeria,* I, December 1956,43-47.

Biobaku, S.O. *The Egba and their neighbours 1842-1872.* London, 1957.

Biobaku, S.O. (editor), *Sources of Yoruba history.* Oxford: Clarendon Press, 1973.

Biobaku, S.O. "The wells of West African History", *West African Review,* 24 January 1953, 18-19.

Bloch, Maurice. "Astrology and writing in Madagascar", in Jack Goody (ed.), *Literacy in Traditional Societies.* Cambridge: Cambridge University Press, 1968, 277-297.

Bodurin, P.O. (editor). *Philosophy in Africa.. Trends and Perspectives.* Ile Ife, 1985.

Braudel, Fernand. *The Mediterranean and the Mediterranean world in the Age of Philip II.* (tr. Sian Reynolds), 2 volumes. *[Le Mediterranee et le Monde Mediterraneen a l'Epoque de Philippe II,* 1949] Fontana/Collins: 1972, 1975, 1981.

Braudel, Fernand. *On History.* (tr. Sarah Matthews), [*Ecrits sur l'histoire*]. London: Weidenfeld and Nicolson, 1980.

Breasted, James Henry. *The Dawn of Conscience.* New York: Charles Scribner's sons, 19331968.

Brett, Michael. "The Arab conquest and the rise of Islam in North Africa", in J.D. Fage (ed.), *The Cambridge History of Africa.* Vol. 2, *From c. 500 BC to AD 1050.* Cambridge: Cambridge University Press, 1978, 490-555.

Bull, Ludlow. "Ancient Egypt", in *The Idea of History in the Ancient Near East,* edited by Julian Oberman *et al.* New Haven; Yale University Press, 1955, 3-33.

Butterfield, Herbert. *The Origins of History.* edited with an introduction by Adam Watson. New York: Basic Books, Inc. 1981.

Buttner, Thea. "Aspects and Roots of African historiography: The encounter or dialogue with Western historical writing and thinking", *Storia della Storiografia,* 19, 1991, 111-116.

Cerulli, E. "Ethiopia's relations with the Muslim World", in *General History of Africa III. Africa from the 7th to the 11th century.* ed. M. El Fasi & I. Irbek, 1988, 575-585.

Chanaiwa, David. "Historiographical traditions of Southern Africa", *The Historiography of southern Africa,* Proceedings of the experts meeting held at Gaborone, Botswana from 7-11 March 1977. Unesco 1980, 25-44.

Chittick, Neville. "The coast before the arrival of the Portuguese", in B.A. Ogot (ed.), *Zamani: a survey of East African History.* Nairobi, 1968, 1973, 98-114.

Chittick, Neville. "Kilwa and the Arab settlement of the East African coast", in J.D. Fage & R.A. Oliver (eds.), *Papers in African Prehistory.* London, 1970, 1974, 239-256, from *Journal of African History, IV,* 2,1963, 179-190.

Chittick, Neville. "The 'Shirazi' colonization of East Africa", Fage & Oliver (eds.), *Papers in African Prehistory.* London, 1970, 1974, 257-276, from *Journal of African History, VI, 3, 1965, 263-273.*

Clarke, Peter B. *West Africa and Islam: A study of religious development from the 8th to the 20th century.* London: Edward Arnold, 1982.

Collingwood, R.G. *The Idea of History.* London, 1946.

Curtin, Philip D. (ed.). *Africa Remembered: Narratives by West Africans.* Madison: The University of Wisconsin Press, 1967.

Curtin, Philip D. "Recent trends in African historiography and their contribution to history in general", in *General History of Africa. I. Methodology and African Prehistory.* J. Ki-Zerbo (ed.), Unesco, 1981, 54-71.

Curtin, Philip D. *The Image of Africa: British Ideas and Action, 1780-1850.* Madison: The University of Wisconsin Press, 1964.

Davidson, Basil. *Old Africa Rediscovered.* London: Victor Gollancz Ltd, 1960.

Davies, W.V. *Reading the Past, Egyptian Hieroglyphs.* University of California Press / British Museum, 1987.

Dayrell, E. "Further notes on 'Nsibidi' signs with their meanings from the Ikom District, Southern Nigeria", *Journal of the Royal Anthropological Institute,* Vol. 41, 1911, 521-540 + 3 plates.

Dayrell, E. "Sorne 'Nsibidi' signs", *Man,* Vol. 10, 1910, 113-115.

Dentan, R.C. (ed.). *The Idea of History in the Ancient Near East.* Yale University Press, 1955.

Dike, K. O. "African History and Self-Government", *West Africa,* No 37: Feb. 28, 1953, 177-78; March 14, 1953, 225-26; March 21, 1953, 251.

Dike, K.O. "African history twenty-five years ago and today", *Journal of the Historical Society of Nigeria,* Vol. 10, No 3, 1980, 13-22.

Dike, K.O. "The study of African History", *Proceedings of the First International Congress of Africanists, Accra, 1962.* London: Longman, 1964.

Dike, K.O. *Trade and politics in the Niger Delta 1830-1885: An introduction to the economic and political history of Nigeria.* Oxford, 1956.

Dike, K.O. & J.F. Ade Ajayi. "African historiography", *International Encyclopaedia of the Social Sciences.* Vol. 6, 1968, 399-400.

Dike, K.O. & F. I. Ekejiuba. *The Aro of south-eastern Nigeria 1650-1980: a study of socio-economic formation and transformation in Nigeria.* Ibadan: University Press Ltd., 1990.

Dike, K.O. & F.I. Ekejiuba. "Change and persistence in Aro oral history", *Journal of African Studies,* Vol. 3, No 3, 1976, 277-296.

Diop, Cheikh Anta. *Anteriorite des civilisations negres: Mythe ou verite historique?* Paris: Presence Africaine, 1967.

Diop, Cheikh Anta. *Civilization or Barbarism? An authentic anthropology.* Paris: Presence Africaine, 1981. New York: Lawrence Hill Books, 1991.

El Fasi, M. & I. Hrbeck. "Stages in the development of Islam and its dissemination in Africa", *Unesco General History of Africa, III, Africa from the 7th to the 11th century,* 1988, 56-91.

Ekwulo, S.A. *Elulu Ikwere: Ikwere Proverbs.* Port Harcourt: Rivers State Council for Arts and Culture, 1975.

Erman, Adolf. *The Ancient Egyptians: A sourcebook of their writing.* [tr. Aylward M. Blackman (1927). Introduction William Kelly Simpson (1966)]. Harper Touchbooks, The Academy Library, New York, 1966.

Fage, J.D. "The development of African historiography", *Unesco General History of Africa, 1, Methodology and African Prehistory.* J. Ki-Zerbo (ed.), 1981, 25-42.

Fahnbulleh, Fatima M. "The seminar on standardization of the Vai script", *University of Liberia Journal,* January 1963, 15-37.

Falola, Toyin (ed.). *African Historiography: Essays In honour of Jacob Ade Ajayi.* Ikeja: Longman, 1993.

Finnegan, Ruth. *Oral Literature in Africa.* Nairobi, Oxford University Press, 1970, 1976, 1977.

Freeman-Grenville, G.S.P. *The East African Coast: Select documents from the first to the earlier nineteenth century.* Oxford: Clarendon Press, 1962.

Frend, W.H.C. "The Christian period in Mediterranean Africa, c. AD 200 to 700", J.D. Fage (ed.), *The Cambridge History of Africa, Vol. 2: From c. 500 BC to AD 1050.* Cambridge: Cambridge University Press, 1978. 410-489.

Gardiner, Sir Alan. *Egypt of the Pharaohs: An Introduction.* London: Oxford University Press, 1961.

Gardiner, P. (ed.). *The Philosophy of History.* Oxford, 1974.

Gaur, Albertine. A *History of writing.* London: The British Library, 1984, 1987.

Gelb, I.J. A *study of writing: The foundations of grammatology.* Chicago: The University of Chicago press, 1963.

Goodman, Lenn Evan. "Ibn Khaldun and Thucydides", *Journal of the American Oriental Society.* Vol. 92, No 2, 1972, 250-270.

Goody, Jack (ed.). *Literacy in Traditional Societies.* Cambridge, 1968.

Goody, Jack. "Restricted literacy in northern Ghana", in *Literacy in Traditional Societies,* edited by Jack Goody. Cambridge, 1968, 198-264.

Greenberg, Joseph H. *The Languages of Africa.* Bloornington: Indiana University, 1963.

Greenberg, Joseph H. "Linguistic evidence for the influence of the Kanuri on the Hausa", *Journal of African History, 1,* 2, 1960, 205-212.

Griaule, M. *Conversations with Ogotemmeli.* Oxford, 1948\1965.

Haley, Alex. *Roots.* New York: Doubleday, 1976.

Hall, H.R. "The eclipse of Egypt", *The Cambridge Ancient History.* Cambridge 1970, Vol. HI, editors: J.B. Bury, S.A. Cook, F.E. Adcock, 251-269.

Harden, Donald. *The Phoenicians.* Penguin Books, 1980.

Harris, Joseph E. *Africans and their history.* New York: Mentor Books, 1972.

Hasan, Yusuf Fadl. "The penetration of Islam in the Eastern Sudan", in I.M. Lewis (ed.), *Islam in Tropical Africa.* London: Oxford University Press, 1966, 144-159.

Hasan, Y.F. & B.A. Ogot. "The Sudan, 1500-1800". in B.A. Ogot (ed.), *Unesco General History of Africa, V. Africa from the 16th to the 18th century.* 1992, 170-199.

Hau, Kathleen. "A royal title on a Palace Tusk from Benin (Southern Nigeria)", *Bulletin de l'IFAN*. Vol. XXVI. ser B, Nos. 1-2, 1964, 21-39.

Hau, Kathleen. "Evidence of the use of pre-Portuguese written characters by the Bini", *Bulletin de l'IFAN*, Vol. XXI, ser. B, Nos. 1-2, 1959, 109-154.

Hau, Kathleen. "Oberi Okaime script, texts and counting system", *Bulletin de l'Institut Fondamental d'Afrique Noire*, Vol. XXVI ser B, Nos. 1-2, 1961, 291-308.

Hau, Kathleen. "Pre-Islamic writing in West Africa", *Bulletin de l'IFAN*, Vol. XXXV, ser B, No 1, 1973, 1-45.

Hau, Kathleen. "The ancient writing of southern Nigeria", *Bulletin de l'IFAN*, Vol. XXIX, ser B, Nos. 1-2, 1967, 150-189.

Heintze, Beatrix & Adam Jones (eds.). *European sources for sub-Saharan Africa before 1900: Use and Abuse.* Paideuma, No. 33, 1987. Stuttgart: Franz Steiner Verlag Wiesbaden for Frobenius Institut, Frankfurt.

Herodotus. *The Histories.* (tr. Aubrey de Selincourt, revised by A.R. Burn). Penguin Books, 1954, 1972.

Hiskett, M. "The 'Song of Bagauda': A Hausa King List and Homily in verse", *Bulletin of the School of Oriental and African Studies* , XXVII, 1964, 540-567; XXVIII 1965, 112- 135,363-385.

Hodgkin, Thomas. "The Islamic literary tradition in Ghana", in I.M. Lewis (ed.), *Islam in Tropical Africa.* London, 1966, 42-462.

Hodgkin, Thomas. (ed.). *Nigerian Perspectives: An historical anthology.* London: 1960.

Holt, P.M. "Egypt, the Funj and Darfur", in Richard Gray (ed.), *The Cambridge History of Africa Vol. 4: From c. 1600 to c. 1740.* Cambridge, 1975, 14-57.

Horton, Robin. *The Gods as Guests: An Aspect of Kalabari Religious Life.* Lagos, 1960.

Horton, Robin. "The Kalabari Ekine society: a borderland of religion and art", *Africa,* Vol. 33, No 2, 1963, 44- 114.

Idris, R. "Society in the Maghrib after the disappearance of the Almohads", *Unesco General History of Africa, IV,* 1984, 102-116.

Ifemesia, Chika (ed.). *Issues in African Studies and National Education: Selected Works of Kenneth Onwuka Dike.* Awka: Kenneth Onwuka Dike Centre, 1988.

Iggers, Georg & Harold T. Parker (eds.). *International Handbook of Historical Studies; Contemporary Research and Theory.* Westport: Greenwood Press, 1979.

Ikime, Obaro (ed.). *Groundwork of Nigerian History.* Ibadan: Heinemann Educational Books Ltd. for the Historical Society of Nigeria, 1980.

Ilevbare, J.A. *Carthage, Rome, and the Berbers.* Ibadan: University of Ibadan Press, 1980.

Isma'il, O.S.A. "Some reflections on the literature of the Jihad and the Caliphate", Y.B. Usman (ed.), *Studies in the History of the Sokoto Caliphate.* Zaria: 1979, 165-180.

Jay, Martin & Jane Flax. "Forum", review of *Postmodernism, or, the Cultural Logic of Late capitalism* by Frederic Jameson. Durham: Duke University Press, 1991, in *History & Theory,* 32, 3, 1993, 296-310.

Jewsiewicki, Bogumil & David Newbury (eds.). *African Historiographies: What History for Which Africa?* Beverly Hills: Sage Publications, 1986.

Jones, Adam. *Raw, Medium, Well Done: A critical review of editorial and quasi-editorial work on pre-1885 European sources for sub-Saharan Africa, 1960- 1986.* Madison: African Studies Program, University of Wisconsin, 1987.

Kagame, A. *La philosophie Bantu-Rwandaise de l'etre.* Brussels, 1956.

Kani, Ahmed M. "Aspects of historiographical development in the Sokoto Caliphate up to 1860", Congress of the Historical Society of Nigeria, Sokoto, May 1991, 10 pages.

Kani, Ahmed M. "The rise and influence of scholars in Hausaland before 1804", *Kano Studies*, NS 1981, 47- 69.

Kiebel, C.B. "Memory sticks and other mnemonic devices", *The Nigerian Field*, Vol. 55, Parts 3- 4, October, 1990, 91- 98.

Kimambo, I.N. & A.J. Temu (eds.). A *History of Tanzania.* Nairobi: East African Publishing House, 1969.

Kimambo, I.N. *A political history of the Pare of Tanzania, c. 1500-1900.* Nairobi: East African Publishing House, 1969.

Klein, Martin. "The development of Senegalese historiography", in B. Jewsiewicki & D. Newbury (eds.), *African Historiographies*, 1986, 215- 223.

Ladurie, E. Le Roy. *Montaillou: Cathars and Catholics in a French village 1294- 1324.* (tr. Barbarce Bray), Penguin Books, 1980, 1981.

Ladurie, E. Le Roy. *The Territory of the Historian. [Le territoire de l'historien* 1973, tr. Ben & Sian Reynolds]. The Harvester Press / University of Chicago, 1979.

Law, Robin. "For Marx But with reservations about Althusser: a comment on Bernstein and Depelchin ", *History in Africa, Vol.* 8, 1981, 247- 25 1.

Leclant, Jean. "The present position in the deciphering of Meroitic script", *The peopling of ancient Egypt and the deciphering of Meroitic script.* Paris: Unesco, 1974, 107- 119.

Levtzion, Nehemia. *Ancient Ghana and Mali.* London: Methuen & Co. Ltd., 1973.

Levtzion, N. & J.F.P. Hopkins (eds.). *Corpus of early Arabic sources for West African history.* London: Cambridge University Press, 1981.

Lewicki, T. *Arabic external sources for the history of Africa to the south of Sahara.* London: Curzon Press Ltd., 1969 / Lagos: African Universities Press/Pilgrim Books Ltd., 1974.

Lewicki, T. "The role of the Sahara and Saharians in relations between north and south", *Unesco General History of Africa. III: Africa from the 7th to the IIth century,* 1988, 276- 313.

Lewis, Herbert S. "The origins of the Galla and Somali", *Journal of African History,* 7, 1, 1966, 27- 46.

Lewis, I.M. (ed.). *Islam in Tropical Africa: studies presented and discussed at the 5th International African Seminar, Ahmadu Bello University, Zaria, January 1964.* London: Oxford University Press for the International African Institute, 1966.

Lewis, I.M. "Literacy in a nomadic society: the Somali case", Jack Goody (ed.), *Literacy in traditional societies,* 1968, 265- 276.

Lewis, I.M. "The Somali conquest of the Horn of Africa", *Journal of African History,* 1, 2, 1960,213-229.

Lovejoy, Paul E. "Nigeria: the Ibadan school and its critics", B Jewsiewicki & D. Newbury (eds.), *African Historiographies,* 1986, 197- 205.

Macgregor, J.K. "Some notes on Nsibidi", *Journal of the Royal Anthropological Institute,* vol. 39, 1909, 209- 219.

Mahdi, Muhsin. *Ibn Khaldun's Philosophy of History: a study in the philosophic foundations of the Science of Culture.* Chicago: The University of Chicago Press, 1964, 1971.

Makdisi, George. "The diary in Islamic historiography: some notes", *History and Theory,* vol. 25, no 2, 1986, 173- 185.

Marks, Shula. "The historiography of South Africa: recent developments", B, Jewsiewicki & D. Newbury (eds.), *African Historiographies,* 165- 176.

Mauny, Raymond. "Trans-Saharan contacts and the Iron age in West Africa", *The Cambridge History of Africa, Vol. 2, From c. 500 BC to AD 1050* edited by J.D. Fage, 1978, 272-341.

Mbodj, Mohamed & Mamadou Diouf. "Senegalese historiography: present practice and future perspectives", B. Jewsiewicki & D. Newbury (eds.), 1986, 207- 214.

Mekouria, T.T. "The Horn of Africa", *Unesco General History of Africa, III, Africa from the 7th to the 11th century,* ed. M. El Fasi & I. Urbek, 1988, 558- 574.

Miller, J.C. (ed.). *The African Past Speaks: Essays in Oral Tradition and History.* Wm. Dawson / Archon Books, 1980.

Momigliano, A. "The place of Herodotus in the history of historiography", *History,* XLIII, 1958, I-3.

Mudimbe, V.Y. *The invention of Africa: Gnosis, philosophy and the order of knowledge.* Bloomington, Indianapolis, London, 1988.

Musa, I.U.A. "The rise of Muslim Sudanic historiography in Bilad as-Sudan: a tentative analysis", 23rd Congress of the Historical Society of Nigeria, Zaria, April, 1978.

Oberman, Julian. "Early Islam", *The Idea of history in the ancient Near East,* R.C. Dentan (ed.). New Haven, 1955. 238- 376.

O'Fahey, R.S. & J.L. Spaulding. *Kingdoms of the Sudan.* London: Methuen & Co. Ltd., 1974.

Ogot, Bethwell A. A *History of the southern Luo.* Nairobi: East African Publishing House, 1967.

Ogot, Bethwell A. "Some approaches to African History: Presidential Address to the annual conference of the Historical Association of Kenya", *Hadith 1,* 1968, I- 9.

Ojoade, J.O. "God in Nigerian proverbs", *The Nigerian Field,* vol. 43, 1978, 171- 177.

Ojoade, J.O. "Some Itsekiri proverbs", *The Nigerian Field*, vol. 45, no 213, 1980, 91- 96.

Ojoade, J.O. "Proverbs as a mirror of Birom life and thought". *The History of Plateau State of Nigeria*. E. Isichei (ed.), London, 1982, 85- 89.

Ojoade J.O. "Proverbial evidence of African legal customs". *International Folklore Review*, vol. 6, 1988, 26- 38.

Ojoade, J.O. "Some Kuteb aphorisms", *The Nigerian Field*. vol. 42,1982,52- 61.

Okpewho, Isidore. *The Epic in Africa*. New York, Columbia University Press, 1979.

Okpewho, Isidore (ed.). *The Oral Performance in Africa*. Ibadan, Spectrum Books, 1990.

Olusanya, G.O. (ed.). *Studies in Yoruba history and culture. Essays in honour of Professor S. O. Biobaku*. Ibadan: University Press Ltd., 1983.

O'Neil, W.M. *Time and Calendars*. Manchester: Manchester University Press, 1975.

Opuogulaya, E.D.W. *The culture of the Wakirike (The Okrika People)*. Port Harcourt: Rivers State Council for Arts and Culture, 1975.

Palmer, H.R. (ed. & tr). *The history of the first twelve years of the reign of Mai Idris Alooma of Borno, 1571-1583, by his Imam, Ahmad Ibn Fartua. Together with the 'Diwan of the Sultans of Borno and 'Girgam' of the Maigumi*. Lagos: Government Printer, 1926; London: Frank Cass & Co. Ltd. 1970.

Palmer, H.R. *Sudanese Memoirs: Being mainly translations of a number of Arabic manuscripts relating to the Central and Western Sudan*. London: Frank Cass & Co. Ltd., 1967, 3 volumes.

Parker, Richard A. *The Calendars of Ancient Egypt.* The Oriental Institute of the University of Chicago. Studies in Ancient Oriental Civilization No 26. Chicago: The University of Chicago Press, 1950.

Parry, J.H. *The establishment of the European hegemony: 1415-1715.* New York: Harper & Row, Publishers, 1961, 1966.

Popper, Karl R. *The poverty of Historicism.* New York: Harper & Row, Publishers, 1964.

Preiswerk, Roy, & Dominique Perrot. *Ethnocentrism and History: Africa, Asia and Indian America in Western Textbooks.* New York, London, Lagos: Nok Publishers, 1978.

Quirke, Stephen. *Who were the Pharaohs? A history of their names with a list of cartouches.* British Museum / Dover Books, Inc., New York, 1990.

Rabb, Theodore K & Robert I. Rotberg (eds.). *The New History: The 1980s and Beyond: Studies in Inter-Disciplinary History.* Princeton:Princeton University Press, 1982.

Rader, Melvin. *Marx's Interpretation of History.* New York: Oxford University Press, 1979.

Ranger, T.O. (ed.). *Emerging themes of African History: Proceedings of the International Congress of African historians held at University College, Dar es Salaam, October 1965.* London: Heinemann Educational books Ltd., 1968.

Redford, Donald B. *Pharaonic king-lists, Annals and Day-books: a contribution to the study of the Egyptian sense of history.* SSEA Publication IV, Benhen Publications, Mississauga, 1986.

Ricoeur, Paul. *Time and Narrative.* 3 volumes. *[Temps et Recit,* 1983, tr. Kathleen McLaughlin and David Pellauerl.] London: University of Chicago Press, 1985, 1988, 1990.

Rodney, Walter. *How Europe Underdeveloped Africa.* London: Bogle-l'Ouverture Publications, 1972, 1976, 1978.

Rosenthal, Franz. *A History of Muslim Historiography.* 2nd Edition, Leiden: E.J. Brill, 1968.

Rosenthal, Franz (tr.). *Ibn Khaldun. The Muqaddimah: An Introduction to History.* 3 volumes. Princeton: Princeton University Press, 1958, 1967.

Saad, Elias N. *Social history of Timbuktu: The role of Muslim scholars and notables 1400- 1900.* Cambridge; Cambridge University Press, 1983.

Salama, P. "The Sahara in classical antiquity", *Unesco General History of Africa. II. Ancient Civilizations of Africa,* G. Mokhtar (ed), 1981, 513- 532.

Sanders, Edith R. "Hamitic hypothesis, its origin and functions in time perspective", *Journal of African History, 10,* 4, 1969, 521- 532.

Sarder, Ziauddin. *The future of Muslim Civilisation.* London: Croom Helm, 1979.

Saunders, J.J. "Rashid al-Din, the First Universal Historian", *History Today,* Vol. XXI, no 7, July 1971, 465- 472.

Seligman, C.G. *Races of Africa.* New York: Oxford University Press, 1966 (1930, 1939, 1957).

Simpson, William Kelly (ed.). [trs. R.O. Faulkner, Edward F. Wente Jr, and W.K. Simpson]. *The Literature of Ancient Egypt: An Anthology of Stories, Instructions, and Poetry.* New Edition. New Haven & London: Yale University Press, 1973.

Slater, Henry. "Dar Es Salaam and post-nationalist historiography of Africa", B. Jewsiewicki & D. Newbury (eds.), *African Historiographies,* 1986, 249- 260.

Smith, Abdullahi. "The early states of the Central Sudan", in J.F. Ade Ajayi & Michael Crowder (eds.), *History of West Africa,* 2nd Edition, London: Longman Group Ltd., 197 1, 1976,152-195.

Stoianivich, Traian. *French Historical Method: The 'Annales' Paradigm.* Ithaca, 1976.

Sumner, Claude. "Ethiopia: Land of diverse expressions of philosophy, birthplace of modern thought", *African Philosophy,* Claude Sumner (ed.). Addis Ababa, 1980, 393- 400.

Talbi, M. "The independence of the Maghrib", *Unesco General History of Africa II, Africa from the 7th to the 11th century,* 1988, 246- 275.

Tamrat, Taddesse. "Ethiopia, the Red Sea and the Horn", *The Cambridge History of Africa, Volume 3, from c. 1050 to c. 1600,* Roland Oliver (ed.), 1977, 99- 182.

Tamrat, T. "The horn of Africa: the Solomonids in Ethiopia and the states of the Horn of Africa", *Unesco General History of Africa. IV, Africa from the 12th to the 16th century.* D.T. Niane (ed.). 1984, 423- 454.

Taylor, John H. *Egypt and Nubia.* Harvard University Press for British Museum, 1991.

Tempels, P. *Bantu Philosophy.* Paris: Presence Africaine, 1945/1959.

Temu, Arnold & Bonaventure Swai. *Historians and Africanist History: a critique. Post- colonial historiography examined.* London: Zed Press, 1981.

Thompson, L.M. "Afrikaner nationalist historiography and the policy of apartheid", *Historians in Tropical Africa.* Salisbury: University College of Rhodesia and Nyasaland, 1962, 371-386.

Trimingham, J. Spencer. A *History of Islam in West Africa.* London: Oxford University Press, 1962.

Unesco. *The Historiography of Southern Africa: Proceedings of the Expert Meeting held at Gaborone, Botswana, from 7 to 11 March 1977.* Paris: Unesco, 1980.

Usman, Yusufu Bala. "History and the basis for Nigerian unity", *For the liberation of Nigeria.* London: Beacon, 1979, 32- 39.

Usman, Yusufu Bala. *The Transformation of Katsina, 1400-1883.* Zaria: Ahmadu Bello University Press Ltd., 1981.

Vansina, Jan. *Living with Africa.* Madison: The University of Wisconsin Press, 1994.

Vansina, Jan. *Oral Tradition: A Study in Historical Methodology.* Chicago, 1961/1965.

Vansina, Jan. *Oral Tradition as History.* Madison & London: 1985.

Vansina, Jan. *Paths in the Rainforests: Towards a history of political tradition in Equatorial Africa.* Madison: The University of Wisconsin Press, 1990.

Verhaegen, Benoit. "The method of 'Histoire Immediate': its application to Africa", B. Jewsiewicki & D Newbury (eds.), *African Historiographies,* 1986, 236- 248.

Waddell (tr.). *The Aegyptiaca of Manetho: Manetho's history of Egypt.* Harvard & London, 1971.

Walsh, W.H. *An Introduction to Philosophy of History.* London, 1951.

Ward, William A. "The present status of Egyptian chronology", *Bulletin of the American Schools of Oriental Research,* no 288, November 1992, 53- 66.

Whiteley, Wilfred. *Swahili: The rise of a national language.* London: Methuen & Co. Ltd., 1969,1973,1974,1975.

Wilks, Ivor. "The transmission of Islamic learning in the Western Sudan", *Literacy in Traditional Societies,* edited by Jack Goody. Cambridge, 1968, 162- 197.

Wilson, John A. "Egypt", *The intellectual adventure of ancient man: An essay on speculative thought in the Ancient Near East.* H. & H.A. Frankfort (eds.). Chicago: University of Chicago Press, 1946.

Wiredu, Kwesi. "The concept of Truth in the Akan language", in P.O. Bodurin (ed.), *Philosophy in Africa.* Ile-Ife, 1985, 43- 54.

Wolf, Erie R. *Europe and the People Without History.* Berkeley: University of California Press, 1982.

Wrigley, C.C. "Historicism in Africa: Slavery and State Formation", *African Affairs,* Vol. 70, no 279, 1971, 113- 124.

INDEX

A

Abbasid caliphate 95
'Abdallabi (Arab sultanate) 134, 136
'Abd al-Mu'rnin 109
'Abd al-Rahman al-Sa'di 122
'Abd al-Wahid al-Marakushi 109
'Abd al-Qadir b. al-Mustafa 104, 132
Abdullahi b. Fudi 131
Abhbar Hadhihi al-Bilad al-Hausiyya wa al-Sudaniyya 132
Abraham 96
Abu'l-Fida 105
Abu Muhammad 'Abd Allah al-Jijani 110
Abu Salih 111
Abu Shama of Damascus 104
Abydos 49
An Account of N'gazargamu 127
Adam 96, 152
Aegyptiaca 17, 18, 169
Aelian 75

Africa 2
ancient civilization of 207
Africa from the Seventh to the Eleventh Century 207
Africa from the Sixteenth to the Eighteenth Century 208
Africa from the Twelfth to the Sixteenth Century 208
Africa in the Nineteenth Century Until 1880 208
Africa: Islamic tradition 99, 100
Africa since 1935 208
Africa South of the Sahara 19
Africa Under Colonial Domination 1880-1935 208
African ethno-philosophy 21
African historiography 1, 2
African Historiographies: What History for Which Africa? 209
African philosophy of history 19
Africa tradition 157, 211
Africanist 205

Africanus, Julius 75
African written tradition 8
Afrikaner nationalist 199
Afrika Zamani 194, 207
Afroasia 4, 5, 106
Afroasiatic family 5
Afroasiatic language 111
Agricultural calendar 66
Ajayi, J.F.A. 193, 208
Akhbar 97
Akhenaten 71
Ala (earth spirit) 22
al-'Araki, Mahmud 135
al-Ahzar 105
al-Bakri 109, 116, 119, 120
al-Barnawi, Muhammad b. 'Abd al-Rahman 131
al-Bayan al-Mughrib 110
al-Bukhari 153
al-Durar al-Hisan fi Akhbar Muluk al-Sudan 123
al-Hakam, Ibn 'Abd 103
Alexander the Great 17, 49, 169
Alexandria 17
Alexandria Library 74
al-Farabi 154
al-Hassan (Mallam) 125
Ali 95
'Ali al-Qifti 104

al-Idrisi 116, 139
al Juz'al-talit-min Kitab al-Bayan al-Maghrib 110
al-Kahina 108
al-Katsinawa, Muhammad 131
al-Mghili, Muhammad b. 'Abd al-Karim 130
a--Maghrib al-Adna 107
al-Magrhib al-Aqsa 107
al-Makin 104
al-Mann bi'l-Imama 109
al-Maqrizi 105
al-Mas'udi 139
Almohad 109
Alooma, Mai Idris 127
Almoravid Movement 116, 117
Almoravids 109, 120
al-Mujib 109
al-Muquadimmah 105, 110
al-Musabbihi 104
al-Qadi Iyad 109
al-Qalqashandi 126
al-Sabbagh (Dan Marina) 131
al-Sultana al-Zarka 134
al-Tahirb b. Ibrahim al-Fallah 131
Althusser 205

al-Umari 121
Alwa (Christian Kingdom) 134
al-Zuhri 109, 120
Ama Oba-ama 27
Ama lugu-ama 27
Ama-nama-ama 27
Ama-nyana-oru 22, 23, 24
Ama-owu-ama 27
Ama-teme-suo 22, 23
Ama-Xosa: Life and Customs 201
Amenemhet (King) 77
Amenemope 77
Amennakhte 77
Amenophus (King) 82
America 5
Amin, Samir 208
Amun (hidden god) 61, 71
Ancient Near East 5
Angola 7, 19, 197, 199
Anii 77
Ankersmit, F.R. 158, 166
Annals 71
Annales d'Histoire Economique et Sociale 165
Annales, Economies, Societies, Civilization 165
(Anonymous): *A History of Mombassa* 142
Antony (monk) 102
Apostle Mark 104
Apuleius 107
Arab Banu Hilal 110
Arabic script 84
Arabs 4, 5, 18
Aristotle 153
Arusha Declaration 204
Asabiyah (group feeling) 150, 151
Asabiyya (group consciousness) 110
Ashanti 31
Ashar al-Ruba fi Akhbar Yoruba 133
Asia 4
Association des Historiens Africains 194
Association des Historiens du Senegal 194
Athanasius 102
Atum (sun-god) 60, 61, 64, 71
Avienus 106
Averroes 154
Avicenna 154
Axum (kingdom) 111
Azania 138

B

Baba, Ahmad 123
Babylonia 47
Baghdad 96, 153
Baghayughu, Muhammad 123
Baisani 97
Bakr, Abu 95
Bala, Kahnie 89
Bamum script 89, 91
Bana 97
Banadir coast 140
Banbi 118
Bangladesh 99
Bantu 6
Bantu language 137
Bantu movement 197
Barbary of Morocco 107
Barghawata 108
Barmandana (King) 121
Barth, Heinrich 127, 183
Basra 153
Bedouin civilization 149, 150
Beja 134
Belekole, J. 89
Bello, Muhammad (Sultan) 131, 133
Bello, Mahmud ibn Muhammad 133
Benin Empire 186
Berber script 86
Berbers 5, 51, 106, 107, 116, 150
Berkeley, George 162
Berlin Conference 174
Bernstein, Henry 205
Beti, Mongo 188
Bible 17
Biobaku, S.O. 191, 193
Birom 30
Bishop Frumentius 111
Black Africa Rediscovered 184
Black Problems (The) 201
Blemmyes 51
Bloch, Marc 165
Boahen, A.A. 191, 195, 208
Boer 199
Book of Consolation of the History of Kilwa (The) 141
Borno 131, 132, 135
Botswana 197, 198
Bowdich 183
Braudel, Fernand 165, 218
British Empire 200
Brown University iv

Butrus b. al-Rahib 104
Bruce, James 183
Buganda 186
Bukeke, Dualo 88
Bull, Ludlow 83
Bulletin de l'Institut Fondamental d'Afrique Noire 90, 194
Bunyoro-Kitara 186
Burkhardt 167
Burundi 137
Bushmen 7, 180
Butterfield 82
Bwana Kitini 143
Bwana Simbi *see* Mkuu, Muhammad bin Bawana
Byzantine (period) 18, 106

C

Cairo 135, 153
Caliph 'Umar 99
Cambridge History of Africa 184, 208
Camel nomads 134
Canadian Journal of African Studies 209
Canon, Turin 70
Cape Coast 187
Carthage 5, 18, 106
Carthaginian script *see* Punic script
Casely-Hayford, J.C. 187
Catalogo dos governadores de Angola 173
Cattle nomads 134
Central Africa 6
Central Sudan 19, 125
Centre d'Etudes et de Reserches Documentaires sur l'Afrique Centrale (CERDAC) 196
Cesaire, Aime 188
Ceuta 172
Chad 5
Chaka 201
Chanaiwa 199, 200, 201
Chancellor College (Zomba) 198
Chinaware 140
Chinese 140
Christian Byzantine 102
Christianity 96
Chittick 140
Chronological Repertory 113
Cicero 169
Cissoko, S.M. 194
Civil calendar 67
Clarence-Smith, W.G. 218, 219

Claudius Ptolemy 67
Clement 102
Collingwood, R.G. 20, 158, 163, 165
Colonial rule 7
Comoros 137
Condorcet 162
Confessions 170
Congo 7
Congo Basin 137
Congo River 6
Congress of British West Africa 187
Copernicus 67
Coptic church 87
Coptic language 50
Coptic Monophysite Christian tradition 102
Coptic religion 18
Coptic script 84, 87
Cordoba 153
Cosmas Indicopleustes 138
Cretan 53
Criticism of the Native Bills 201
Croce 167
Crowther, Samuel Ajayi 187
Cuneiform 52
Curse of Ham 199
Curtin, Philip 179, 187, 189

Cush *see* Kush
Cushitic 5
Cyprian 107

D

Damas, Leon 187
Damascus 96
dar al-Harb 134
dar al-Islam 134
dar al-Mu'ahadal Aman 134
Dar es Salaam School of Tanzania 189, 204, 205
Dar Fur 134, 135, 136
Darwin 164, 179
Dashre (The Red Land) 47
Davidson, Basil 184
Day-book 73
de Barros 141
De Civitate Dei 160, 170
Delafosse, Maurice 184
Demotic script 85
Depelchin, J. 205
Derrida 213
Descartes, Rene 113, 161
Deutscher Akademischer Austauucherdienst iv
Dibalami, Mai Dunarna 127
Dike, K.O. 191, 192, 193
Diogenes Laertius 75

Diop, Alioune 187
Diop, Cheikh Anta 188, 195
Diwan 128
Dongola (Dunkala) 134
Dubois, W.E.B. 187
Duein fubara 23, 24
Dunqas, Umara (King) 134
Dupuis 183
Dyula 124, 125

E

East Africa Coast 137, 202
   select documents on 142
Eastern Sudan 19, 133, 135, 136
Edo 90
Efik 90
Egba 187
Egba and Their Neighbours 191
Egberi (story, fable) 27
Egharevba, Jacob U. 186
Egypt 4, 15, 46, 153, 157
Egyptian hieroglyph 85
Egyptian scripts
   Coptic 53, 55
   Demotic 53, 54
   Hieratic 53, 54
   hieroglyphics 53
Ekine (Sekiapu Society) 25
Ekoi 90
Ekpo (secret society) 90
el-Fasi, M. 207
el-Kenisa 51
Elemu kura egberi 27
Elephantine 47
Enlightenment (The) 161, 162
Ethiopia 4, 7, 18, 111, 174
Ethiopian dynasty 46
Ethiopic writing 84, 86, 91
Ethnology 25
Etymologicum Magnum 76
Euphrates 5
European colonial rule 140
Eusebius 75
Eutychius 103

F

Fadl-Allah, Rashid al-Din 143
Fage, John 184
Falasha Jews 111
Fanon, Frantz 204, 213, 220
Fari, Sidi 130
Fars 140
Fatmid period 104

Fatwa (legal opinion) 98
Febvre, Lucien 165
Fez 109
First cataract 50, 51
Foucault 219
Freeman-Grenville, G.S.P. 142, 143
Frobenius, Leo 183
Frobenius Institute iv
Frumentius (Bishop of the Ethiopian Church) 102
Funj (Fundj) 133
Funj Chronicle 135, 136
Funj Sultanate 134, 135
Futa Toro 135

G

Gaborene 198
Gadabuursi script 88
Gao 121
Garamantes 115
Garazawa (Sarki) 129
Garvey, Marcus 187
Gawalu 89
Geb (earth-god) 60, 63, 64
Gebre-Masqual (Lalibela) 112
Ge'ez/Ethiopic script 111

General History of Africa 184, 198, 202, 207, 208
Germaus 140
Gerze 89
Ghana 119, 120, 124, 186, 188
Gibbon 162
Girgam 133
Gold Coast 187
Goody, Jack 94
Great Ennead 60, 61, 64
Great Pyramid of Giza 49
Greeks 4
Greek tradition 18, 159
Griaule 19
Griffith, Francis L. 86
Griots 118
Groundwork of Nigerian History 191
Guinea 124
Guinea Coast 7
Guyana 187

H

Habar (Khabar) 98
Hadith 12, 14, 153, 202
Hadithi I 202
Halfaya 136
Halicarnassus 159

Ham 149
Hamburg University 89
Hamites 180
Hanno 106
Hanzuan 141
Haratin 116
Hardedef 77, 78
Harkhuf 114
Hat-Hor (goddess) 62
Harweris 71
Hau, Kathleen 90
Hausa 5, 124, 125
Hausaland 132
Haywat, Waida 113
Hecataeus 65, 74, 159, 168
Hegel, Georg Wilhem Friedrich 162, 163, 167, 181
Heliopolis 16, 65
Heliopolitan theology 60, 61, 64
Hempel 165
Herder 163
Hermes see Thoth
Hermopolis see Khmum
Herodotus 15, 16, 47, 64, 65, 106, 115, 116, 157, 159, 168, 178, 195
Hierapolis 58
Hieroglyphics 53
Himilco 106
Histoire immediate 197
Historia 159
Historians and Africanist History 204
Historical Association of Kenya 202
Historiography 1
Historiography of Southern Africa 198
History, Philosophy of 20, 76
History of Ilorin 133
History of Kua, Juani Island, Mafia 143
History of Pate 142
History of Swaziland 298
History of the First Twelve Years of the Reign of Mai Idris Alooma of Bornu 128
History of the Maghrib 144
History of Walasma 114
Hittite 53
Hnum (patron god of potters) 61
Hodgkin, Thomas 184
Homer 159
Homeric epics 14
Hopkins, A.G. 208

Horn of Africa 18
Horus 61, 71
Hory 77
Hottentotts 7, 180
How Europe Underdeveloped Africa 204
Hud 96
Hume, David 162
Hykssos 49, 82

I

Ibibio 90
Ibn 'Abd-al-Hakam 104
Ibn Abi Zur'al-Fasi 110
Ibn al-Athir 109, 110
Ibn al-Qattan 109, 110
Ibn al-Shabushti 104
Ibn Banna 97
Ibn Battuta 118, 139
Ibn Fartuwa 127, 128
Ibn Idhari al-Karrakushi 109, 110
Ibn Isharku 128
Ibn Iyas 105
Ibn Khaldun, al-Rahmah 105, 109, 110, 117, 120, 143, 144, 145, 146, 148, 150, 153, 154, 160, 171, 178

Ibn Rushdi 109
Ibn Shaddad Batal al-Din 104
Ibn Sahib al-Salak 109
Ibn Taghribirdi 105
Ibn Tumart 109
Ibn Zulak 104

Ida al-Nasakh man Akhadhtu min al-Shuyukh 131
Idea of History 83
Idu (festival) 24
Ifrikiya 107, 108
Igbo 22, 90
Iginiga (*Newbouldia laevis*) 22
Ikwerre (of the Niger Delta) 31
Ilm 'al-Akhnar 97
'Illm al-Tarikh 97
'Imad al-Din al-Isfahani 104
Imhotep 77, 78
India 99
Indonesia 99
Infaq al-Maysur fi Tarikh Bilad al-Tahur 131
Institute of African Studies 193

International Congress of the
    Historical Sciences 165
Instruction of Amenemope
    80
Ipuwer 77, 81
Irjets 51
Isesi (King) 79
Ishmael 96
Ishmaniya script 88
Islamic Maghrib 107
Islamic tradition 8, 12, 42,
    93
Isnad al-Shuyush
    wa'l-'Ulama 125
Isong (secret society) 90
Isthmus of Sinai 50
Itsekiri 29
Ivory Coast 124

Jenne-Timbuktu 124
Jesus 96
Jewsiewicki, Bogumil 197,
    209
John, Bishop of Nikiou 104
Johann Wolfgang Goethe
    University iv
Johnson, Samuel 186
Johnston, Harry 184
Josephus 75
Journal of African History
    183
*Journal of the Historical
    Society of Nigeria* 191
Judaism 96
Julian calendar 68
Juz'min Kitab Nazm
    al-Juman 110

J

J. William Fulbright Foreign
    Scholarship Board iv
Jabavu, Davidson Don
    Tengo 201
Jabavu, Tengo 200
Jacobite Church 104
Jamala (camel nomads)
    134
Jami'-al-Tuwurkh 143

K

Kabila 110
Kagame 19
Kagwa, Apolo 186
Kaires 77, 78
Kalabari 23
Kamil fi'l-tarikh 110
Kanbalu (Qanbalu) 139
Kanem-Borno 126, 123, 128,
    134
Kano 123, 128, 129

Kano Chronicle 136
Kant 163
Kanuri 132
Kapelle/Kpelle script 89
Karamoko 124
Karimi, Abdu 130
Karnala, Kisimi 88
Kashta 52
Ka'ti, al-Hajj al-Mutawakkil 122
Ka'ti, Ismail 122
Katsina 128, 130
Kayrawan 108, 109
Kebra Negast 111, 113, 114
Keira (Kayra) Sultanate 135
Keita, I.D. 214
Keme 47
Kenadiid, Ismaan Yusuf 88
Kenya 4, 137
Khakheperr-sonbu 77, 78, 81
Kharijites 108
Khartoum 51
Khety 77, 78
Khmun 60
Khoisan 180
Khonsu 71
Khufu 49
Kibala 141
Kieran, J.A. 202
Kifayat a-Muhtaj 123
Kikuyu 31
Kilwa Chronicle 140, 141
Kilwa Kisiwani 139
Kimambo, Isaria 203
King-lists 69
Kings (*see under individual names*)
Kinshasha 196
Ki-Swahili 137, 138
Kitab al-'Ibar 110, 145, 154
Kitab Ghunja 125
Kitab ila Ma'arifat Umara Kasna 130
Kitab Tartib Umara Kashma 130
Kitini, Bwana 143
Ki-Zerbo, Joseph 195, 207
Koelle, S.W. 89
Kongo Kingdom 174
Kordofan 134, 135
Kua 143
Kufah 153
Kule (drum praise poetry) 25, 27
Kumma 51
Kush 49, 51
Kuteb (Central Nigeria) 31
Kwaluseni 198

L

Ladurie, Emmanuel le Roy 166
Land-charters 136
Lesotho 197
Levant 4
Levi-Strauss, C. 212, 213
Liberal revisionist 200
Liberia 7, 174
Libu tribe 80
Libyan (Siwa, Bahriya, Farafa, Dahkla and Kharga) 50
Libyco-Berber 115
Literature of pessimism 81, 82
Locke, John 162
Lot 96
Lotus 61
Lovanium University 196
Luanda 173
Lumumbashi school (of thought) 196, 197
Lucas (Rev) 188
Lunar calendar 66
Lusaka 198
Ly, Abdoulaye 195
Lybian script 84, 86, 91
Lychus 75

M

Michiavelli, Nicolo 160, 161
Machinga 142
Mafia 137
Maghrib 6, 18, 105, 107, 108, 116, 117, 135
Mahmud ibn 'Abdallah 125
Mahram 126, 128
Mai Umme (Humai) 126
Makhuratne, Phinias 198
Malalas 75
Malawi 198
Mali 124, 132, 188
Maliki school (of thought) 135
Malikite school (of thought) 109
Mamluk period 105
Man Who Was Tired of Life 81
Mandakha 141
Mandella era 202
Mandinke (of Mali) 117
Manetho 16, 46, 47, 48, 59, 70, 71, 73, 169, 185, 217
Manetho's *Aegyptiaca* 73, 75, 76, 81

Mani, 'Mu'alim Muhammad 126, 127
Manja (King) 88
Mauny, Raymond 184
Martinique 188
Marx, Karl 163, 167
Marxism 164, 165
Marxist 177
Masani, Muhammad dan 131
Masmuda Berbers 108
Matamandalin 141
Matsebula, J.S. 198
Mazrui, Ali A. 208
Mecca 96
Medina 96
Mediterranean 5
Mediterranee et le Monde Mediterraneen a la Epoque de Phillipe II 165
Medjayu 51
Mekhoa le Macle au Basotho 201
Memeptah 50
Memphis 52, 64
Memphite theology 59, 64, 68
Mende script 88, 89
Meroe 52, 85, 111
Meroitic script 52, 53, 84, 85, 86, 91
Merykara/Merkare (King) 80
Mesopotamia 47, 53
Meshwesh 49
Metahistory: The Historical Imagination of Nineteenth Century Europe 166
Methodology and African Prehistory 207
Mfecane Revolution 197
Michelet 167
Middle East 5
Miocene Age 47
Mkuu, Muhammad bin Bwana 143
Moeti oa Bochbela 201
Mofolo, Thomas Mokopu 201
Mogadishu 139
Mohammed (Prophet) 12, 95, 97, 99
Mohlomi Journal of South African Historical Studies 198
Mokhtar, O. 207
Mombassa 141
Montesquieu 162
Morocco 108

Moses 96
Mozambique 137, 197, 199
Mranga 142
Mtakata 142
Mudimbe 21
Muhammad, Baba Guru al-Hajj 123
Muquaddimah 143, 144, 145, 146, 148, 154, 155
Muriri wa Bari 141
Musa, Mansa 121
Mustafa, al-Hajj Muhammad ibn 125
Muyawamat 97
Mwa 141
Mwa Kiswani 142
Mwinehande bin Juma (Shaikh) 143

N

Nachtigal, Gustav 183
Nail al-Ibthihaj 123
Nairobi school (of thought) 203
Namibia 197, 199
Napata 52, 85
Narmer (Menes) [King] 58
Narrative tradition 218
Nasamonians 115

National Archives of Nigeria 193
National University of Lesotho 198
Native disabilities in South Africa 201
Native life in South Africa 201
Nawazil (of the Western African Sudan) 98, 130
Nazan al-Juman 109
Neferti 77, 78
Nefer-tem 61
Negrillos 180
Negritude 188, 194
Negroes 180
Negus Nagast (King of Kings) 112
Nehasyu 51
Nembe 22, 24, 26
Neolithic age 47
Nephtys 60, 64
Netjerikhet of Djoser 49
Newbury, David 209
Newton, A.P. 181, 182
Niane, D.T. 208
Nietzsche 167
Niger Delta region of Nigeria 21
Nigeria 190

Nigerian scripts 90
Nile 4, 5, 47
Nilo-Saharan languages 111
Njimi 127
Nkosi Sikeleli: I-Africa 201
Nkrumah, Kwame 187, 188
Noah 96
Northern Africa 5
Nsibidi signs 90, 93
Nubia 49, 51, 52, 133, 134
Nubian Church 87
Nubian dynasty 46
Nubian kingdom 85
Numidian script 86
Nupe 36
Nut (sky-god) 60, 63, 64
Nuu/Nun (Nw/Nwn) 60, 61, 63
Nuur, Sheikh Abdurahman 88
Nuwet/Nunet 61
Nyakatura 186
Nyoja (King) 89

O

Obenga, T. 196
Oberi Okaime script 91, 92, 93

Ogdoad 61, 64
Ogot, Bethwell Alan 202
Okpo 23, 24
Okrika 23
Olduvai 4
Oliver, Roland 184
Omani rule 140
On (creation myth) 60
Opu-gbololo-ongu-tugu 24
Oral history 13, 14
Oral tradition 8, 11, 12, 13, 14, 42
   Definition of 11
Oral Tradition: A Study of Historical Methodology 183
Ora Maritima 106
Origen 102
The Origin of Species 164, 179
The Origin of History 82, 83
Osarsiph 82
Osiris 60, 64
Othman 95

P

Pachomius 102
Padmore, George 187
Pakistan 99

Paleolithic age 47
Palermo Stone 57, 72
Palmer, Richard 128, 184
Papyri 15
Pate Sultans 143
Paths in the Rain Forest (Vansina) 214
Pemba 137, 139, 141
Perham, Margery 191
Periplus of the Erytraean Sea 106, 138
Persia (Iran) 99
Person, Yves 184
Piocene Age 47
Piy (Piye, Piankhi) 52
Piyay 77
Pharaoh Necho II 106
Phapta 138
Philae 47, 53, 55
Philosophia perennis 19
Philosophy of History 163
Phoenicia 5
Phoenicians 106
Paatje 186, 201
Plato 75, 153
Philadelphus (Ptolemy II) 16
Pleistocene age 47
Plutarch 75
Polybius 160
Popper 165

Porphyrius 75
Portuguese 138, 140
Positivism 164
Practice of History in Africa 3
Presence africaine 188, 195
Prince Henry of Portugal 171
Proto-Elamite 53
Protosinaitic 53
Ptah 59, 61, 64
Ptahhemdjehutty 77, 78
Ptahhotep 77, 78, 79
Ptolemy, Claudius 67, 138, 149
Ptolemy II (Philadelphus) 16
Ptolemy's *Geography* 138, 139
Punic heritage 106
Punic script 84, 86
Punt (Pwene) 50
Pwene (Punt) 50
Pygmies 7, 180

Q

Qane (oral culture) 113
Qataa'if al Jinan al a'Ahwal Ard al-Sudan 132
Qayrawan 153

Qissat Salagha Tarikh Ghunja 125
Quaque, Philiip 187
Qunbuluibn Mukhtar 122
Quraysh 127

R

Rabis, Warjabi B. 119
Races of Africa 180
Rahaman, Abdu 129
Ranger, Terence 203
Ranke 167
Ras Mkumbuu 138
Raudal al-'Afkar 132
Rawal al-Qirtis 110
Re 61, 62, 63, 71
Red Sea 50
Redford 83
Reindorf, Carl 186
Rennaisance 161
Ribla 110
Ricoeur 167
Rockefeller Foundation v
Rodney, Walter 214, 204
Roma 198
Roman script 85
Romans 4, 18
Romantic movement 162
Rome 5

Rosetta stone 54
Rousseau, Jean Jacques 162, 213
Rubusana, Waiter B. 200
Rumfa (Rimfa), Muhammadi 129, 130
Rwanda 137

S

Sahara 4, 6, 114, 137
Sai, Akiga 186, 187
Saifawa/Sefawa 127
St Anthony 169
St Augustine 36, 107, 160, 169, 170
St Mark 102
Sahih 153
Sahidic script see Coptic script
Salah al-Din 104
Salih ibn Tarif 96, 108
Samir Amin's Institut Africain de Development at de Planification 194
Sanad/Isnad (line of transmission of knowledge) 123
Sanhaja 109, 116
Sankore Mosque 122

Satju 51
Sawirus (Severus) b. Muqaffat (Bishop) 103
Sayf b. Dhi Yazan 127
Sboyet (Instruction) 99
Scholia 75
Sebennytis 16
Science of Culture 144
Scorpion (King) 58
Sedentary civilization 149, 150
Sefkhet-abwy 71
Sekese, Azariehe 201
Sekiapu (Ekine) 25
Seligman, C.G. 180
Seminant 92
Semites 180
Semitic 5
Semma 5
Senegal 135, 187, 194
Senghor, Leopold Sedar 183, 187, 188, 194
Sennar (Sinnar) 133, 134, 135
Septuagint 102
Seshat 71, 73
Seth 60, 64
Sethy I (Sety I) 61
Setyu 50
Shabako (King) 52, 59, 69

Shabitko 52
Shaka Zulu Mfecane 19
Shauga 141
Shaykh 'Uthman 121
Shekhemkhet (King) 58
Shem/Sam 96
Shilluk 134
Shirazi (Persian) 138, 140, 142
Shu (god of air/atmosphere) 60, 63, 64
Sinnar 136
Siwa 50
Smith, Abdullahi 193
Snefru 49, 58
Societe des Historiens Zairos 196
Socrates 153, 159
Sofala 139
Soga, John Henderson 201
Soga, Tiyo 200
Sokoto caliphate 128, 131, 133
Sokoto jihad 130
Somalia 137
Somali scripts 87
Song of Bagauda 132
Song of the Harper 77
Songhai 188

Songhay 117, 118, 121, 128, 132
Soninke (of Ghana) 117
Sontoga, Enoch 200
Spain 99
South Africa 4, 6, 186
South-Eastern Bantu 201
Southern Africa 197
Southern Asia 99
Soyinka, Wole 188
Step Pyramid of Nekjerikhet 58
Stigand, C.H. 142
Stone age 47
Sudan 6
Sudanese Memoirs 128
Sumeria 47
Sumerian 53
Sumner 113
Sunnite Islam 109
Suotugu (place of creation) 22
Susenyos (Emperor) 113
Swahili 134, 143
    Chronicles 140, 141
    Histories 142
    Region 6
    Tradition 18
Swai 189, 204, 206
Swaziland 197, 198

T

Tabaco, Zolu 89
Tabagot 98
Tabaqat 136
Tabari 98
Tacitus 160
Tahargo 52
Taj al-Din fi Ma Yajib 'ala al-Muluk 130
Takrur 119
Tamia, D. 89
Tanbih al-Ikhwan ala Ahwal Bilad al-Sudan 131
Tanganyika 142
Tanutamani 52
Tanzania 4, 137
Tarikh 43, 97, 99, 191
Tarikh al-Dawalatain 110
Trikh al-Fatash fi-Akhbar Wa-'l-juyush Wa-Akabir al-Nas 122, 123
Tarik ahl Wala 125
Tarikh al-Sudan (History of Sudan) 122, 123
Tarikh Arbab Hadna al-Bald al-Musamma 128
Tarikh Daghabawi 125
Tarikh Mai Idris qa Ghazawatihi 127

Tarikh Mai Idris 127
Tarikh Umara Bauchi 133
Tassili n-Ajjer 115
Tazyin al-Warayat 131
Tefenet (wife of Shu) 60, 64
Tempels 19
Temu, Arnold 189, 203, 204, 206
Tertulian 107
Thagaste 169
Theban tradition 70
Thebes 52, 61, 64
Theodoretus 75
Theophilus 75
Thoth (god of writing) 52, 60, 61, 71, 92
Thutmoses I 51, 70
Thutmoses III 51, 70
Thucydides 155, 159, 160
Tifinagh 116
Tigris 5
Timbuktu 122, 123, 124
Time and Narrative 167
Tiv 186
Tjehnyu 50
Tjembu 50
Tocqueville 167
Toma script 89, 92, 93
Tombe 89

Trade and Politics in the Niger Delta 191, 192
Traders (Djallaba) 134
Trevor-Roper, Hugh 181, 182
Tripoli 126
Tripolitania 108
Troglodytes 115
Tuareg 115
Tunis 153
Tunisia 107
Turdetanian script 86
Turkey 99
Turin Canon 70
Turin Papyrus 59

U

Udofia, Akpan Akpan 91
Uganda 137, 186
Ujamaa 204
Ukba ibn Nafi 108
Ukpon, Michael 91
Ukpotio (secret society) 90
Ukwa (secret society)
'Umar 95
'Umar, Jubril b. 131
Umayyad Arab 135
Unesco 184, 198, 207
Unguja 139

United States Information Agency iv
Universal History from the Creation Centred on the History of the Arabs 144
University of al-Azhar 103
University of Botswana 198
University of Dar es Salaam 203
University of Dakar 194
University of Ibadan 176, 190
University of Khartoum 176
University of Legon 190
University of Nairobi 202
University of Makerere 176
University of Port Harcourt iv
University of Swaziland 198
University of Timbuktu 43
University of Wisconsin-Madison iv
University of Zambia 198
Upper Volta 124
Urvoy, Yves 184
Usman, Yusuf Bala 193
'Uthman b. Muhammad b. Fudi 131

V

Vai script 88, 89, 91, 92
Vanda invasions 107
Vansina, Jan 183, 214, 215, 216, 217, 218
Vellut 197
Velten, C. 142
Vico 162
Voltaire 161, 163
Von Ranke, Leopold 164

W

Wadai 134
Wad Dayfallah 136
Wallerstein, Immanuel 208
Walsh 165
Wamba 205
Wangara-Dyula 125
Wangarawa 129
Wuqwaq 139
Wawae/Wawat 51
Wen-nefer 77
Western Europe 5
Western Sudan 5, 19, 117, 120, 122, 135
Western tradition 9, 42, 157
White, Hayden 158, 166, 219

'White Man's Grave' 180
Wido 93
Wilson, John 84
Wiredu, Kwesi 33
Wisdom Literature 77, 80
Wogbe, Momolu Duwau 89
Wright, John 187
Writing
    Cuneiform 5
    Ethiopic 8
    Hieroglyphics 5, 8
    Meroitic 8
World spirit (Weltgeist) 163
World War II 174, 175

Y

Yaqob, Zara 113
Yahya b. Abi Bkar 120
Yaji (Sarki) 129
Yakob, Zera (Emperor) 113
Yanbu 141
Yoruba 90, 133, 186

Z

Zaawo, Jaa 89
Zambia 197
Zana (Braha) [King] 111
Zaire 137, 196
Zaire River 6
Zaite, Abdurahamna 129
Zamani: A Survey of East African History 202
Zanj/Zenj 139
Zanzibar 137
Zazzau (Zaria) 128, 131
Zeila 139
Zerkeshi 110
Zimbabwe 188, 197, 199
Zomba 198